Street by Street

GW00602824

EAST KENT
PLUS RYE
Enlarged Areas Ashford, Canterbury, Dover, Folkestone, Margate, Ramsgate

Ist edition May 2001

© Automobile Association Developments Limited 2001

This product includes map data licensed from Ordnance Survey® with the permission of the Controller of Her Majesty's Stationery Office. © Crown copyright 2000. All rights reserved. Licence No: 399221.

All rights reserved. No part of this publication may be reproduced, stored in a retrieval system, or transmitted in any form or by any means– electronic, mechanical, photocopying, recording or otherwise – unless the permission of the publisher has been given beforehand.

Published by AA Publishing (a trading name of Automobile Association Developments Limited, whose registered office is Norfolk House, Priestley Road, Basingstoke, Hampshire, RG24 9NY. Registered number 1878835).

Mapping produced by the Cartographic Department of The Automobile Association.

A CIP Catalogue record for this book is available from the British Library.

Printed by G. Canale & C. s.p.a., Torino, Italy

The contents of this atlas are believed to be correct at the time of the latest revision. However, the publishers cannot be held responsible for loss occasioned to any person acting or refraining from action as a result of any material in this atlas, nor for any errors, omissions or changes in such material. The publishers would welcome information to correct any errors or omissions and to keep this atlas up to date. Please write to Publishing, The Automobile Association, Fanum House, Basing View, Basingstoke, Hampshire, RG21 4EA.

Ref: MX099

ii

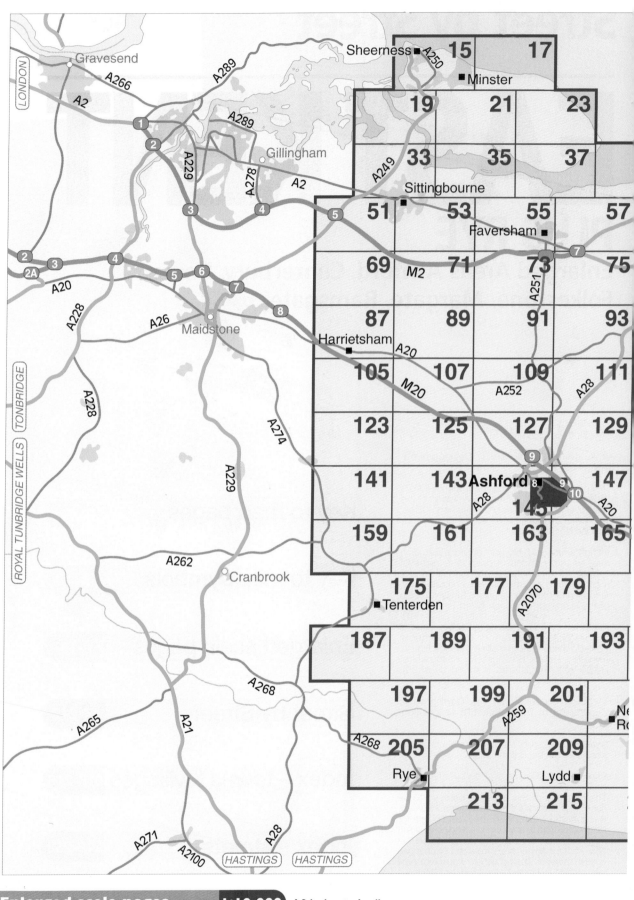

Gravesend

LONDON

A266

A289

A2

A289

A229

A278

A2

Gillingham

Sheerness

A250

15

17

Minster

19

21

23

A249

33

35

37

Sittingbourne

51

53

Faversham

55

57

7

69

M2

71

73

A251

75

2
2A
3
4
5
6
7
8

A20

A228

A26

Maidstone

Harrietsham

A20

87

89

91

93

A228

A274

105

M20

107

109

A252

111

A28

123

125

127

129

A229

A262

Cranbrook

A265

A21

A228

141

143 Ashford

A28

8

9

145

10

147

A20

159

161

163

165

175

Tenterden

177

A2070

179

187

189

191

193

197

199

201

Ne
Ro

A259

A268

A265

A21

A268

205

207

209

Rye

Lydd

213

215

A271

A2100

A28

HASTINGS

HASTINGS

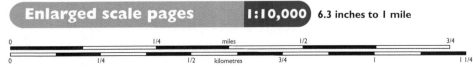

Enlarged scale pages   **1:10,000**   6.3 inches to 1 mile

0   1/4   miles   1/2   3/4

0   1/4   1/2   kilometres   3/4   1   1 1/4

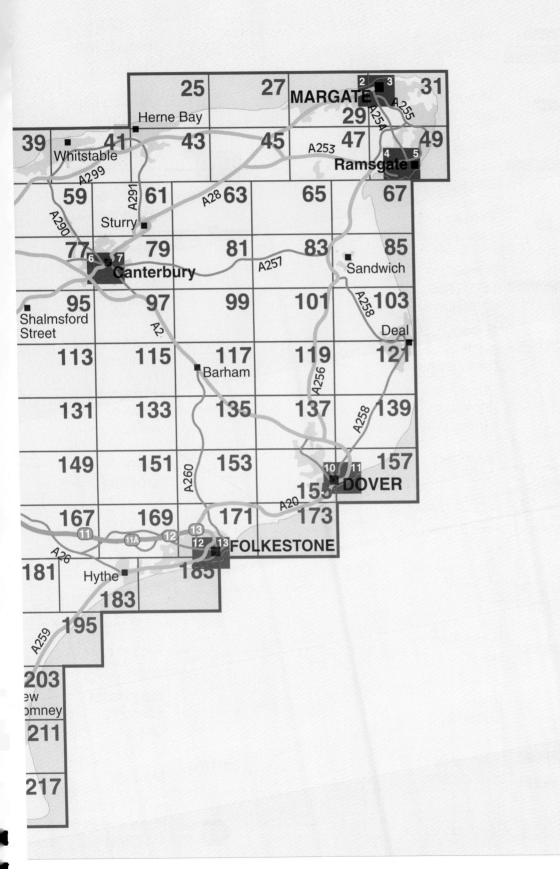

Junction 9	Motorway & junction
Services	Motorway service area
	Primary road single/dual carriageway
Services	Primary road service area
	A road single/dual carriageway
	B road single/dual carriageway
	Other road single/dual carriageway
	Restricted road
	Private road
← ←	One way street
	Pedestrian street
	Track/ footpath
	Road under construction
⊏------⊐	Road tunnel
P	Parking

P+🚌	Park & Ride
🚌	Bus/coach station
	Railway & main railway station
	Railway & minor railway station
⊖	Underground station
⊖	Light railway & station
++++++++++++++	Preserved private railway
LC	Level crossing
•—•—•—•—	Tramway
- - - - - - -	Ferry route
....	Airport runway
— · — · — · —	Boundaries- borough/ district
▼▼▼▼▼▼▼▼▼▼	Mounds
93	Page continuation 1:17,500
7	Page continuation to enlarged scale 1:10,000

River/canal
lake, pier

Toilet with
disabled facilities

Aqueduct
lock, weir

Petrol station

465
▲
Winter Hill

Peak (with
height in
metres)

PH Public house

Beach

PO Post Office

Coniferous
woodland

Public library

Broadleaved
woodland

i Tourist Information
Centre

Mixed
woodland

Castle

Park

Historic house/
building

Cemetery

Wakehurst
Place NT

National Trust
property

Built-up
area

M Museum/
art gallery

Featured building

† Church/chapel

City wall

Country park

A&E Accident &
Emergency
hospital

Theatre/
performing arts

Toilet

Cinema

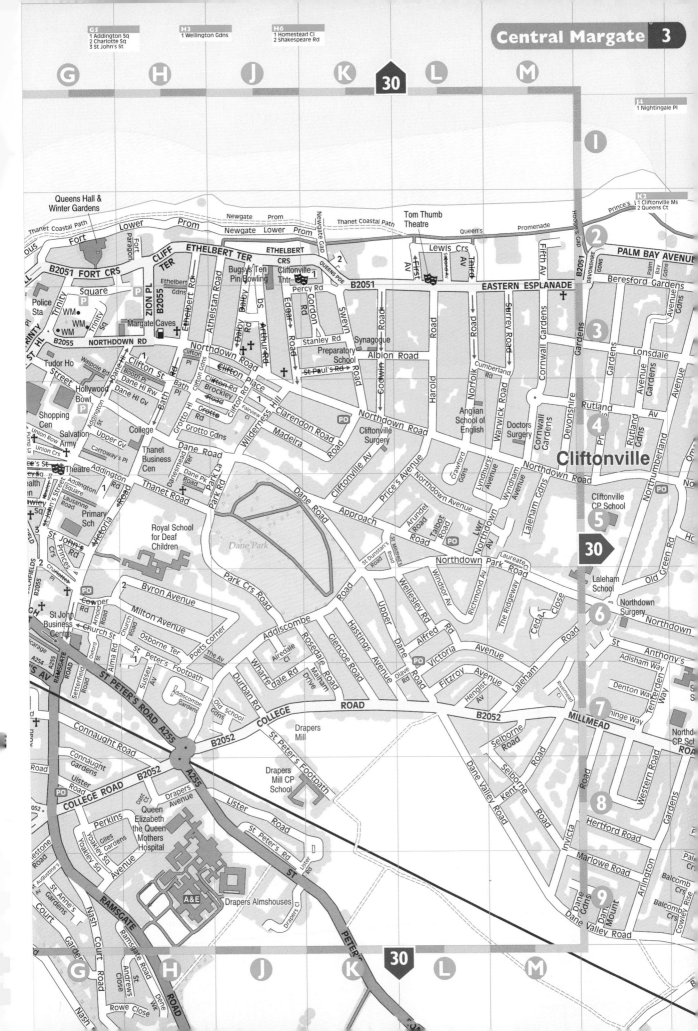

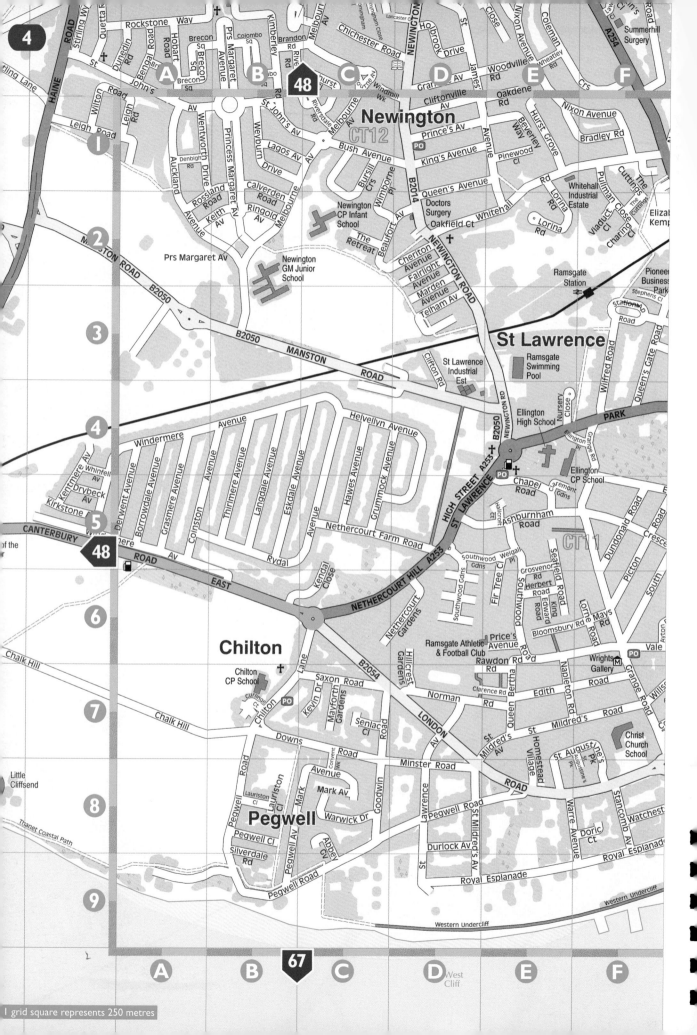

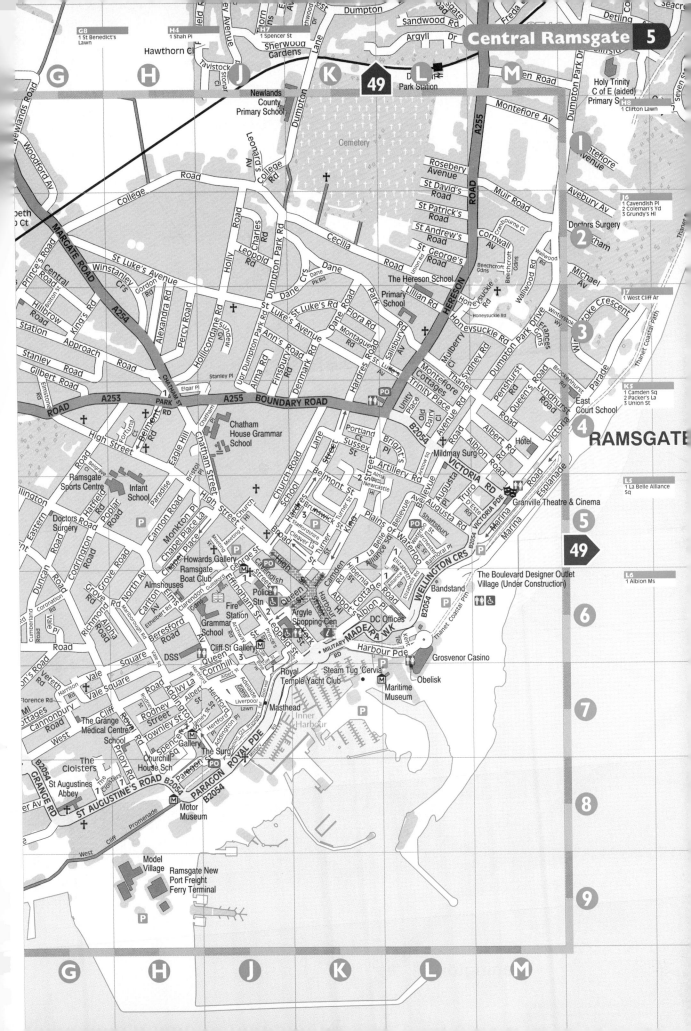

G8 1 St Benedict's Lawn
H4 1 Shah Pl
H7 1 Spencer St

G H J K **49** L M

Hawthorn Cl
Newlands County Primary School

Holy Trinity C of E (aided) Primary S
H8 1 Clifton Lawn

Dumpton Park Station

Cemetery

Montefiore Av
Montefiore Avenue

I

Rosebery Avenue
St David's Road
St Patrick's Road
St Andrew's Road
St George's Road

Muir Road

Avebury Av
Doctors Surgery

I6 1 Cavendish Pl 2 Coleman's Yd 3 Grundy's Hl

2

College Road

The Hereson School

Michael Av

Cornwall Av

I7 1 West Cliff Ar

Cecilia Road

Honeysuckle Rd
Honeysuckle Rd

HERESON ROAD

Penshurst Rd
Dumpton Park Drive
Frances Gdns
Brockenhurst Rd

Thanet Coastal Path

Crescent

3

St Luke's Avenue
Charles Rd
Leopold Rd
Holly Rd
Dumpton Park Rd

Primary School
Lillian Rd

Mulberry Cl
Montefiore Cottages
Trinity Place

Queen's Road
Lyndhurst Road
Albert Rd
East Court School

KS 1 Camden Sq 2 Packer's La 3 Union St

4

Winstanley Crs
Gordon Rd
Alexandra Rd
Percy Road
Hollicondane Rd
Ann's Road
St Luke's Rd
Flora Rd
Montague Rd
Dane Crs

A254 MARGATE ROAD
A255

Central Rd
Prince's Rd

Stanley Pl
Elgar Pl
A253 PARK ST/RD
A255 BOUNDARY ROAD

Unity Place
Dairy Cl
Portland Ct
Bright's Pl

Sydney Rd
Avenue Rd
Victoria Rd
Hotel

RAMSGATE

Chatham House Grammar School

VICTORIA RD
Mildmay Surg
Augusta Rd
Truro Rd
D'Este Rd

Marina
Granville Theatre & Cinema

L5 1 La Belle Alliance Sq

5

Chatham Street
Church Street
Broad
Artillery Rd
Sussex St
Belmont St
Brunswick St
Turner St
King St
Plains Of Waterloo
La Belle Alliance Rd

Bandstand

VICTORIA PDE
Marina
Balmoral Pl

49

The Boulevard Designer Outlet Village (Under Construction)

L6 1 Albion Ms

Ramsgate Sports Centre
Infant School
Doctors Surgery
Hatfield Rd
Poplar Road
Cannon Road
Monkton Pl
Chapel Place La
Chapel Place
Howards Gallery
Ramsgate Boat Club

Cleaver La
Camden Rd
Hibernia St
Abbot's Hl
Cottage Rd
Albion Rd

WELLINGTON CRS

Thanet Coastal Path

6

High Street
Eagle Hill
Bristol Rd
Paradise
Almshouses
North Av
Carlton Av
Clarendon Rd
Fire Station
Grammar School
Police Stn
Queen St
Harbour Hl

Argyle Shopping Cen
DC Offices
MADEIRA WALK

Grosvenor Casino

Belgrave Rd
Fortuna Ct
Belmont Rd
George Street
Meeting St
High Street
Leopold St
Prince's St

MILITARY RD
Harbour Pde

Obelisk

Eastern Road
Codrington Road
Grove Road
Richmond Rd
Alpha Road
Duncan Road
Cumberland Rd
Coronation Rd
Vale Rd
Marlborough Rd
Beresford Road
Ethelbert Rd
Cliff St Gallery
DSS
Queen Sq
Cornhill

Steam Tug 'Cervia'
Royal Temple Yacht Club
Maritime Museum

7

Florence Rd
Cannonbury Rd
Cannonbury Road
Vale Square
Royal Rd
Vale Square
Ivy La
Rodney Street
Addington Street
Albert St
Hertford St
Adelaide Pl
Liverpool Lawn
Masthead

Inner Harbour

8

The Grange Medical Centre
Townley St
Spencer Sq
Churchill House Sch
The Surg
St Augustines Abbey
The Cloisters

PARAGON ROYAL PDE
B2054
Gallery

GRANGE RD
ST AUGUSTINE'S ROAD
B2054

Motor Museum

West Cliff

9

Model Village
Ramsgate New Port Freight Ferry Terminal

Promenade

West Cliff

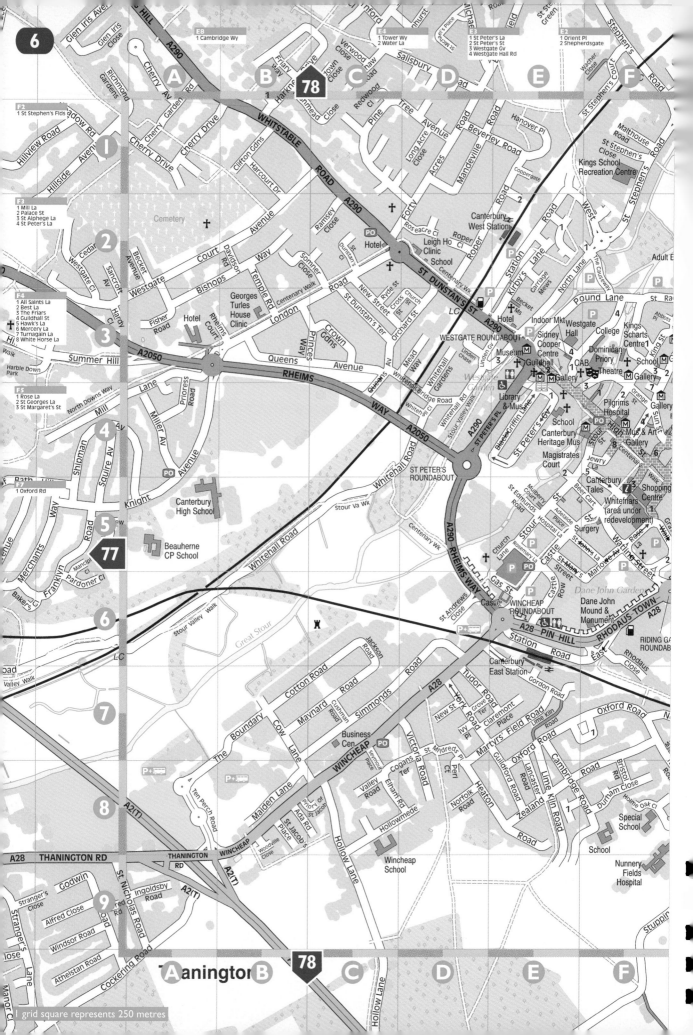

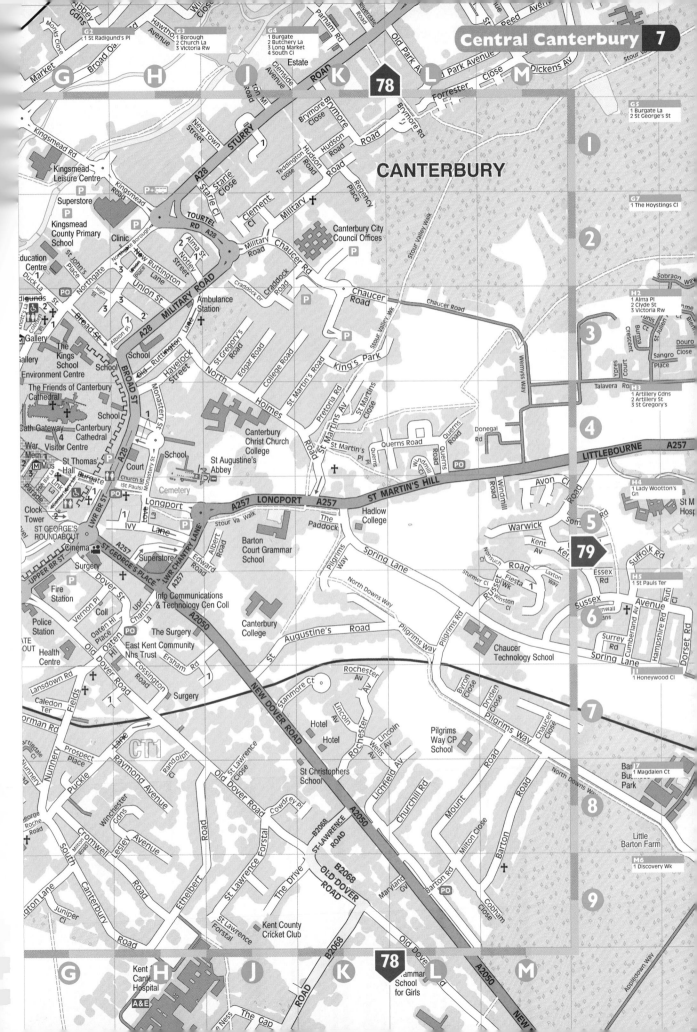

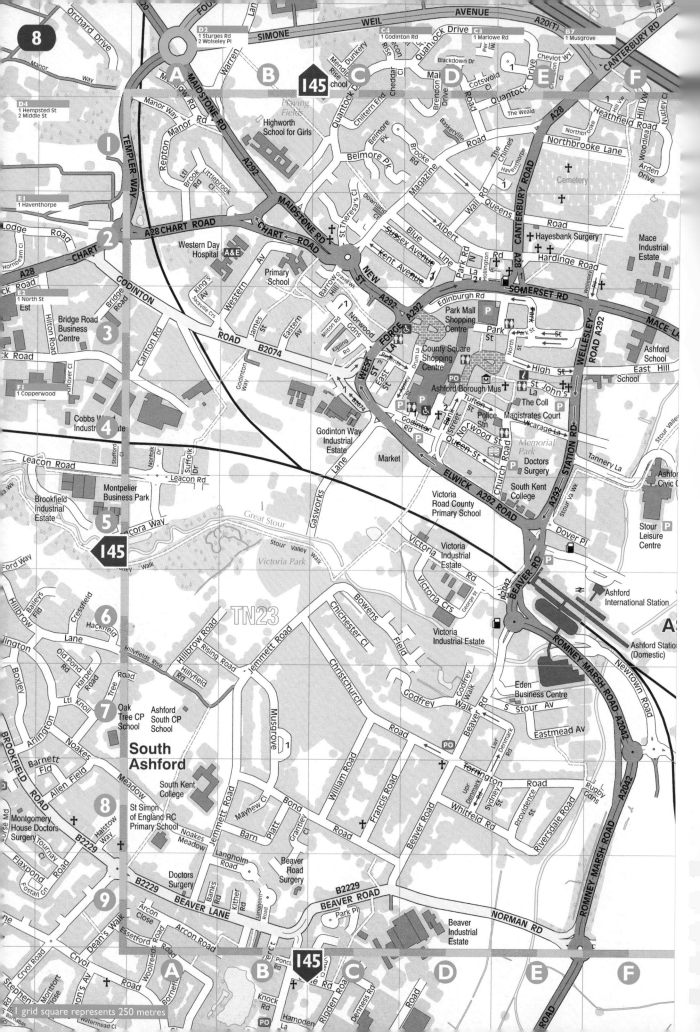

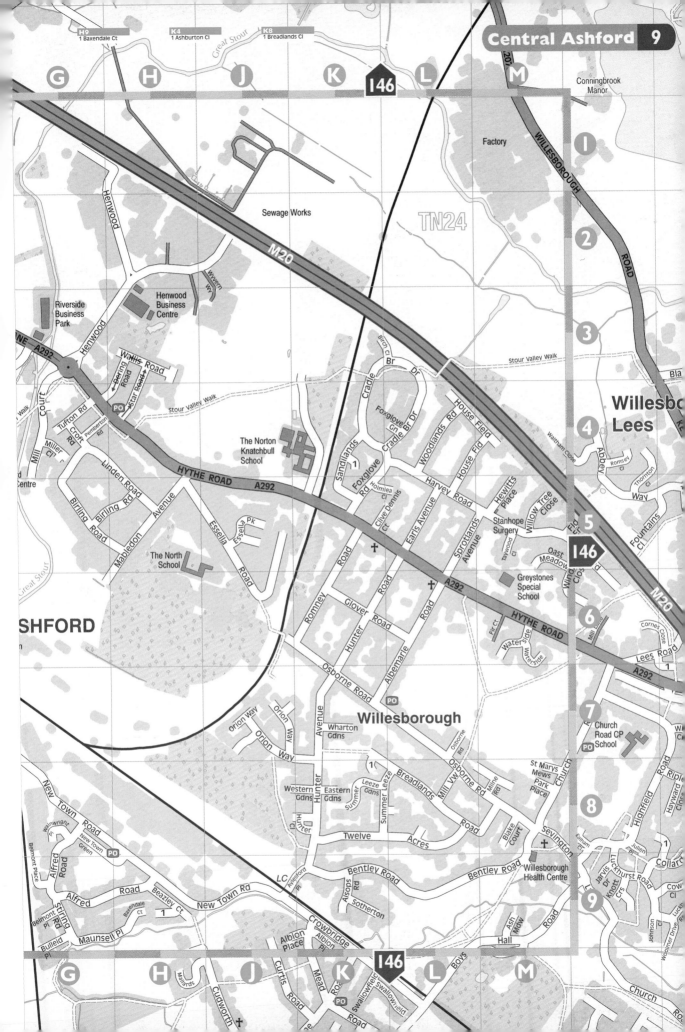

H9
1 Baxendale Ct

K4
1 Ashburton Cl

K8
1 Breadlands Cl

G H J K **146** L M

Conningbrook Manor

Factory

WILLESBOROUGH ROAD

1

2

TN24

3

Sewage Works

M20

Riverside Business Park

Henwood Business Centre

Henwood

Wyvern Wy

A292

Wallis Road

Dering Road

Star Road

Croft Rd

Pemberton Rd

Tufton Rd

Miller Cl

Mill Court

Stour Valley Walk

PO

HYTHE ROAD A292

The Norton Knatchbull School

Cradle Br Dr

Birch Cl

Br Dr

Stour Valley Walk

Waltham Close

Willesborough Lees

4

Abbey

Romsey Cl

Thornton Cl

Bla

Way

Linden Road

Birling Road

Birling Rd

Avenue

Mabledon

Essella Road

Essella Road

Essella Pk

Sandilands Rd

Foxglove Cl

Foxglove Gn

Holmlea

Clive Dennis Ct

Harvey Road

Earls Avenue

Woodlands Rd

House Fld

House Field

Hewitts Place

Stanhope Surgery

Willow Tree Close

Taywood

5

146

Eli

Oast Meadow

Wind Clo

Fountains Cl

The North School

Romney Road

Glover Road

Hunter Road

Road

Sprotlands Avenue

A292

Greystones Special School

Fir Ct

HYTHE ROAD

Mill Lane

6

Cornes Close

Lees Road

A292

1

Great Stour

SHFORD

Centre

Waterside

Waterside

Osborne Road

PO

Albemarle Road

Willesborough

Wharton Gdns

Osborne Rd

St Marys Mews Park Place

Church Road

Church Road CP School

PO

7

Orion Way

Orion Way

Orion Way

Avenue

Hunter

Western Gdns

Eastern Gdns

Hunter Ct

Leeze Gdns

Summer Leeze

Summer Leeze

Breadlands Road

Mill Vw Rd

Osborne Rd

Milne

Blake Court

Enham Cl

Julien

8

New Town Road

Wainwright Pl

New Town Green

PO

Alfred Road

Belmont Place

String Rd

Belmont Pl

Bulleid Pl

Maunsell Pl

Alfred Road

Beazley Ct

Baxendale Ct

1

New Town Rd

LC

Aylesford Pl

Twelve Acres

Alsops Rd

Sotherton

Bentley Road

Bentley Road

Willesborough Health Centre

Sevington

Jarvis Dr

Luckhurst Road

knott Crs

Cow Cl

Collart

Luck

Johnson

Woolmer Drive

Highfield Road

Hayward Close

Ripple Road

Wi

C

1

9

Crowbridge Road

Albion Place

Albion

Mallards

Cudworth

Curtis Road

Mead Rd

Swallowfield

Swallowfield Road

PO

Hall

Ash Mdw

Road

Church

Boys

G H J **146** K L M

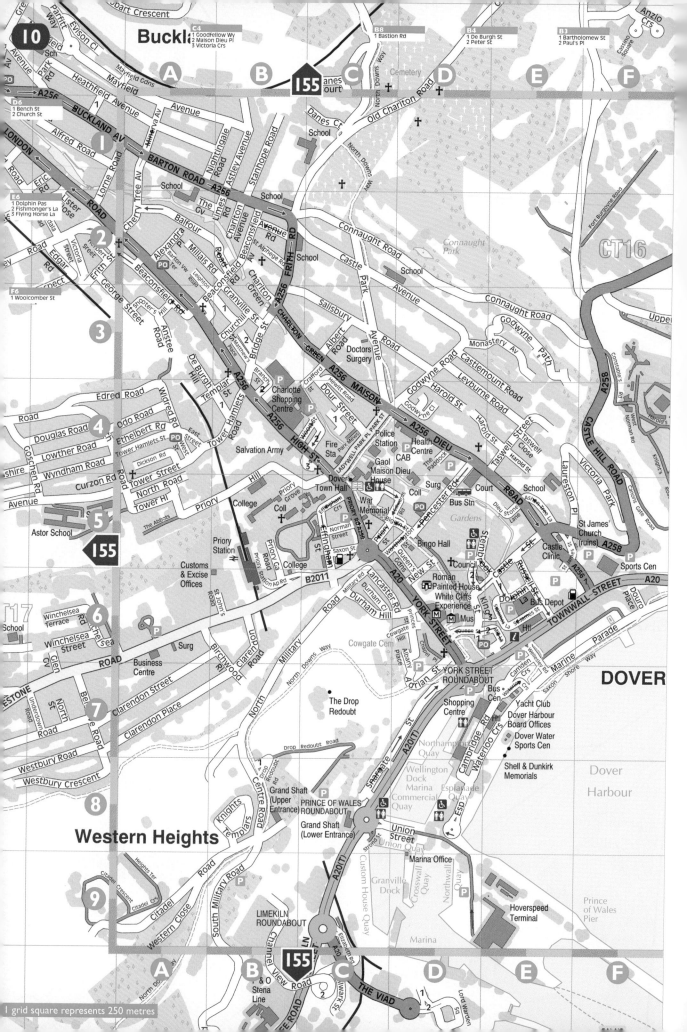

156

G   H   J   K   L   M

I

2

3

4

5

156

6

7

8

9

G   H   J   K   L   M

156

Alamein Close

Kohima Place

JUBILEE WAY

A258

Upper Road

Upper Road

Upper Road

Edinburgh Hill

Bleriot Memorial

Upper Road

JUBILEE WAY — A2(T)

Saxon Shore Way

Cliff Road

Saxon Shore Way

Saxon Shore Way (East)

Back Road

Camber Way

Fan

The

Keep

Godwin Road

Road

P

Mortimer Road

East Roman Ditch

P

P

Pharos

Dover Castle

Queen Elizabeth

Road

Police Station

Athol Ter

Saxon Shore Way

JUBILEE WAY (ELEVATED ROAD) A2(T)

Dock Exit Road

Dock Road

P

Eastern Docks

East

Cliff

Marine Pde

A2(T)

A20

Saxon Shore Way East Ramp

Cliff Road

Exit Road

CALAIS

Upper Road

Cliff Road

Saxon Shore

Saxon

La

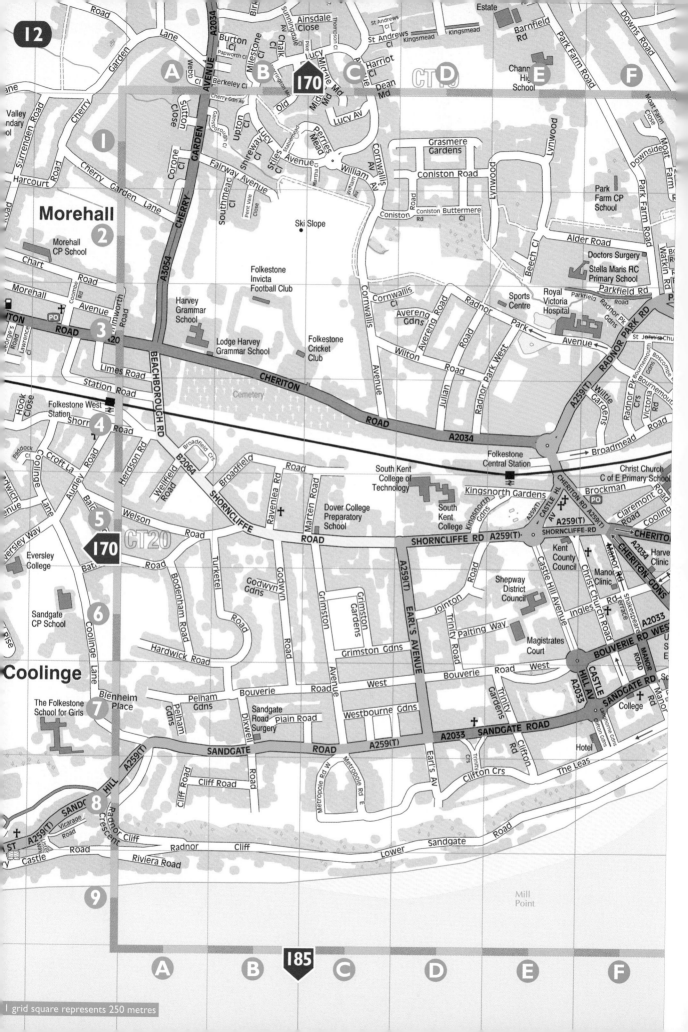

1 grid square represents 250 metres

FOLKESTONE

BOULOGNE

A B C D E F

1

Garrison
Point

2

Blue
Town

Jacob's
Bank

SHEERNESS

Anchor Lane

Main   Road
Archway   Road
Road
High   St
Charles   St
West Street
Chapel   St

Duke of Clarence
Trading Estate

BRIDGE
RD

Sheppey
College

Beach Street

A250   HIGH ST

Broadway

Sheppey
Little
Theatre

Doctors
Surgery

Marine Pa

3

River Medway

Sheerness-
on-Sea
Station

Mile Town

Railway Road

Russell Street

Cross Street

Delamark Road

BROADWAY

Alma
Street

Broadway

Berridge Road

Invicta Road

James   Street

Clyde Street

Richmond Road

Jefferson Road

Richn

Hope Street

Rose Street

St Edwards
School

Om Medical
Centre

Rose
Street
CP School

Granville Road

TRINITY   ROAD

A250

PO

Unity Street

Coronation Road

St Helen's

Nursery
Close

4

West Swale

A249(T)

New Road
Industrial Est

Mile Town
Industrial Pk

Regis Business
Park

New Road

Thames Avenue

Estuary Road

Cecil Avenue

George's Avenue

Victoria

St Agnes
Gardens

Maple St

Sheerness
Clinic

HIGH STREET

A250

Marine Town

5

West
Minster

A249(T)

BRIELLE   WAY

New Road

Dorset Road

Regis
Industrial
Estate

Nelson
Close

The
Lappel

Queen's

Coats Avenue

PO

Hawthorn Avenue

Almond Tree Close

St George's Avenue

Davie
Close

School

Wheatsheaf
Gardens

South View Gardens

Halfway

6

Cromwell
Road

Linden
Drive

Elmbridge Drive

Chillam Cl

Appledore
Avenue

Boxley

Bradhurst
Close

Detling
Close

Hartlip
Close

Holm
Place

Isle of Sheppey
Cemetery

7

B2007

Whiteway Road

BRIELLE   WAY

St Peter's Close

QUEENBOROUGH

Primary
School

A250

Sunnyfield's

Eastern
Avenue

Hilda Rd

Western Avenue

Rosemary Avenue

Holmside Avenue

Ferndale Close

8

West
Point

North Road

Coronation
Crescent

Jubilee
Crescent

Foxley
Road

Chalk Road

Queenborough

South Street

West   Street

Queenborough
Yacht Club

RAILWAY   TERRACE

High
Street

The
Surgery

Moat Way

Castle
Street

Barler
Place

Yevel

A249(T)

Dumergue Avenue

Castlemere
Avenue

Park Avenue

Edward Road

Queenborough
CP School

Sterling Road

Belgrave Road

Bartletts

Uplands Way

The Close

Ashley
Close

Elm
View Cl

19

Queenborough
Station

MAIN   ROAD

B2007

A B C D E F

1 grid square represents 500 metres

G H J K L M

1

2

3

4

16

5

6

7

8

Sheppey Yacht Club

Barton's Point

Marine Parade

The Commodore Catamaran Yacht Club

Marine Parade

Barnsley Close

Seager Road

Beckley Road

Cheyney Middle School

nd County School

Minster Marshes

Scrapsgate

The Leas

Minster Drive

Scarborough

Southsea

Augustine Drive

Minster Drive

Drive

Avenue

Avenue

Scarborough

sexburga

Drive

Wards

Seaside

Road

Scarborough

Westcliff Drive

Clovelly Drive

Clondale Road

Hill

Roamer Close

Aston Close

Howard

Seathorpe Avenue

Lynmouth Drive

The Glen

Woodland Drive

The Glen

Chase Road

Highview

Norwood Rise

Sheppey Community Hospital

Princes Avenue

Imperial Avenue

Stanley Avenue

Baldwin Road

Ripney Hill Farm

Sheerness Golf Club

Drove Road

Power Station Road

St Katherine Road

William Right Drive

Buddle Drive

Danley Road

Halfway Houses

Danley Middle School

Sheppey Rugby FC Club

Elliott Park School

Marian Avenue

Scrapsgate Road

Marina Drive

Johnson Road

The Broadway

Kent Avenue

Waverley Avenue

Hillside Road

MINSTER

Whybornes Chase

Love Lane

Brecon Chase

Union Road

The Glen

Minster Abbey

Museum

Queens Road

Cliff

Appleford Drive

Mills Close

Salmon Crescent

Noreen Avenue

Sunnyside Avenue

Queenborough Drive

Abbeyview

Shurland Avenue

Shiva Medical Centre

Saxon Avenue

Glenwood Drive

Drive

Belleuve Road

Minster In Sheppey CP School

Orchard Grove

Abbey Close

CHAPEL ST

Tams Gardens

Lynsted Rd

Belmont Rd

Fleet Road

ROAD

Doctors Surgery

PO

Banner Way

Raleigh Way

Admirals Walk

Highfield Road

Southdown Road

Selwood Close

de Gardens

Hill Cres

B2008

MINSTER

ROAD

Minster College

Silverdale Avenue

Porter Close

Darlington Drive

Sanspareil Avenue

Summerville Avenue

PO

Fleetwood Close

Dreadnought Av

Nautilus Drive

Barton Hill Drive

Blatcher Close

MINSTER ROAD

Worcester Close

New Road

Copland

New Road

Bramston Road

Prince Charles Avenue

B2008

Chiddingfold Close

Hopsons Place

St George C of E Mi School

Parsonage Chase

Leigh Court

Hilltop Road

Holyrood Drive

Parish Road

Plover Road

Heron Drive

Lapwing Close

Avenue

Scocles

Nelson Avenue

Drake Avenue

Avenue

willis court

Lovell Road

Wain Ct

Thistle Hill Way

Elm Lane

20

Scocles Ct

Blackthorne Road

Orchid Close

Barton Hill

Thistle Hill Way

Scocles

1

2

3

4

◄ 15

5

6

7

8

Royal
Oak Point

Bugsby's
Hole

East
End

Lane

Cliff Gardens

Oak

Mill
Hill Windmill Rise

Oak Avenue

CHEQUERS ROAD

St Georges
C of E Middle
School

Pigtail Corner

Danedale Avenue

Bell

Lane

Farm

Punnetts
Farm

Old Billet Lane

Connetts

Cripps
Farm

Plough Road

Plough Road

Plough Road

Elm Lane

Tadwell
Farm

Kingsborough
Farm

Garretts

Avenue

Avenue

The
Mount

B2008

EASTCHURCH ROAD

Brambledown

Norwood
Manor

21

Avenue

Baldwin Road

Stanley Av

Road

PO

CHAPEL
ST

Tams
Gardens

Boundary

LOWE

1 grid square represents 500 metres

Surf Crs
Dawn Rise
Third Avenue
Sunset Close
Swanley Farm
Third Avenue
First Avenue
Fourth Avenue
Second Avenue
Sixth Avenue
Trouts
Manor Way
Warden Road
Berryfield
Warden Road
Barnland Farm
Thorn Hill
Ware Point
Cliff
Preston Hall Gardens
Sea Approach
St James
Imperial
Knoll Way

A B C D E F

1

2

3

Chetney
Marshes

4

Slaughterhouse
Point

Long Reach

Saxon shore Way

Saxon shore Way

5

The Shade

6

Halstow C

Chetney
Cotts

Barksore
Marshes

7

Bedlams Bottom

Raspberry Hill Lane

Saxon shore Way

Funton Creek

8

Saxon Shore Way

A B C **32** D E F

Iwade CP School
Fans Lane een Close Linkway
Iwade Springvale

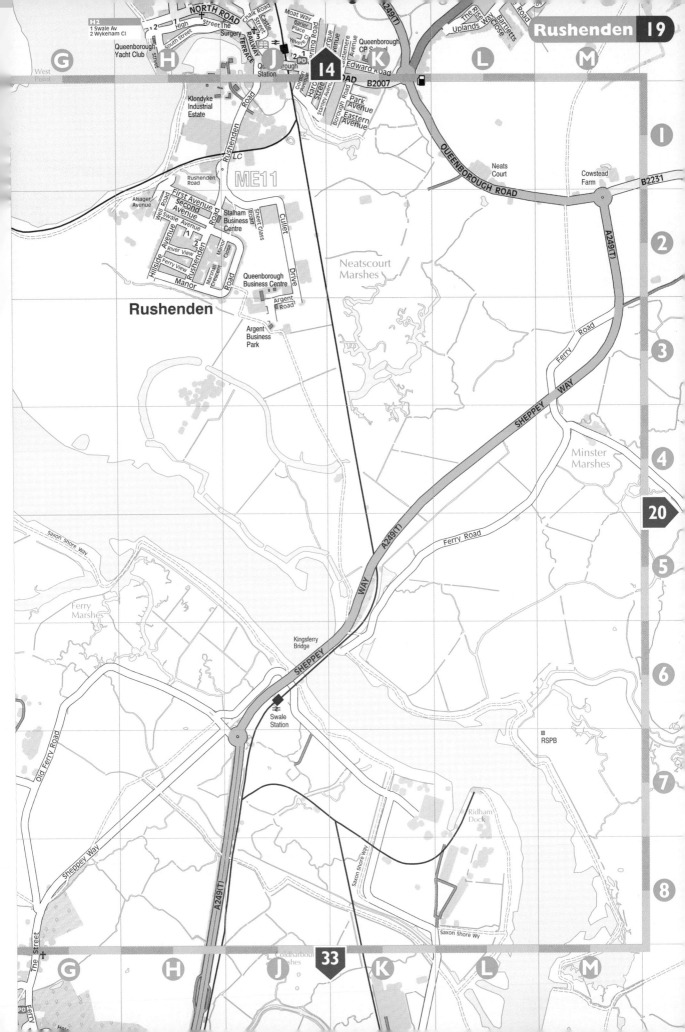

A   B   C   D   E   F

15

I

B2231   LOWER   ROAD   FORTY ACRES HILL   B2231

Ferry Road

Wallend

South Lees

Poors

Windmill Quay Road

19

Southlees Marshes

Stray Marshes

Isle of Sheppey

The Dray

Elmley Island

Elmley Marshes

A   B   C   D   E   F

34

Barton Hill

Scocles Road

Thistle Hill Way

Elm Lane

Elmley Road

Bellflower Avenue

Blackthorne Road

Orchid Close

Scocles Farm

Thistle Hill Way

A.D

Plover Road

Drive

Hilltop Road

Wills Cairn

Lovell Road

Holyrood

Leigh Court

Wain Ct

Heron

5
4
3
2
1

7
6

1 grid square represents 500 metres

A   B   Berryfield   C   17   D   E   F

Warden Road

1 Squires Ct

Warden Road

Barnland Farm

Knoll Way

Empres
Garden
Windso
Garden
Clare
Gar
Le
Ga

1

Warden Road

Eastchurch C of E
Primary School

†

PO
Street

Doctors
Surgery

Anne Boleyn
Close

Church Road

Rayham

Mustards

2

B2231

LEYSDOWN ROAD

Bay
View

3

Mustards Road

Coronation D

St Clements Cl

Danes   Drive

Warden View Gardens

Bay View
Gardens

Cliff View

Gardens

ew Drive

Old Rides Farm

Rides Farm

LEYSDOWN

ROAD

4

New
Rides

Harty Ferry Road

21

5

Capel Hill
Farm

Newhouse

6

7

Capel Fleet

Harty Ferry Road

8

A   B   C   36   D   E   F

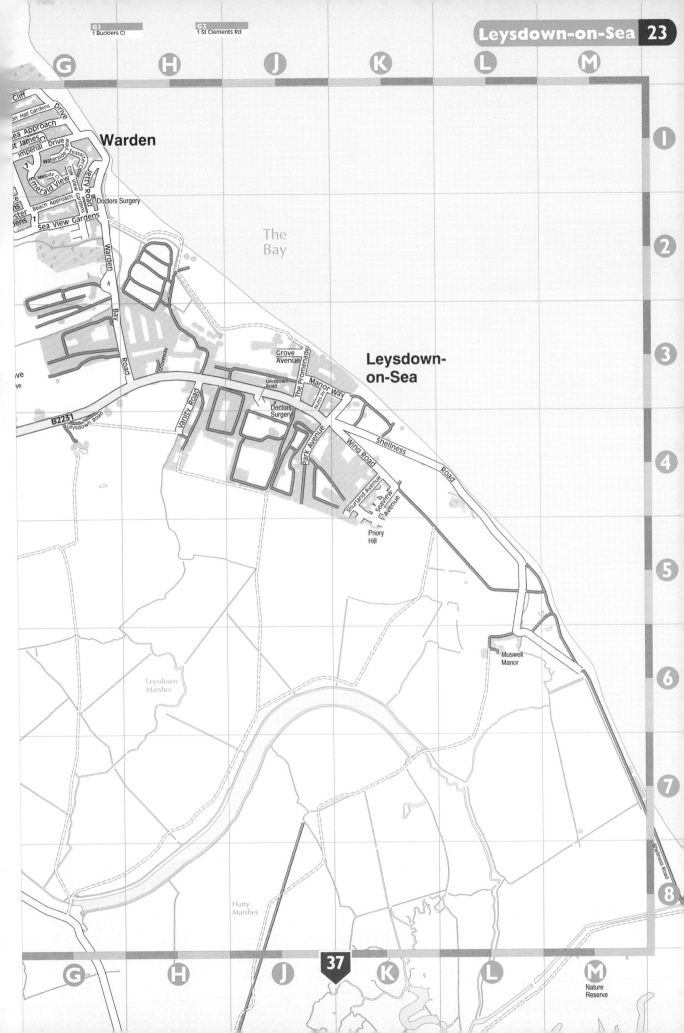

G H J K L M

1

Warden

On Hall Gardens
Sea Approach
St James
Imperial Drive
7
Waterside
Melody
Seasalter Close
Cliff View Gardens
Jetty Road
Emerald View
Beach Approach
ster
ens
7
Sea View Gardens
Doctors Surgery

The
Bay

2

Warden
Bay
Road

4

Groveway

Grove
Avenue

Leysdown-
on-Sea

3

ove
se

B2231
Leysdown Road

Leysdown
Road

The Promenade

Manor Way

Nutts Av

Vanity Road

Doctors
Surgery

9

Park Avenue

Wing Road

Sheliness

Road

4

Snurland Avenue

Seaview
Avenue

Priory
Hill

5

Muswell
Manor

6

Leysdown
Marshes

7

Sheliness Road

8

Harty
Marshes

37

G H J K L M

Nature
Reserve

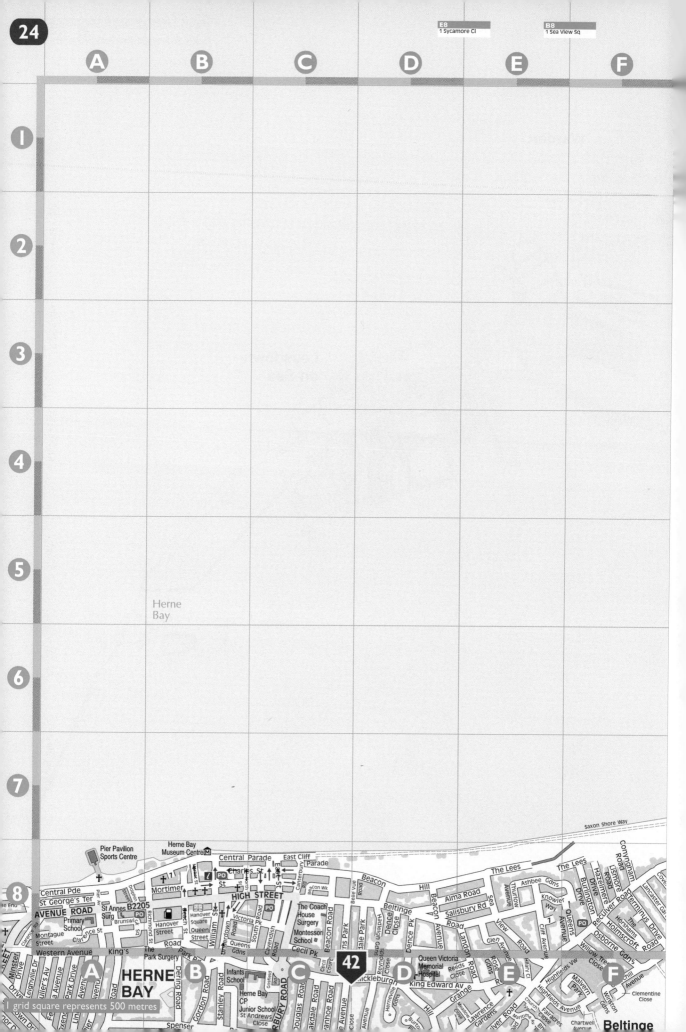

A B C D E F

1
2
3
4
5
6
7
8

Herne
Bay

Saxon Shore Way

Pier Pavilion
Sports Centre

Herne Bay
Museum Centre

Central Parade

East Cliff
Parade

The Lees

The Lees

Conyngham
Road

Central Pde

St George's Ter

Mortimer
St

Charles St

PO

Beacon
Hill

Aima Road

Ashbee Gdns

Thurlow
Avenue

Knowler
Way

Burlington
Drive

Hazelmere
Road

Lismore
Road

HIGH STREET

Beltinge
Road

Salisbury Rd

Sea
View
Road

Cliff
Avenue

Queens
Avenue

Holmscroft
Road

Reculver Road

Terminus Road

Lancaster Rd

Avenue Road

St Annes
Surg

Brunswic
St

Richmond St

Hanover
Square

Victoria Pk

Beacon
Road

Dence
Close

Dence Pk

Landon
Road

Rose
Gdns

Willow Tree
Close

Osborne Gdns

Montague
Street

Clarence St

Hanover
Street

Queen/
Street

Park R

Perdown
Road

Victoria Pk

Queens
Gdns

South
Road

Cavendish
Road

The Coach
House
Surgery

Montessori
School

Glen

Harry Rd

PO

St Andrews
Close

The
Park Surgery

King's

Cecil Pk

Cecil Road

Cecil
Court

Reynolds
Close

Beacon
Avenue

Reeds
Close

Queen Victoria
Memorial
Hospital

Highfields Vw

Highfields Avenue

Chartwell

Western Avenue

Montague
Street

Herne Bay
Primary
School

42

HERNE
BAY

Herne Bay
CP
Junior School

Infants
School

Gosfield
Road

Micklefield

King Edward Av

Grange

Church Rd

Lawrence
Gardens

Winston
Park

Clementine
Close

Beltinge

Spenser

A B C D E F

I grid square represents 500 metres

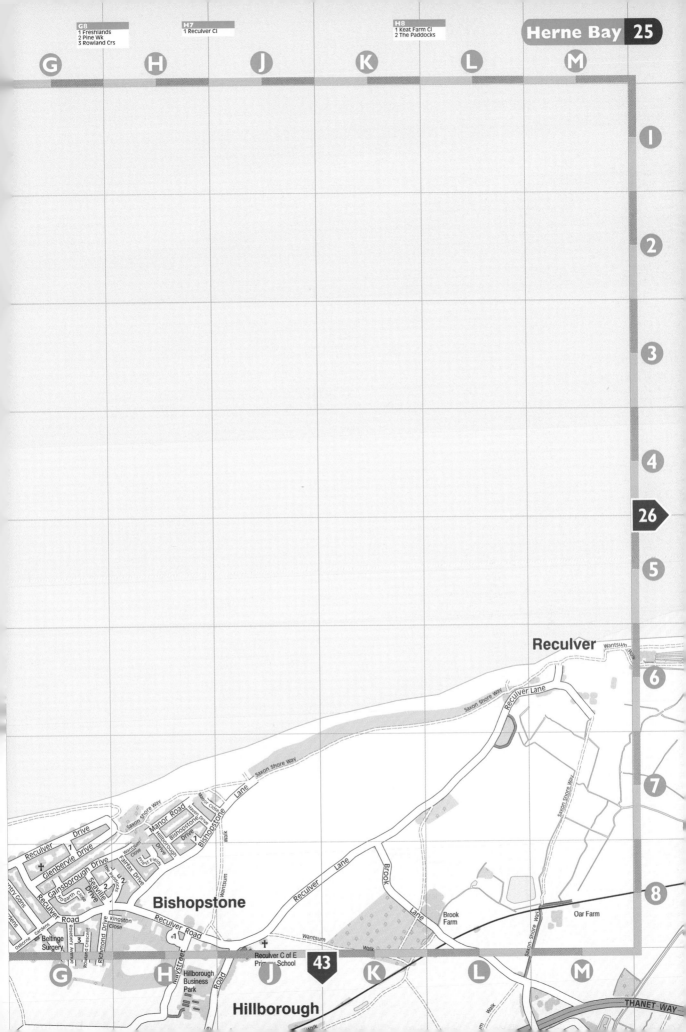

G8
1 Freshlands
2 Pine Wk
3 Rowland Crs

H7
1 Reculver Cl

H8
1 Keat Farm Cl
2 The Paddocks

G H J K L M

1
2
3
4
26
5

Reculver

Wantsum Walk
Saxon Shore Way
Reculver Lane

6

Saxon Shore Way

7

Saxon Shore Way

Recover Lane

Brook Lane

Brook Farm

Oar Farm

8

Manor Road
Manor Close
Haven Drive
Bishopstone Drive
Hillborough Drive
Bishopstone

Reculver Drive
Glenbervie Drive
Gainsborough Drive
Seaville Drive
Fairfax Drive
Hogarth Close
The Paddocks
West Fields
Wantsum Close

Bishopstone

Reculver Road

Beltinge Surgery
Osborne Gardens
Rowland Crescent
Richmond Drive
Kingston Close
Hay Street

Hillborough Business Park

Reculver C of E Primary School

43

Wantsum Walk

Hillborough

G H J K L M

THANET WAY

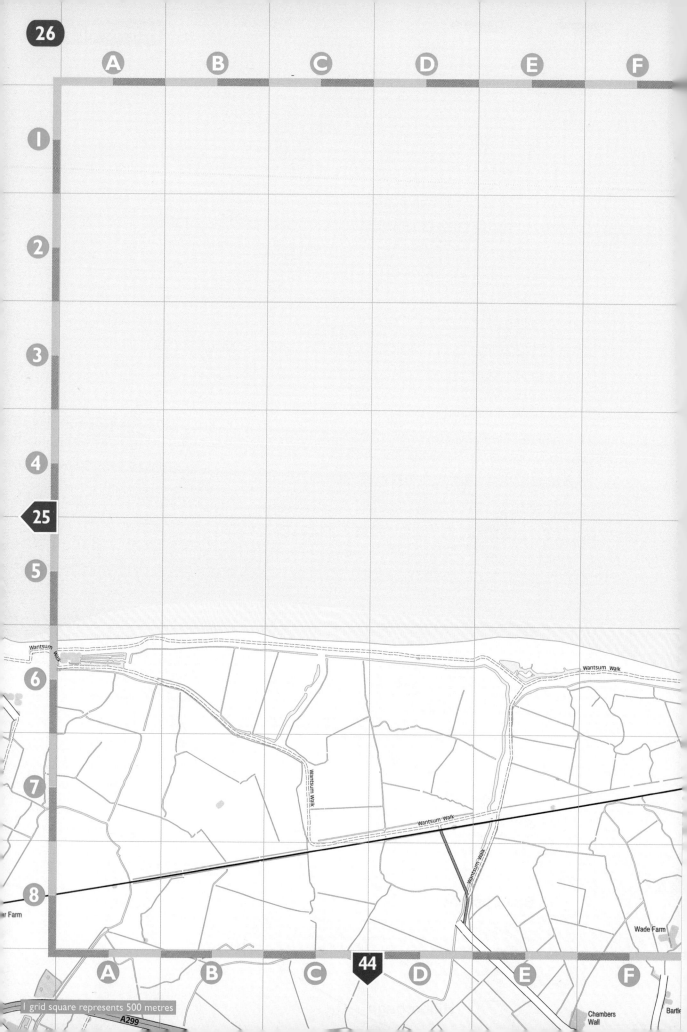

A   B   C   D   E   F

1

2

3

4

25

5

Wantsum Walk

6

Wantsum Walk

Wantsum Walk

7

Wantsum Walk

Wantsum Walk

8

ar Farm

Wade Farm

A   B   C   44   D   E   F

1 grid square represents 500 metres

A299

Chambers Wall   Bartle

G H J K L M

1

2

3

4

28

5

The Parade

Haven View Avenue

Sea V

Harold Road

Alfred Road

Ethelbert Road

Grenham Bay A

Recuiver Avenue

St Mildreds Ave

Minnis
Bay

4

7

+ +

3

The Parade

Queen's Avenue

King's Avenue

Canute Road

Minnis Road

Viking Cl

Ethelbert
Road

2

1

PO

Old Farm Road

Minnis Bay
Sailing Club

Wantsum Walk

Darynton Avenue

Dane   Road

Horsa Road

Ingoldsby Road

6

Wantsum Walk

Plumpudding
Island

LC

7

Wantsum Walk

Wade
Marsh

Great
Brooksend
Farm

8

Wantsum Walk

Shuart

45

Brooks End

G H J K L M

Shuart
Lane

Hale

A28

atts

Better

A   B   C   D   E   F

B5, C6, D6
Street Names for these grid squares are listed at the back of the index

K5, M3
Street Names for these grid squares are listed at the back of the index

1

2

3

Grenham Bay

Epple Bay

Westgate on Sea

4

27

Promenade

Esplanade   Thanet Coastal Path

Sea Road

Cliff Fld   Carlton Rd

The Parade   Thanet Coastal Path   Cliff Road
Hereward Avenue   Sea View Road   Anna Park   Herschell Rd   Beresford   Promenade   Thanet Coastal Path   Epple   Bay
5   Harold Road   Grenville Gardens   Green Road   Spencer Road   Epple Avenue   Dudley Avenue   Carlton Road West   Ryder's Av   Domneva Road
Ethelbert Road   Grenham Bay Avenue   Beach Avenue   Shakespeare Rd   St James's Terrace   Queen Bertha's Avenue   Westgate & Birchington Golf Club

Mimis Road   Recuiver Avenue   St Mildred's Avenue   Cross Road   Ocean Close   A28   Health Clinic   CANTERBURY   Hengist Rd   Linksfield Road
Horsa Road   Ingoldsby Road   Minnis Road   Birchington-on-Sea Stn   Pinnochios Galleria   Alpha   Road   St Davids Cl   The King Ethelbert School   Ursuline Convent School   Chilham Avenue
6   Old Farm   PO   Pembroke Lodge   Mus & Art Gallery   York Terrace   Marilyn Crescent   Ursuline Drive   The Warren   Lymfield Road
Central Surg   Station Road   Woodford Court   Neame Road   Wilbrough   Hoser Gardens   Anne Close   Edward Drive   Birchington   Dunstan Avenue   Allen Avenue   Dane End Close   Golden Acre Lane   Linksfield Drive

Gordon Square   Kent Gardens   Westfield   Road   Doctors Surgery   Barrington Crescent   Mountfield Way
Lincoln Gardens   Devon Gardens   Lancaster Gardens   Hereford Gardens   Charlesworth Drive   Birch Hill Court   Dovedale   Sutherland Drive   Brandon Way
Essex Gardens   Manor Drive   A28   B2048 Road   Farrar Cornford The Parkway   Laming Road   Park Road   Quex Park

7   Mill Lane   Mill Row   Norrie Rd   N Phillips Road   Sewell Close   Stone Barn Avenue   Woodland Avenue   Silver Avenue
Birchington Primary School   Holton Close   PARK   King's Road

PO   Nottingham Road   Sherwood   Alexandra Rd   Quex View Rd   Brunswick Road   LANE   Waterloo Tower   Shottendane Road
Great Brooksend Farm   Broadley Avenue   Park Avenue   King Edward Road

8

Brooks End   College Farm   CANTERBURY ROAD BIRCHINGTON   46   Q28 ACOL HILL   Hill

A   B   C   D   E   F

1 grid square represents 500 metres

A28

F7
1 Pippin Cl

F1
1 Meadow Cl

E8
1 Ashington Cl
2 Wentworth Dr

D8
1 Gainsborough Cl

A   B   C   18   D   E   F

Iwade CP
School

Fans   Evergreen
Lane   Close

Iwade

Springvale
Sheerstone
Meadow Rise

I

Funton

Saxon Shore Way

Coleshall

2

Orchard
Farm

School Lane

Culnells

3

Sheppey Way

Pheasant
Farm

Stickfast Lane

Cambray
Farm

4

Lane

Howt
Green

Belmor

Great
Norwood

Parsonage

Nether
Toes

A249(T)

5

High Oak Hill

Little
Norwood

Parsonage

Sheppey Way

Upper
Toes

Oak
Hill

Lane

Parsonage

Lane

Quinton

Avenue

Lane

6

Bobbing

Road

Cold
Harbour

Cold Harbour

Harbour

✝
Bobbing CP
School

The Meads Avenue

Vicarage Rd

Knightsfield
Road

Laxton
Way

Worcester
Grove

7

Lane

Cold Harbour Lane

Cold

Bobbing
Court

Road

B2006

STAPLEHURST RD

Windmill
Road

Cherry Grove

Derby
Grove

Howard
Road

Keycol

Rook

Grove Dairy
Farm Business
Centre

Bobbing Hill

MAIDSTONE

SHEPPEY WAY

Grove
Park CP
School

Hilton Dr

Milton
Regis

Hythe Rd

Road

A2   KEYCOL HILL

Ladyfields
Close

A249(T)

Key Street

Wellington Rd

Clive Road

Gayhurst
Drive

Sittingbourne
Industrial Park

8

Gore Court
Cricket
Club

Gibbons
Rd

Chatsworth Dr

Kenilworth Ct

Sandford Road

Chadby

Rowenden

Lonsdale

Drive

Springfield Rd

Eastwood
Road

Waterloo Rd

MAIDSTONE ROAD

Chestnut

Cherry Flds

Grove Pk Av

Brier Rd

Newlands

Avenue

Warwick Cs

Prentis Cl

A2   LONDON

Bourne
Gv

Staplehurst

Cavell Way

Well Winch Rd

Chalkwell

CHALKWELL ROAD

Doctors
Surgery

A   B   C   51   D   E   Sydney
Avenue   Adelaide Drive   F

Westlands
Secondary
School

Somerset
Close

Lydbrook
Close

Tavistock
Close

London
Road
Trading Est

Chestnut

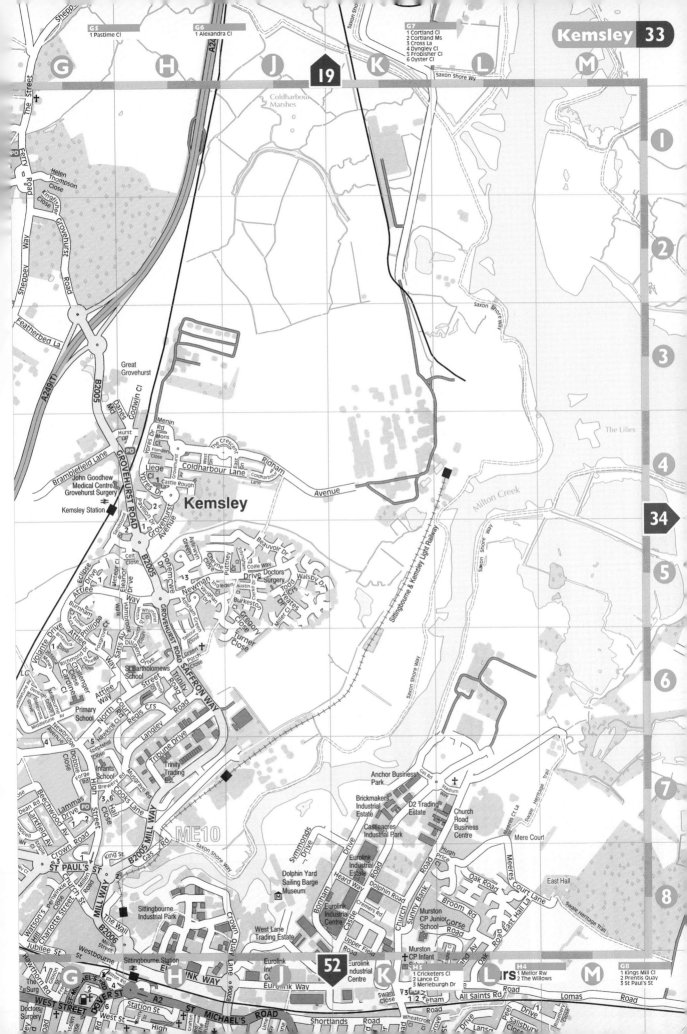

G5
1 Pastime Cl

G6
1 Alexandra Cl

G7
1 Cortland Cl
2 Cortland Ms
3 Cross La
4 Dyngley Cl
5 Frobisher Cl
6 Oyster Cl

G
H
J
K
L
M

19

Coldharbour Marshes

Saxon Sho
Saxon Shore Wy

The Lilies

1
2
3
4
34
5
6
7
8

Helen Thompson Close

Kingfisher Close

Sheppey Way

Ferry Road

Grovehurst Road

Featherbed La

B2005

A249(T)

Great Grovehurst

Danes Mdw

Godwin Cl

Menin Rd
Mons Ct

Yares Dr
Flanders Close

Hurst Lane

Bramblefield Lane

John Goodhew Medical Centre
Grovehurst Surgery

Kemsley Station

Liege Cl

Ypres Dr

Castle Rough

Grovehurst

West Cl
East Cl

The Crescent

Ridham

Coldharbour Lane

Coldharbour Lane

Kemsley

Avenue

Milton Creek

Saxon Shore Way

Eclipse Drive

Attlee

Meteor Cl

Celt Close

Eleanor Dr

Way

Aylewyn Green

Cheyne Close

Puttney

Colfe Way

Beauvoir Dr

Doctors Surgery

Walsby Dr

Ingleden

Austin Cl

Todd Crs

Yeates

Drive

Newman

Doremewe

Burnham

Phillippa

Attlee Dr

Fairway

Richmond Cl

Challenger Cl

Caratacus

Millbourne Av

Cardel Cl

Denbigh Green

Greenbank

Middletune Av

Burkesto Cl

Gregory Close

Turner Close

Green

Porch Close

Miller Cl

Vaughan

St Bartholomews School

Volante Drive

North Court

Regis Crs

Primary School

Trinity Road

SAFFRON WAY

Hawkins Cl

Langley

Sittingbourne & Kemsley Light Railway

Saxon Shore Way

Spotshill Close

Tribune Drive

Trinity Trading Est.

Newbridge Avenue

Dobble Close

Infants School

Brewery Rd

Forge Rd

Musgrave Rd

Cooks Lane

Hall Close

High Street

ME10

Beechwood Drive

Larkfield Av

Chappell

Crown Road

Dean Rd

King St

B2005 Mill Way

Gas

Saxon Shore Way

Anchor Business Park

Brickmakers Industrial Estate

Castleacres Industrial Park

D2 Trading Estate

Church Road Business Centre

Cot Rd

Stadium

Meeres Ct La

Mere Court

Swale Heritage Trail

East Hall

Swale Heritage Trail

MILL WAY

B2006

St Paul's St

The Wall

Sittingbourne Industrial Park

Crown Quay Lane

Symmonds Drive

Dolphin Yard Sailing Barge Museum

Bonham Drive

Heard Way

Eurolink Industrial Estate

Eurolink Industrial Centre

Cremers Rd

Dolphin Road

Castle Road

Church Road

Sunny Bank

Hugh Price

Murston CP Junior School

Oak Road

Broom Rd

Gorse Road

Meeres Court Lane

East Hall La

West Lane Trading Estate

Jubilee St

Westbourne St

Watson's

Charlotte Street

Periwinkle Cl

Mill Close

Millen Rd

Sittingbourne Station

LINK WAY

Eurolink Ind

Eurolink Industrial Centre

Eurolink Way

Murston
CP Infant

Swan Close

52

G
H
J
K
L
M

The Surg

Doctors Surgery

WEST STREET

DOVER ST

ST MICHAEL'S ROAD

Station St

West St

High

Shortlands

Road

A2

Peham

All Saints Rd

Lime Grove

Wheatcroft

Roseberry

Salisbury

Lomas Road

H4
1 Mellor Rw
2 The Willows

G8
1 Kings Mill Cl
2 Prentis Quay
3 St Paul's St

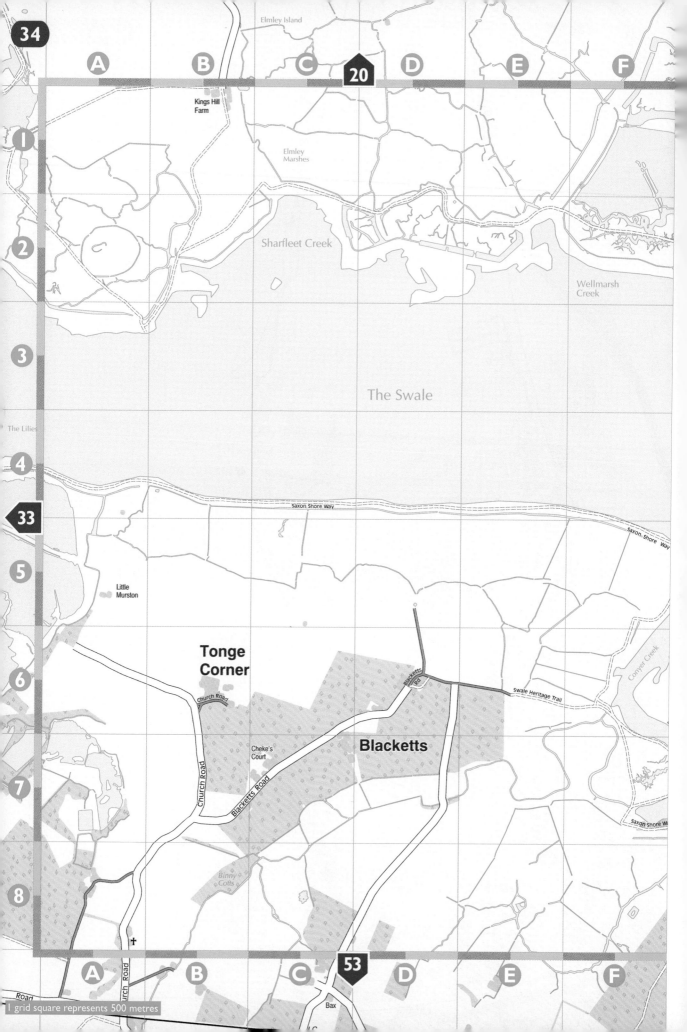

A   B   C   **20**   D   E   F

Elmley Island

Kings Hill Farm

Elmley Marshes

1

2

Sharfleet Creek

Wellmarsh Creek

3

The Swale

The Lilies

4

Saxon Shore Way

33

Saxon Shore Way

5

Little Murston

6

Tonge Corner

Church Road

Blacketts Rd

Swale Heritage Trail

Conyer Creek

Cheke's Court

Blacketts

Church Road

Blacketts Road

7

Saxon Shore Way

Binny Cotts

8

†

A   B   C   **53**   D   E   F

Church Road

Road

Bax

1 grid square represents 500 metres

G H J K L M

21

36

I
2
3
4
5
6
7
8

Bells Creek

Dutchman's
Island

Spitend
Marshes

Peg Fleet

Spitend Point

Fowley Island

South Deep

Conyer

Conyer Road

Teynham Level

The
Moorings

Brunswick
Field

Conyer Road

G H J K L M

Teynham
Street

54

Teynham
Court

Luddenham
Marshes

A   B   C   22   D   E   F

1

2

3

Mocketts

4

35

The Ferry
Inn

Harty Ferry Road

5

6

7

Nature
Reserve

Uplees

Uplees Road

Howletts

8

A   B   C   55   D   E   F

Poplar Hall

Court
Ledge

1 grid square represents 500 metres

G   H   J   23   K   L   M

Harty
Marshes

Nature
Reserve

1

Elliots
Farm

2

Isle of
Harty

3

4

38

5

Sayes
Court

The Swale

6

Saxon Shore Way

7

Cleve
Marshes

8

Nagden
Marshes

Saxon Shore Way

Graveney
Marshes

A   B   C   D   E   F

2

3

4

5

6

Seasalter
Sailing
Club

Faversham Road

7

Graveney
Marshes

8

A   B   57   C   D   E   F

grid square represents 500 metres

G   H   J   K   L   M

nkerton Bay

I

WHITSTABLE   2

A M F Bowling   Beach

Whitstable Yacht Club

HARBOUR STREET   Westgate Ter   Whit Cen

Cromwell   Reserv   Whit

Sea Wall   3

Horsebridge Road

Peter's St   Albert Street   Diamond

Harbour Gallery   Regent St   Warwick Road   Acton Road   Road

Lower Island

HIGH STREET   PO   School   Hamilton Road   Wheat

Waterloo Rd   Middle Wall   Kg Edward St   Beresford

Marine Gap   Argyle Rd   Cromwell Rd

Playhouse Theatre   Salts   Whitstable Mus & Gallery

Infant School   Cl   4   Statron

Daniel's Ct   Collingwood Road   Nelson Road   The Oxford Street Health Clinic   Whitstable County Junior School

Island Wall   West Cliff   Belmont Road   40

Whitstable & Seasalter Golf Club

Clifton Road   PO   Swinfield   Vale Rd   5

CANTERBURY ROAD   Harwich Rd   Hillview   Green Lane   Grimsell Road   Norman Rd   Gosselin St

Alexandra Road   Glebe Way   Suffolk Rd   Essex Rd   Kent Rd   Maugham Court   Saddleton

Maugham Court   Gordon   Paddock View   6

Stanley Rd   Hunters

Seasalter

Seasalter Beach   Lane   Meteor Av   Valkyrie Av   Columbia Avenue   Joy Lane County Infant School   Dove Close   Vulcan Close   Grosvenor Rd   Windmill Rd   Stanley Rd   Duncan Down

Joy   Medina   Shamrock   Cypress   Shearwater Avenue   B2205   Bayview Road

Admiralty Wk   Fairway Crs   Florence Avenue   Britannia Av   Kingfisher Close   Pierpoint Rd   Millers Court

Parade   George's Cl   Somerset Close   Field View   Osprey Cl   Grimthorpe Avenue   Clovelly Road

Preston   Bowwer St   Mary's Grove   Ashley Dr   Hazlemere Road   Dorset Cl   Norview Rd   Martindown Road   Spring Wk   7

Hodgson Road   Eden Rd   Sandpiper Road   Swallow Av   The Hts   Meadow Walk   BORSTAL HILL   Benacre Road

Allan Road   Miller Rd   Macdonald Parade   Doctors Surgery   Sunset Close   Sherwood Drive   Lamb's Wk

Wauchope Rd   Faversham Road   The Grange   Anthony   Sheppey View   Long Reach Cl   PO

Lucerne Drive   Kimberley Grove   Roberts Rd   Ladysmith Grove   Jayne Walk   CT5   South View Road   Clapham Hill   7

Bridge Country Leisure Club   Seasalter Cross   Freeman's Close   Church   Wrak Hill   Montpelier Avenue

Lane   THANET WAY   A299   A290   8

A299   Wellington Street   Marlborough Road

Seasalter Level   Willow Road   Royal Av   Willow Road   **Clapham Hill**

Ladysmith Road   CLAPHAM HILL   A290   Bogshole

Seasalter Way   Pilgrims   alk Lane

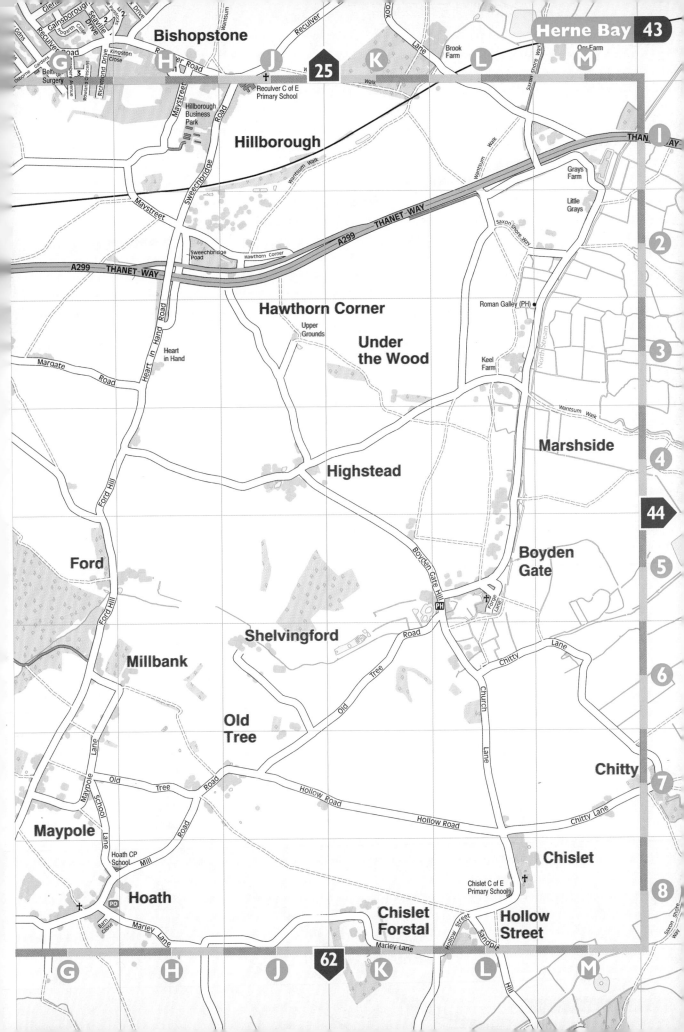

Bishopstone

G   H   J   25   K   L   M

Reculver

Reculver C of E
Primary School

Hillborough Business Park

Hillborough

Brook Farm

Walk

Orr Farm

Maystreet

Sweechbridge Road

Wantsum Walk

Saxon Shore Way

THAN... ...AY   1

A299   THANET WAY

Grays Farm

Little Grays

Saxon Shore Way

2

A299   THANET WAY

Sweechbridge Road

Hawthorn Corner

North Stream

Hawthorn Corner

Upper Grounds

Roman Galley (PH)

Margate   Road

Heart in Hand Road

Heart in Hand

Under the Wood

Keel Farm

3

Wantsum   Walk

Marshside

4

Highstead

44

Ford Hill

Ford

Boyden Gate Hill

Boyden Gate

5

PH

Forge Lane

Shelvingford

Road

Chitty   Lane

6

Millbank

Old   Tree   Road

Church   Lane

Chitty   7

Old Tree

Maypole Lane

Old   Tree   Road

Hollow Road

Hollow Road

Chitty Lane

Maypole

Hoath CP School

Mill   School   Lane

Hollow Road

Chislet

Hoath

PO

Barn Close

Marley Lane

Chislet C of E
Primary School

8

Chislet Forstal

Marley Lane

Hollow Street

Sandpit

Hollow Street

Saxon Shore Way

G   H   J   62   K   L   M

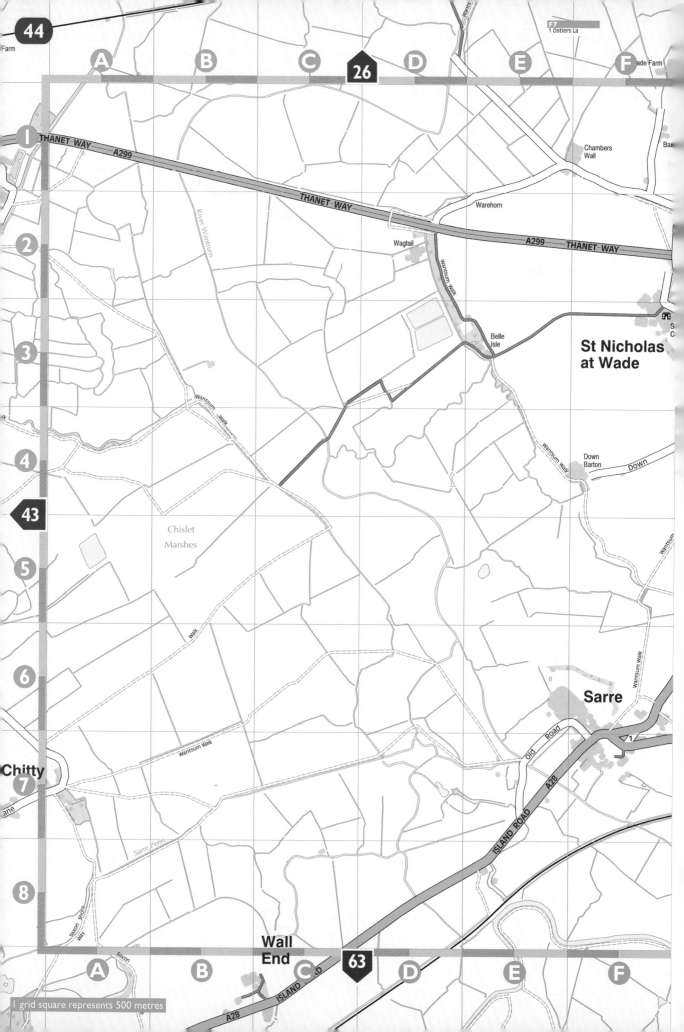

H3
1 Musgrave Cl
2 Tollemache Cl

L8
1 Primrose Wy

M4
1 The Green

Chal Farm

G

H

J

29

K

L

M

1

Two Chimneys

Woodchurch Road

Westgate Avenue

Queendown Road

Castle Mayne Avenue

Trafalgar Road

St Margarets Road

Vincent Farm

Vincent Road

Flete Farm

2

B2050

Woodchurch Road

Manston Road

MANSTON ROAD

Cheeseman's Farm

Grange Lane

Preston Road

3

Alland Grange Lane

Esmonde

2 1

R A F Manston History Museum
M

B2050

Alland Grange

Beaumont Cl

Bell-Davies Drive

Saint Catherine's Grove

Spra

4

B2190

Kent International Airport

Manston Court Road

Manston

1

High Street

PO

B2050

ON

48

5

Bush Farm

A253

Wy Cottage Hill

Way Hill

Way

Thorne Hill

Thorne Farm

King Arthur Road

Arundel Road

Windsor Road

6

Grinsell Hill

Cliff View Road

Foads Hill

Sea View Road

CANTERBURY ROAD W

Clive Road

LC

7

Cliffs End

1 2

1

Earlsmead Crescent

H pIO

Noyes Close

Del's

1

Lane

Cliffs

End

Meverall Avenue

Mount Green Avenue

SANDWICH ROAD

8

Sevenscore

Cottington

LC

LC

St Augustines Golf Club

St Augustines Cross

Cottington Road

Beech Grove

PO

Nicholas Drive

Foads

Cliffs End Grove

Oakland Court

Walmer Gardens

G

H

J

66

K

L

M

M8
1 Greystones Rd

M7
1 Richardson Wy
2 Sceales Dr

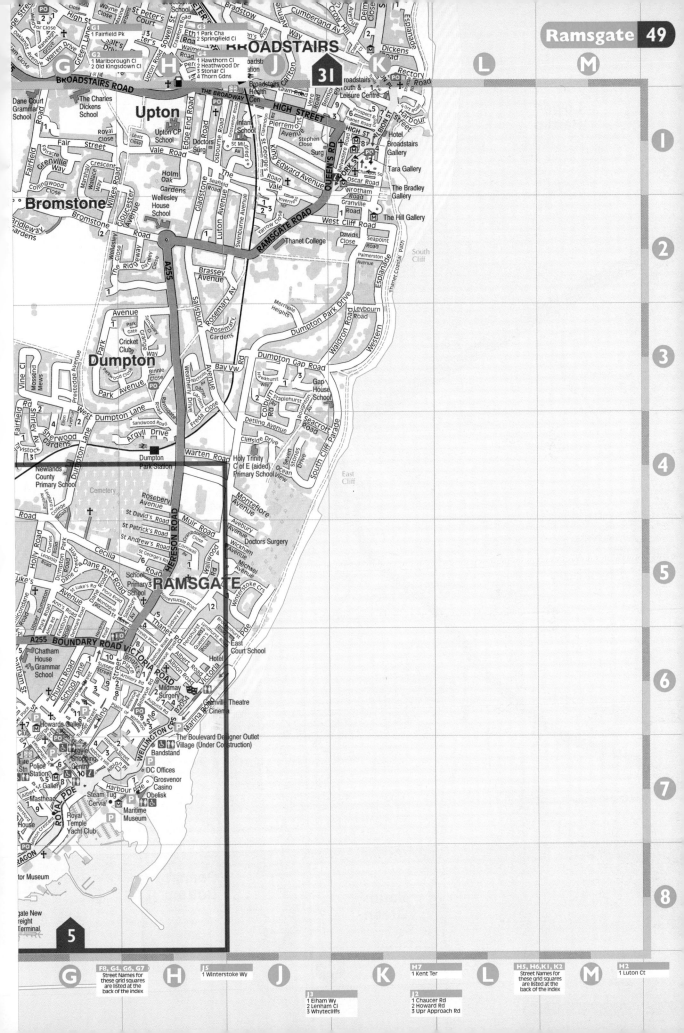

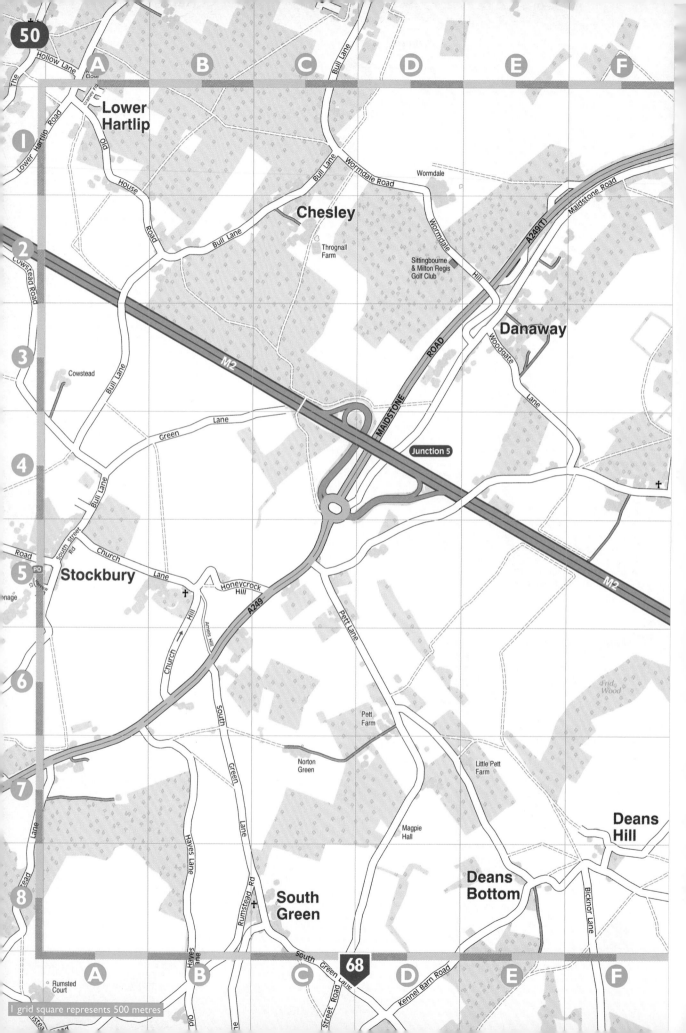

The
Hollow Lane
Lower Hartlip Road
Old House Road

Lower Hartlip

A   B   C   Bull Lane   D   E   F

1

Bull Lane
Wormdale Road
Wormdale

Chesley

Thrognall Farm

Wormdale Hill

Sittingbourne & Milton Regis Golf Club

A249(T)

Maidstone Road

Cowstead Road

2

Danaway

Bull Lane

Cowstead

M2

Woodgate Lane

3

Green   Lane

MAIDSTONE ROAD

4

Junction 5

Bull Lane

South Street Rd

Church   Lane

Road

PO

Stockbury

5

Honeycrock Hill

Church Hill

Arnels Hill

A249

Pett Lane

M2

Parsonage

6

South Green Lane

Frid Wood

Pett Farm

7

Haves Lane

Norton Green

Little Pett Farm

Deans Hill

Lane

Rumstead Rd

Magpie Hall

Deans Bottom

8

South Green

Bicknor Lane

Rumsted Court

A   B   South   C   68   D   Kennel Barn Road   E   F

South Green Lane

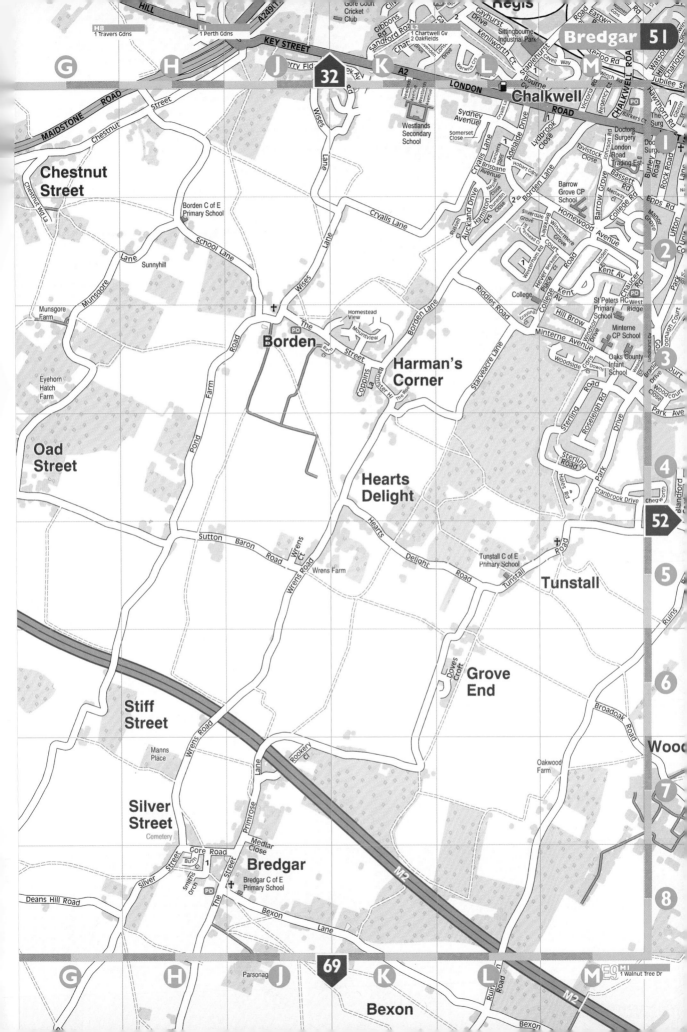

L3 1 Morello Cl
M3 1 Cherry Tree Cl
Binny Cotts

G   H   J   `34`   K   L   M

Bax

LC

LC

I

Scraps Hill

Lower Road

Church Road

Hempstead Lane

Lower Road

Teynham Station

Barrow Green

2

Bapchild

THE STREET

A2

Teynham

Orchard Vw

Baker

Harrys Ct

Roper Road

The Crescent

Conver Rd

Osier

Domeday Close Dr
Lords Close Dr
Wihtred Road
Panteny Lane

Honeyball Wk

Broada Cre

Roundel Close

3

Dully Road

LONDON

ROAD

Radfield

Frognal Lane

Frognal Close

Teynham Parochial
C of E (Controlled)
Primary School

Belle Friday Cl

Station

Rivers Road

Amber

Bradfield

Nutberry Close

Avenue

Haywood

Little Dully

Claxfield Road

Frognal Gdns

Donald Moor Av

New Gardens

Cherry Gdns

Nobel Close

Teynham Medical Centre

PO

†

Doctors Surgery

Cellarhill

A2

4

LONDON

`54`

Upper Newla

Batteries Close

Lynsted Lane

Cellar Hill

Nouds Road

5

Nouds

Dully House

Wood

Street

Claxfield Road

Batteries Farm

Lynsted Lane

Bogle

Road

Nouds Farm

6

Dully Road

Lynsted CP School

†

Tenacre

Nouds Lane

Tickham

Tickham Lane

7

The Street

The Vallance

Aymers

Lynsted

Park Farm

Mill

Lane

Loyterton

8

Ludgate

Ludgate Road

Monks Farm

Kingsdown

Lynsted Park

A B C 35 D E F

I

Teynham
Street

Teynham
Court

Conyer Road

Swale Heritage Trail

Luddenham
Marshes

2
arrow
reen

Osier Road

Conyer Road

Osiers Farm

rescent
acre

Roundel
Close

3

Lower Road

Swale Heritage Trail

Deerton
Street

Swale Heritage Trail

Elverton

The Old
Farmhouse

LC

4

LONDON

ROAD

Lower
Newlands

Mockbeggar

LC

Stone Farm

Lower Road

53

uds Rd

5

Lewson

Upper
Newlands

Norton Road

Norton Ash

LONDON   ROAD

A2

Nouds

Street

World's End

Provender Road

6
uds Farm

Norton Road

Lewson
Street

Barbary Farm

Lane

Tickham

Tic

Lane

7

Norton Road

Provender Rd

Faversham Road

8

Coxett Hill

Monks
Farm

A B C 72 D Putt Wood E

Faversham Road

F

J7, M7
Street Names for
these grid squares
are listed at the
back of the index

M2

G H J K L M

36

I 2 3 4 56 5 6 7 8

J4
1 Ivory Cl

J6
1 Sumpter Wy

K3
1 Colegates Ct

K4
1 Maitland Ct
2 Wreight Ct

J5
1 Athol Pl
2 Cremier Pl

56

Queen Elizabeth School

Poplar Hall

Court Lodge

Luddenham Court

Oare

Nash's Farm

Ham Farm

Four Oaks

Luddenham CP School

The Brents

Upper Brents Industrial Estate

Springhead Road
Larksfield
Broomfield Road
Brook Road
Upper Brents

Bysing Wood Road

Davington Primary School

St Mary of Charity C of E Junior & Infant School

Davington

Bysing Wood CP School

Penshurst Rise

Faversham Cottage Hosp

Arden Theatre

Health Cen

Faversham Station

Preston

Wesley Sports Centre

Arthur Salmon Cl

St Nicholas Road

Ospringe C of E School

Osspringe

Osspringe Place

Perry Court

The Abbey School

Beaumont Davy Cl

Westwood Place

Faversham Town Football Club

Preston Park

LONDON ROAD
A2
OSPRINGE STREET
LONDON ROAD
ASHFORD ROAD A251

WESTERN LINK
B2045

G6
1 Elliots Pl
2 Garfield Pl
3 Solomons La
4 William St

H5
1 Conduit St
2 Lammas Ga

L6
1 Beckett St
2 Caslocke St
3 Fielding St
4 Mendfield St
5 Millstream Cl
6 Runnymede Ms
7 Water La

L5
1 Stonedane Ct
2 Woodgate Cl

M5
1 Admiralty Cl
2 Stephens Cl

L7
1 Aldred Rd
2 Ethelred Ct

K6
1 Capel Rd

A8
1 Blenheim Av
2 Worcester Cl

A7
1 Buttermere

A6
1 Bob Amor Cl
2 Ch. Drayson Ct
3 Minster Rd

A **B** **C** 37 **D** **E** **F**

I

Nagden
Marsh

Saxon Shore Way

Graveney
Marshes

Nagden

2

Ham
Marshes

Broom
Street

3

Ham Farm

Sandbanks Road

Saxon Shore Wy

Sand Banks

4

Saxon Shore Way

Upper Brents
Industrial
Est

Vinson

Goosefields

PO

55

Abbey Fields

Abbey
Road

5

Queen Elizabeths
School

Langdon
Court

FAVERSHAM

Fields

Gordon Rd

Gordon
Square

St Mary of Charity
C of E Junior & Infant
School

Cyprus Rd

Westgate Rd

Luton Rd

Abbey

Cole
Rd

Arden Rd

Abbots Road

St Saviour's Cl

Cluny Rd

Cheney Rd

Swale Heritage Trail

Goodnesto

Orchard
Pl

Central
Pk

St John's Rd

Park Road

Millfield

Road

6

ST

B2040 **WHITSTABLE ROAD**

Faversham
Industrial Estate

Graveney Road

Whitstable Road

Cemetery

B2040

Lady Dane Farm

Ewell Farm

Preston

Windermere

Winnerdale

LOVE LANE

Homestall
Lane

Head

Thanet Way

A299

7

Preston
Park

Preston Avenue

Maidenside Avenue

Bramley Avenue

Russet
Avenue

Laxton Way

PO

Homestall

CANTERBURY

Faversham Town
Football Club

8

Selling Road

ROAD

A2

M2

tion 7

Bren   ner

Nash

Canterbury

A **B** **C** 74 **D** **E** **F**

1 grid square represents 500 metres

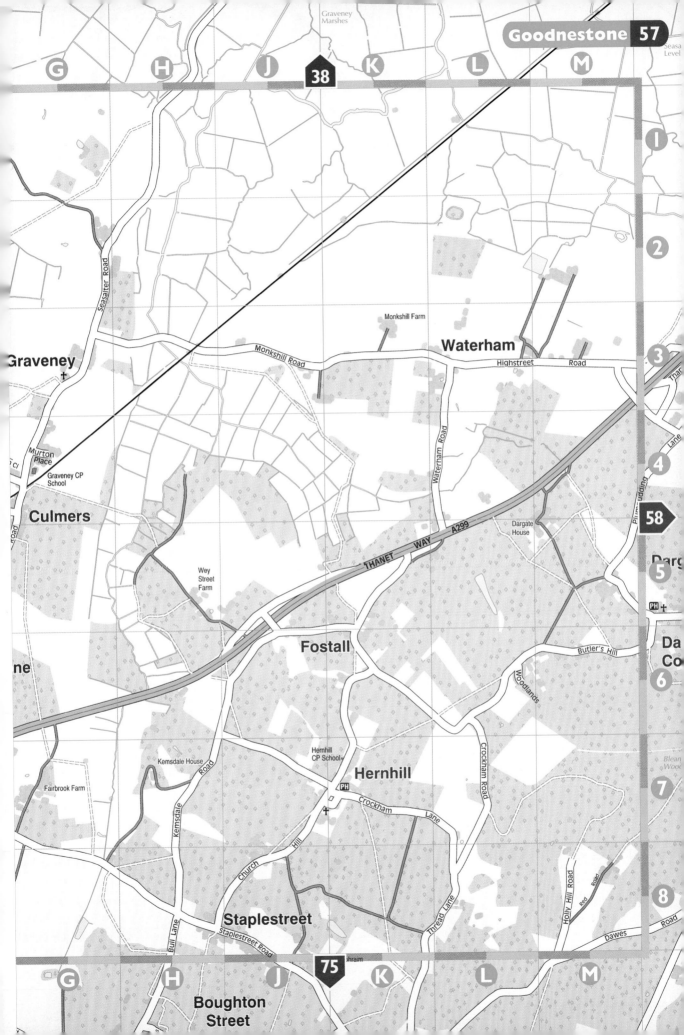

G H J K L M

38

I

2

Graveney Marshes

Seasa Level

Monkshill Farm

Waterham

Monkshill Road

Highstreet Road

Graveney
✝

3

Thar

Murton Place

Graveney CP School

4

Waterham Road

Culmers

Dargate House

A299 THANET WAY

58

5

Dar

PH ✝

Wey Street Farm

Fostall

Butler's Hill

Woodlands

Da Co

6

Kemsdale House

Kemsdale Road

Hernhill CP School ✝

Crockham Road

Blean Wood

7

Fairbrook Farm

Hernhill

PH

✝

Crockham Lane

Thread Lane

Holly Hill Road

Red Road

8

Church Hill

Staplestreet

Bull Lane

Staplestreet Road

hraim

Dawes Road

G H J K L M

Boughton Street

Church Road

Hicks Forstal Road

H6
1 Bournes Cl

H7
1 Delaware Cl

G H J **42** K L M

Knave's Ash

Blean Wood

West Blean House

Wealden Forest Park

Hicks Forstal

Hicks Forstal Road

Rushbourne Manor

I

Buckwell

2

Woodlands Farm

Hoath Road

3

Calcott

Tile Lodge Farm

4

Hersden CP School

Hoades Court

Bredlands Lane

62

Maple Grd

5

HERNE BAY ROAD A291

Hawcroft Farm

Stonerocks Farm

A28

Montgomery Grant Maintained School

Pennington Close

Westbere

6

Sweechgate

Oak

Hawe Lane

Popes Lane

Redcot Lane

Hoath Road

Church Lane

Bushy Hill Road

Walnut Tree Lane

Den Grove Wood

Deansway Av

River View

McCarthy Av

Woodside Rd

Heath View

Delfne Road

Ladywood Rd

St Nicholas Close

Sturry C of E Primary School

Paffard Close

Chestnut Drive

Oakwood Road

Hoades Road

Laburnum Lane

Oak Hill

Oaklands Way

Baps

Westbere Lane

Church Lane

Hillview

Risdon Close

Cemetery

Whatmer Close

Well Close

Westbere Marshes

Broadlands

Park

Meadow Road

Rowan Close

Cedar Close

Hudson Close

Sleigh Road

The Coppins

Road

Twyne Road

Homefield Road

SLAND ROAD

Fairview Gdns

Fairview Gardens

STURRY

7

STURRY HILL A291

A28

LC

Court Sturt Mews

Forge Close

Sturry Station

8

PO

The Junior Kings School

Church La

High Street

Marlow Meadow

Fordwich Road

Brooklands Close

1 2

MILL ROAD

King Street

Spring Lane

PH

The Di

Higham Farm

Stour Valley Walk

G H J **79** K L M

A B C 45 D E F

I

2

Saxon Shore Way

Plucks Gutter

Saxon Shore Way

Saxon Shore Way

Stour Valley Way

3

School Lane

The Street

East Stourmouth

4

The

Stour Valley Way

5

Santon Lane

Santon Farm

Lower Santon Lane

Stour Valley Way

Westmarsh

Molland Lane

6

Wingham Barton Manor

Wass Drove

Paramour Street

Stour Valley Way

Molland Lane

7

Sheerwater

Ware

Fradbrook Lane

Sheerwater Road

Great Knell Farm

8

† **Elmstone**

Hoaden House

Lane

Molland Lane

Church Hill Farm

A B C **82** D E F

Hoaden

Ovenden Farm

I grid square represents 500 metres

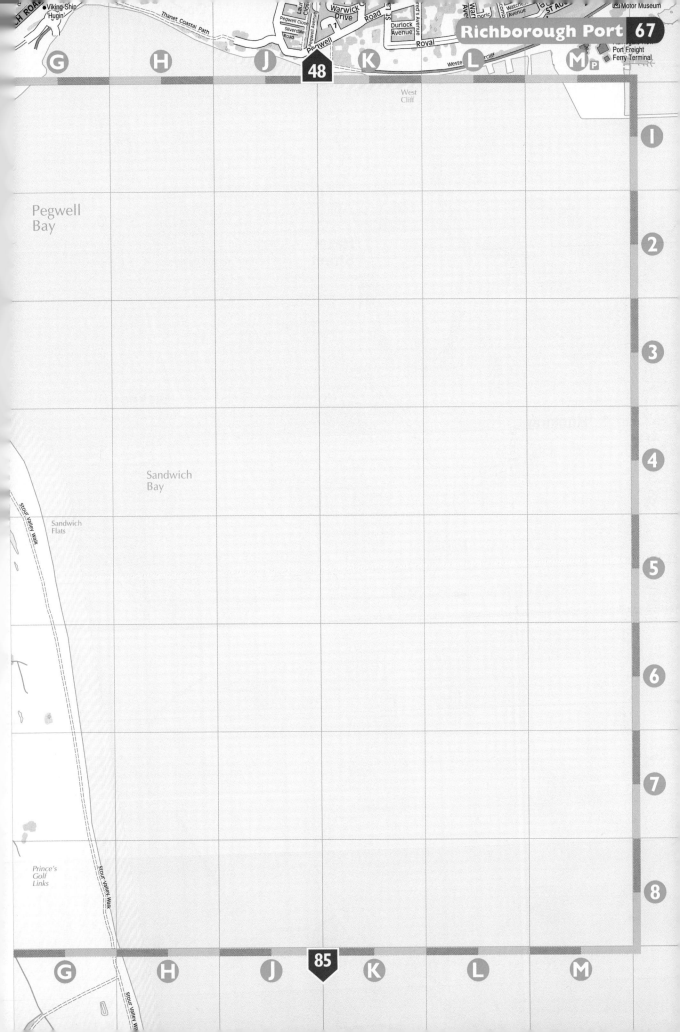

Viking Ship
Hugin

Thanet Coastal Path

Laur
Warwick
Drive
Road
St La
Durlock
Avenue
Royal
Weste
rcliff
Ware
nonic
Avenue
Watch
Avenue
ST AU
Motor Museum

Pegwell Close
Silverdale
Road
Pegwell
Pegwell Avenue

Port Freight
Ferry Terminal

West
Cliff

G   H   J   48   K   L   M P

Pegwell
Bay

Stour Valley Walk

Sandwich
Bay

Sandwich
Flats

Prince's
Golf
Links

Stour Valley Walk

G   H   J   85   K   L   M

Stour Valley Walk

1
2
3
4
5
6
7
8

Deans Hill Road

Silver

Smiths orch

PO

Bredgar C of E Primary School

The Street

Bexon

G

H

J

51

K

L

M

ME9

M2

I

Parsonage Farm

Bexon

Ruins Barn Road

Bexon Lane

2

Blind Mary's Lane

Bashford Barn Lane

Bottom Pond Road

Swanton Street

3

Bottom Pond Road

Trundle Wood

Bottom Pond

High Wood

Norwood

Stock Wood

4

70

5

Bedmonton

Saywell Farm

Frinsted

Copes

6

Kippen

The Street

Dray's Field

Mattinson Place

Wormshill

Yewtree Farm

7

Oorlair

Park Farm

Yoke's Court

8

Madam's Court

Lord's Hill

G

Post

RinglH**tone**

J

87

K

L

M

PH

Ringlestone Road

E9

A   B   C   **52**   D   E   F

Broadoak

Pitstock Farm

Penfield House

I

2

3

Milstead

Horn Hill

Frinsted Road

Broadoak Road

Pond Bottom

Rawling Street

Cheney H

Slough

Penfield Lane

Penfield Road

Pitstock Road

Mintching Wood Lane

Sawpit Road

Kingsdown Road

Dungate

M2   M2

Mintching Wood

Kingsdown Wood

4

69

Milstead Manor Farm

Milstead & Frinsted C of E Primary School

Manor Road

Hollybushes

Bluetown

Great Higham

5

Down Court

6

Kippen

Torry Hill

Little Higham

West End

7

Timbold Hill

Coalpit Lane

Yoke's Court

8

Syndale Bottom

Old Lenham Road

Faversham Road

Wichling

Solomon Temple

Temple Farm

A   B   C   **88**   D   E   F

Wichling Wood

Filmer Wood

1 grid square represents 500 metres

54

A   B   C   D   E   F

Monks
Farm

I

Norton
Road

Rushett

Putt Wood

Faversham Road

Hanslett's
House

Hanslett's Lane

2

Stuppington
Farm

M2

Well
Lane

Hillside

3

College
Wood

Elverland Lane

Eastling Road

Faversham Road

Elverland

71

North
Eastling
Road

4

ampion
urt

North
Eastling
House

Box
Lane

5

Scooks
Farm House

Stalisfield Road

6

North
Court

Newnham Lane

Eastling Road

7

Eastling

Meesen's Close

Eastling Road

The Street

PH

Otterden Road

Kettle Hill Road

Eastling
CP School

Pett
Dane

Stalisfield Road

Belmont

New
York

8

ng Hou

Pinks
Farm

Town
Place

A   B   C   D   E   F

90

Hayward's   Hill

Arnold's Oak
Farm

Ke

55

Faversham Town
Football Club

Perry Court

The Abbey
School

Ashford Rd

West
Place

I

M2

Junction 6

Westwood
Court

2

Whitehill

Little
Brook

Copton

3

Painter's
Forstal

Lorenden

Forstal Road

Eastling Road

Porter's Lane

Selgrove

A251

PH

Bayfield

Plumford

ASHFORD ROAD

The Oaks

Abbots Hill

Water
Lane

Lane

Abbots

Cades
orch

Churchman's
Farm

Kennaways

Plumford Road

Littles
Farm

North Street

74

4

5

Throwley Road

Plumford Road

Gosmere

Pidgeon
Cott

6

Newhouse
Farm

Newhouse Lane

ME13

Wilgate Green Road

Throwley
House (Hotel)

Sheldwich

7

Faversham
Golf Club Ltd

Wilgate
Green

Badgins Road

ASHFORD ROAD

Lees Court

Hunters Way

Sheldwich
CP School

South
Wilderton

Old

Cobrahamsole
Farm

Amos Close

West Barrow

Nursery Lane

Morgan kirby's
Garden

Sheldwich Lees

8

Parsonage Stocks Road

Bagshill
Road

Parsonage
Farm

91

Lords
Farm

Abbots Road

G   H   J   K   L   M

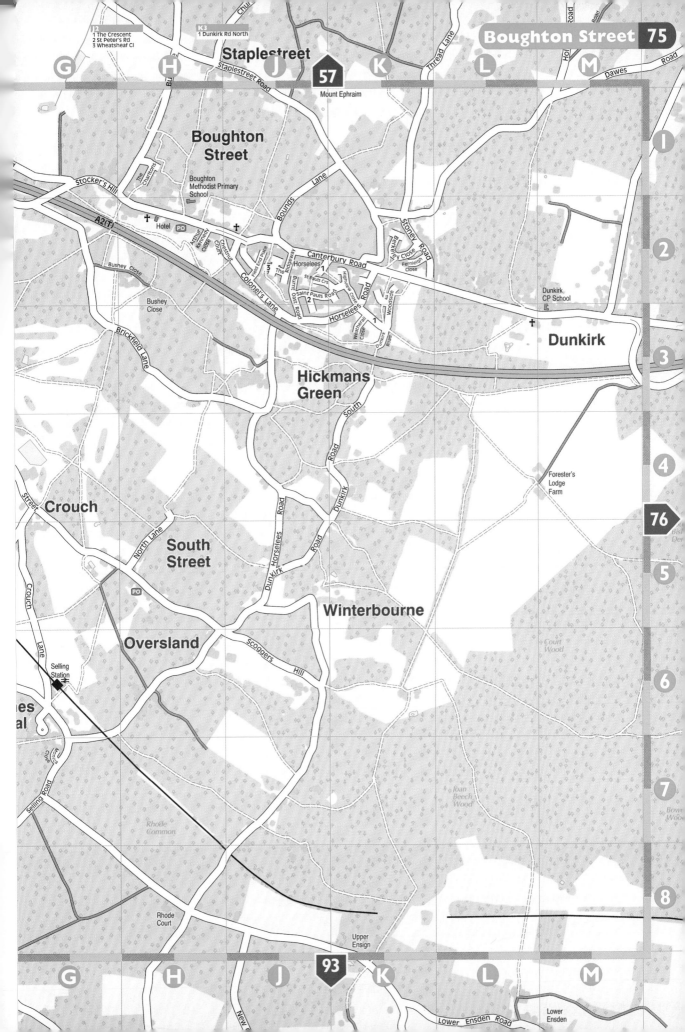

G   H   J   K   L   M

57
Mount Ephraim

76

93

G   H   J   K   L   M

J2
1 The Crescent
2 St Peter's Rd
3 Wheatsheaf Cl

K3
1 Dunkirk Rd North

Staplestreet

Staplestreet Road

**Boughton
Street**

Stocker's Hill

A2(T)

Church Lane

Thread Lane

Holt Road

Dawes Road

Boughton
Methodist Primary
School

Hotel   PO

Arthur Kennedy Close

Chestnut Court

Colonel's Lane

Bushey Close

Bushey
Close

Brickfield Lane

Bounds Lane

Field End Place

The Ridges

Burnt Oast Road

Saint Pauls Road

St Pauls Crs

Horselees

Canterbury Road

Highfield Close

Horselees
Road

Weatherall Close

Dunkirk Road

Stoney Road

Berkeley Close

Fernleigh Close

Woodside

Dunkirk

Dunkirk
CP School

**Hickmans
Green**

South Road

Dunkirk Road

Horselees Road

Dunkirk Road

Forester's
Lodge
Farm

Crouch

North Lane

Crouch Lane

**South
Street**

PO

Oversland

Winterbourne

Scoggers Hill

Selling
Station

Selling Road

Monk's Close

Court
Wood

**es
al**

Joan Beech
Wood

Bower
Wood

Rhode
Common

Rhode
Court

Upper
Ensign

Lower Ensden Road

Lower
Ensden

New Road

I   2   3   4   5   6   7   8

A   B   C   58   D   E   F

Dawes Road

Co

I

Courtenay
Farm

Bossenden
Farm

North
Bishopden
Wood

New Road

Church Wood

2

3   A2(T)

Stumps
Farm

Fishpond
Wood

Denstead Lane

4

75   South
Bishops
Den

Denstead
Farm

5

Denstead
Wood

Petty
France

6

Denstead Lane

Primrose Hill

Chartham
Hatch

7   Bower
Wood

Town Lane

Nightingale
Close

New Town Street

8

Nickle
Farm

North Downs Way

Hatch Lane

A   B   C   94   D   E   F

LC

1 grid square represents 500 metres

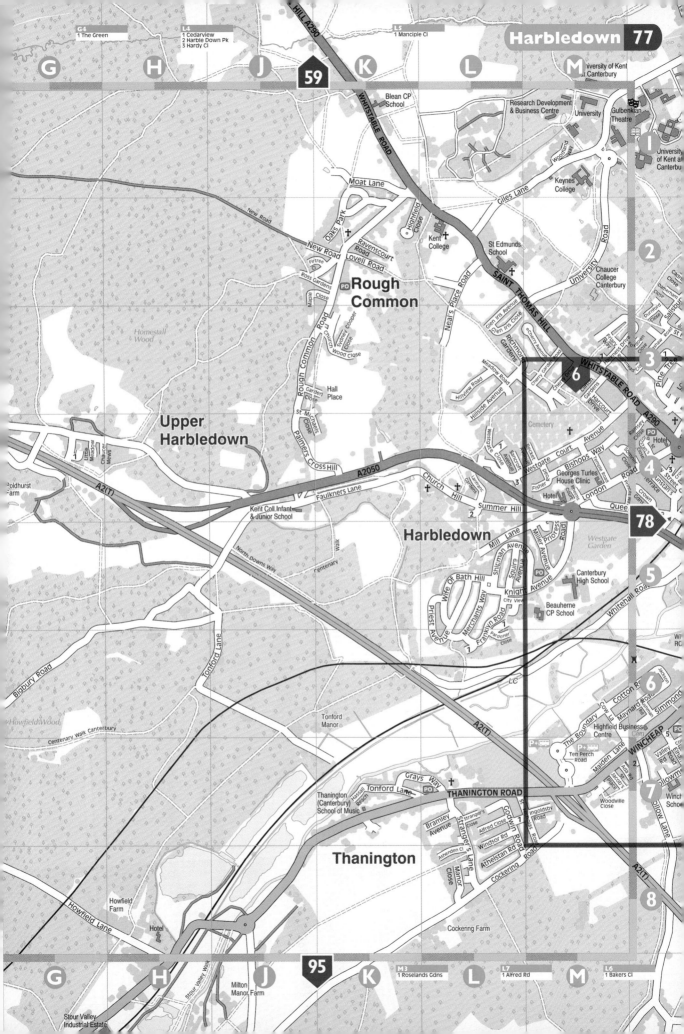

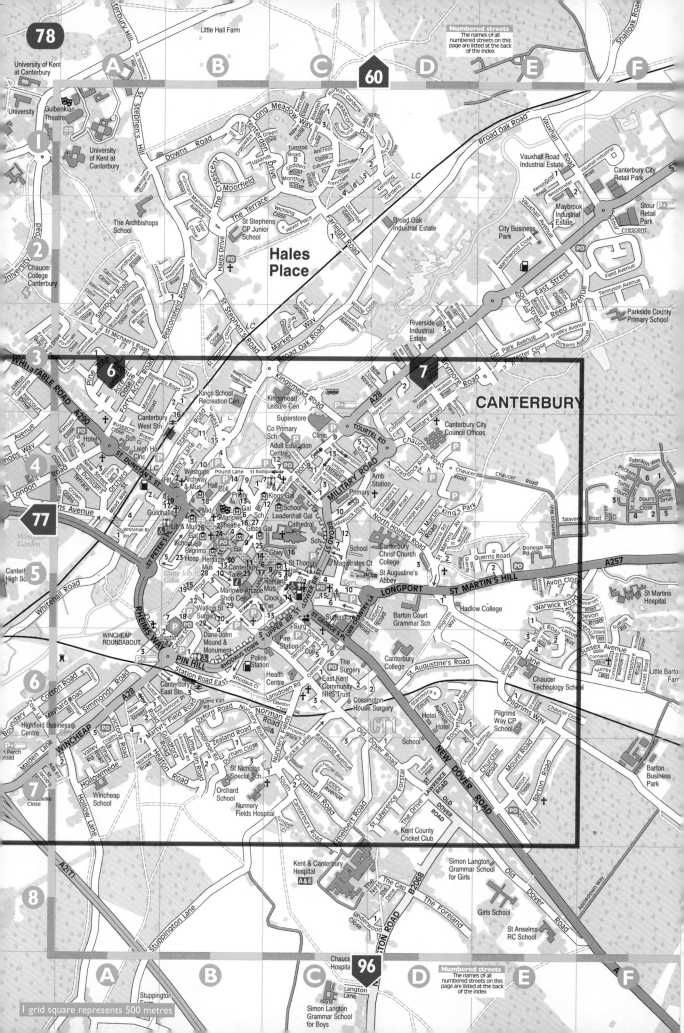

61

80

97

G H J K L M

Sturry Station

H1 1 Marlow Mdw
2 Water Mdw
The Kings School
PO

H1 1 Yew Tree Gdns

Forge Close

Marlow Meadow

Fordwich Road

Brooklands Close

A28 MILL ROAD

MILL

King Street The Drove

PH

High Street

Moat Lane

Well Lane

Spring Lane

Fordwich

Stour Valley Walk

Higham Farm

Stour Valley Walk

Stodmarsh Road

Oldridge Wood

Swanton Lane

Canterbury Christ Church College

Canterbury Golf Club

Polo Farm Sports Club

LITTLEBOURNE ROAD

CANTERBURY ROAD

A257

CANTERB

Bekesbourne Lane

Worcester Lane

The Hoath Farm

Woolton Farm

Howletts Zoo Park

Oakleigh Lane

Bekesbourne Hill

Bekesbourne Hill

Bekesbourne Lane

Bekesbourne Station

School Lane

Hode Farm

Milestone

North Downs

School Lane

Bekesbourne

80

A   B   C   62   D   E   F

Higham Farm

Stodmarsh   Road
Elbridge
House

1   Elmleigh Rd

Burnt House

Hollybush Lane

1 Hillcrest Rd
2 Pineside Rd

Supperton
Farm

Frognall

Stour Valley Walk

Hollybush Lane

Swanton
Farm

Wickham   Court   Lane

Grove Road

The List

The Street

Seaton

Wickhambreaux

Wickhambreaux
C of E Primary
School

Seaton   Road

Seator

Court Hill

Wickham   Road

Wickham Lane

79

Nargate Street

Drill Lane

The Street

Bave   Lane

PH

Ickham

St. Vincent's Close
The Elders
Court Meadows
Court Hill

2
1   Eventhill Road

New Wing Close

Littlebourne C of E
Primary School

Church Road

Nargate St

Wingham   Road

A257

CANTERBURY ROAD   THE HILL   HIGH STREET   Jubilee Road

Littlebourne

Rose Acre Road
Orchard Close
The Maltings

Hotel
PH   PO
Doctors
Surgery

1

School Lane

Treasury Lane
VW

Cherville Lane

The Green

A257

Lee
Priory

A257

Bramling

Lane

Bekesbourne

Bramling Road

Garrington
Farms

A   B   C   98   D   E   F

Bramling
Downs

1 grid square represents 500 metres

G H J K L M

63

82

99

1 Edmund St
2 Miles Ct
3 Sweetlove Pl

1 College Wy
2 Vicarage Gdns

Longmete Road

Rookery Farm

Church Hill Farm

1

2

3

4

5

6

7

8

Wyborne's Charity

Deerson Lane

Deerson Farm

Preston Lane

CT3

Perry

Walmestone

Perry Road

Little Wenderton Farm

Preston Road

Rusham Road

Preston Hill

Broomhill

Britton Farm

Petta Lane

SANDWICH HILL

A257

Wingham Surgery

North Court Close

Oxenden Crs

Palmer Road

1

2

3

PO

Mary's Meadow

St

2

Harris's Av

1

South Court Drive

Wingham

Dambridge Farm

CANTERBURY RD

A257

HIGH STREET

School Lane

2

Wingham Primary School

HIGH STREET

Wingham Green

Mill Road

Wingham Well

B2046

Wingham Business Centre

Wingham Industrial Estate

Popsal Lane

Witherdens Hall

Goodnestone Road

Staple Road

Twi

Neavy Downs

Snakes Hill

ADISHAM

Dene Farm

Crockshard Lane

Crockshard Hill

Goodnestone Road

G H J K L M

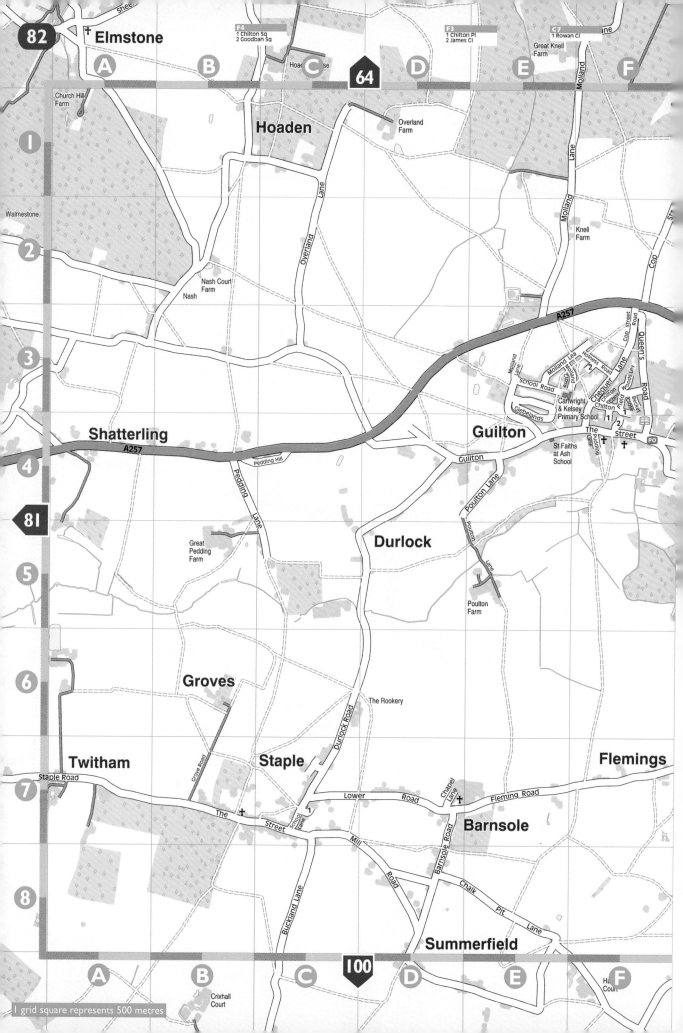

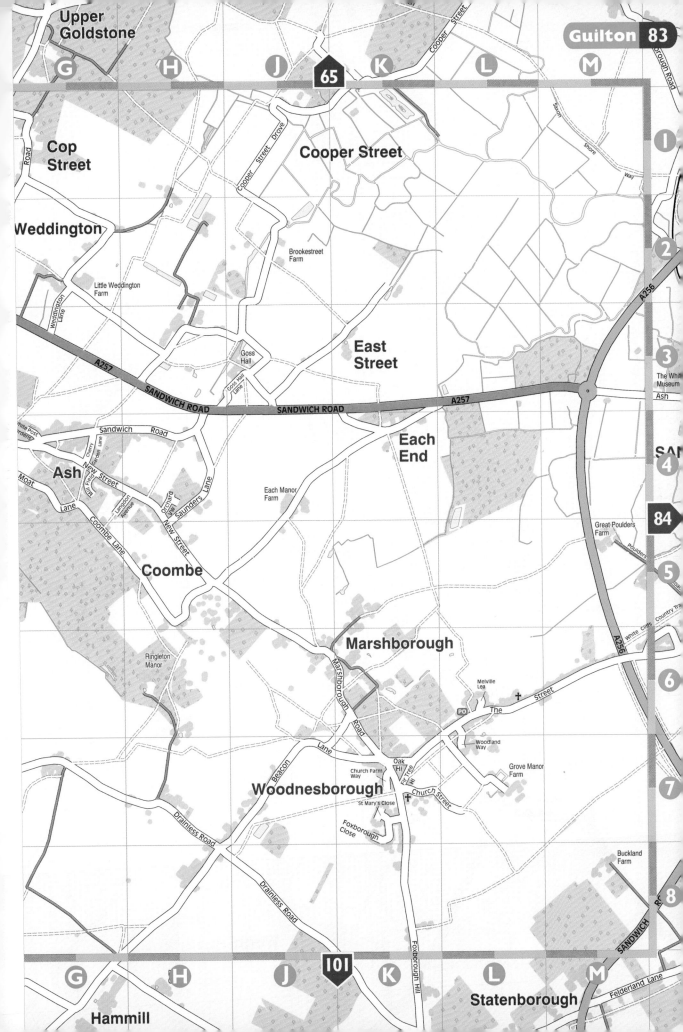

A25

66

A

B

C

Ramsgate Road

D

E

F

1

Richborough Road

Richb
Castle

Saxon Shore Way

Way

A256

Great
Stonar

Richborough Business Park

Stonar
Lake

Broad Salts

2

A256

LC

Richborough Road

Wantsume Lees

Mill Cl

New Downs
Farm

3

83

The Whitemill
Museum

Ash   Road

LC

Strand

The Butts

Infant School

School Rd

Church

Stonar Gdns

Stonar Close

SANDWICH

Delf Street

Harnet St

The Hunt Gallery

Kent Private Clinic
Holos Clinic

Mkt Street Gallery

Moat
Sole

Tannery Lane

Guildhall

Fisher St

Knightrider Street

Stour Valley Walk

White Cliffs Country Trail

Saxon Shore Way

4

The Market
Place Surgery

Delf Stream Gallery

High St

King St

Sandwich Lawn
Tennis Club

LC

Cemetery

Poulders

Jubilee Gdns

Woodnesborough Road

Sandwood Road

New Street

Mill Wall Pl

Manwood Road

St Georges Place

Sir Roger Manwoods
School

St Georges Road

Sandown Road

5

A256

White Cliffs Country Trail

Sunnyside Gdns

Laburnum Av

St

Burch Av

Fordwich Place

Deleside Lees

St George's

Denture
Clinic

St Andrew's

Sandown Lees

Road

Bart's

Sailing & Motor
Boat Club

Sandwich County
Junior School

Stone
Cross
Lees

Hazelwood Meadow

Sandwich
Station

LC

6

CT13

Stone Cross

Dover Road

Deal Road

Sandwich Sports
& Leisure Centre

LC

7

John's Green

The Crescent

A258

Sandwich Technology
School

Coventon Lane

Lane

Blue
Pigeons

Goretop Lane

LC

8

Buckland
Farm

A256

SANDWICH ROAD

DEAL ROAD

White Cliffs Country Trail

Felderland Close

Worth CP
School

PH

Minnis Wy

Street

Temple Way

Worth

Felderland

The Ch

Upton
House

102

A

B

C

D

E

F

derland Lane

grid square represents 500 metres

Prince's Golf Links

Stour Valley Walk

Princes Golf Club

Royal St George's Golf Links

Stour Valley Walk

White Cliffs Country Trail

al St Georges Club

Princes Drive

Sandwich Bay

Sandwich Bay Estate

Avenue

King's

North Road

Guilford Road

Princes Drive

Av

Waldershare

Shawdon Avenue

Francis Avenue

Cambridge Avenue

White Cliffs Country Trail

North Stream

Mary Bax's Stone

PH

G   H   J   67   K   L   M

G   H   J   103   K   L   M

I   2   3   4   5   6   7   8

G7
1 The Old Bailey

H7
1 Church Crs

M8
1 Douglas Rd

G

H

J

69

K

Lord's
Hill

L

M

Madan
Court

1

Black Post

Ringlestone

Ringlestone Road

PH

Wrinsted
Court

2

Merlewood
Farm

Stede Hill

Horsalls

Hogbarn

Hogbarn Lane

Stedehill
Wood

3

West
Stre

4

Flint Barn
Farm

Flint Lane

88

West

W
G

Stede
Court

Flint Lane

Coles
Dane

Stede Hill

Marlow
Farm

5

Lea Farm

Faver's Road

6

Pilgrim's Way

Pilgrim's Way

Marley
Court

Pilgrim's Way

North Downs Way

Marley Road

Pilgrims
Lakes

Harrison Drive

tsham

Lexelands

Harrietsham
Road

Marley Road

Church Lane

St. Welcume's
Way

Norwood

Mercer

Downlands

Old Lane

Dickley Lane

Drive

Ham Lane

7

Church

East

Street

Rectory Lane

Harrietsham
Primary
School

The
Surgery

ASHFORD ROAD **A20(T)**

Dickley
Wood

Maidstone Road

Ford Road

Royton Avenue

Clifton Close

Faversham

The
Square

8

Ham Lane

Ham Lane

Loder
Close

Groveland
Close

Douglas Road

Mitchell
Close

Malthouse
Close

Lenham

Hatch
Road

Beacon
Road

Robins Avenue

Honywood Road

Robins Close

Old School Close

Mill Close

High Street

Church
Square

PO

Globe
Lane

Cen

Old

Boldrewood Farm

105

G

H

J

K

L

Lenham
Station

M

Valley Walk

A   B Syndale Bottom C **70** D Wic E ng F Temple

I

Wichling Wood

†

Faversham Road

Filmer Wood

Ashdown

Ashdown Road

Lord's Wood

Lady Margaret Manor

Greet

2

Payden Street

3

Oakenpole Wood

Maitlands Farm

West Street

West Street

4

87

Flint Lane

Woodside Green

Lone Barn Road

Payden Street

Bunker's Hill

Slade Road

5

Lea Farm

Faversham Road

Tophill Farm

Payden Street

Warre Stree

6

Warren Street

PH

s Way

7

Rayners Hill

Cemetery

Great Pivington Farm

North Downs Way

Hubbards Hill

Highbourne Park

Wa

Royton Avenue

The Square

8

Grovehurst

A20(T)

†

PO

Church Square

Old Ashford Road

ASHFORD ROAD

Glebe Gdns

Walk

Tanyard Farm

A   B   C **106** D   E   F

Nor s Way

East

1 grid square represents 500 metres

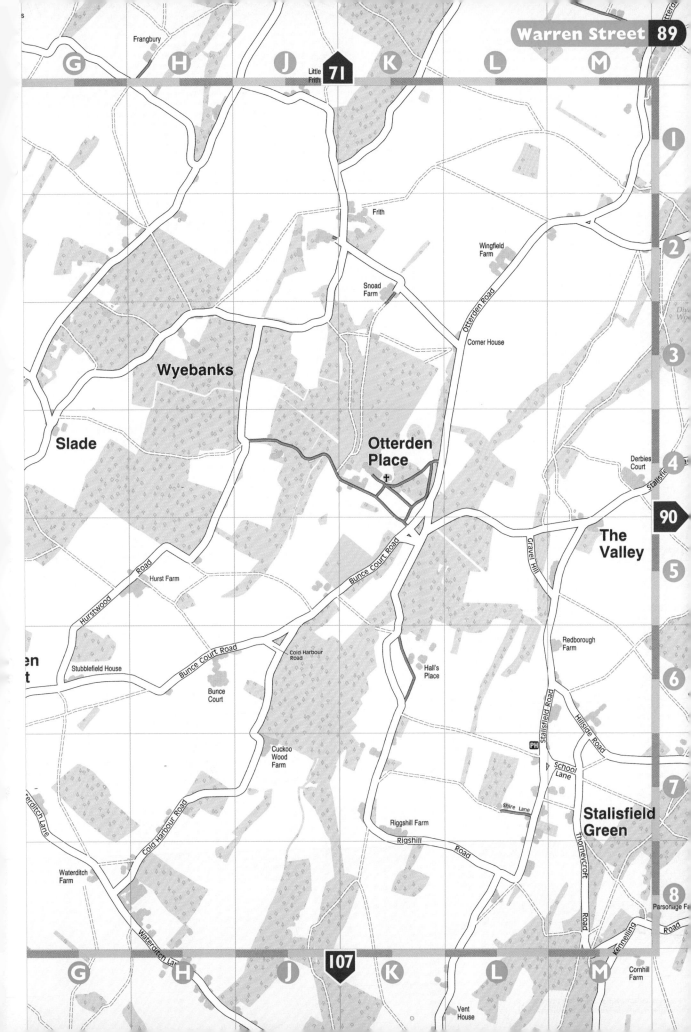

G H J 71 K L M

Frangbury

Little Frith

I

2

Frith

Wingfield Farm

Otterden Road

Snoad Farm

Corner House

3

Wyebanks

Otterden Place

Derbies Court

4

Slade

90

Stalisfie

The Valley

Road

Hurstwood

Hurst Farm

Bunce Court Road

Gravel Hill

5

Redborough Farm

6

Stubblefield House

Bunce Court Road

Cold Harbour Road

Hall's Place

Stalisfield Road

Hillside Road

en t

Bunce Court

Cuckoo Wood Farm

PH

School Lane

Cold Harbour Road

Shire Lane

7

Waterditch Lane

Stalisfield Green

Riggshill Farm

Rigshill Road

Thorneycroft

Waterditch Farm

8

Parsonage Fa

Waterditch Lar

107

Kennelling

Road

Cornhill Farm

G H J K L M

Vent House

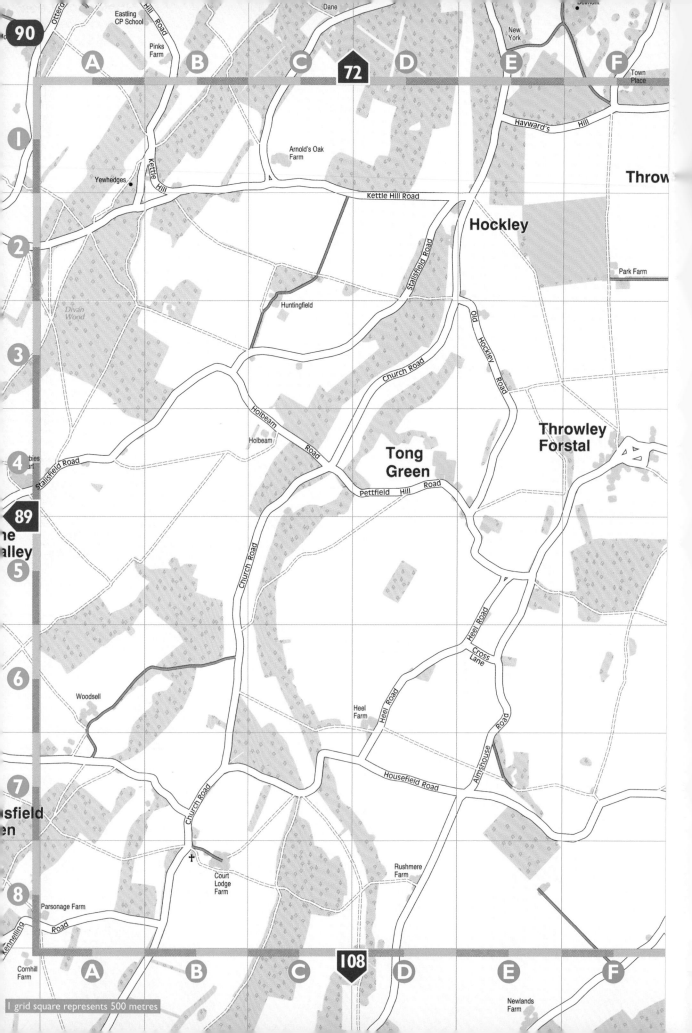

G H J **73** K L M

I

2

3

4

92

5

6

7

8

Parsonage

Bagshill Road

Parsonage
Farm

Throwley Road

Lords
Farm

Dayton Road

Valley
Farm

Leaveland
Court

Badlesmere
Court

Workhouse Road

Bethel
Row

Badlesmere

A251

Leaveland

ASHFORD ROAD

Bell's Forstal

Shottenden Road

Loose Down Road

Dryland
Farm

Cadman's
Farm

Oast Lane

Broomfield
Farm

Pontus

Snoadstreet

FAVERSHAM ROAD

Howlett's
Farm

Pested

Pested

G H J 75 Upper Ensign K L M

I

Lower Ensden Road

Lower Ensden

2

New Cut Road

New Forest Lane

Selling Road

Rhode Court

Stone Stile Farm

Shrimpton Close

Lees Road

Shalm

North Downs Close

Green Lane

Lower Lees Road

PO

Old Wives Lees **3**

Cork Farm

Long Hill

Copas Hill

Cherry Orchard

Spinning Lane

Mulberry Hill

nden

Soleshill Road

North Downs Way

Bowerland Farm

Bowerland Lan

4

94

BURY

Meadow Close

5

A252

Chilham Gallery

Felborough Close

Herds Close

Bagham Road

Bagham Lane

Chilham Station

PH

M

The Street

PO

Chilham

Taylors Hill

Hambrook Lane

School Hill

Chilham Surgery

Branch Road

Arden Grange

Bagham

LC

Mill Lane

St Marys C of E Controlled Primary School

6

Dane Court

Julliberrie Downs

A28

Mountain Street

7

Young Manor Farm

Dane Street

Mountain Street

ASHFORD ROAD

Stour Valley Walk

East Stour Farm

8

North Down

G H J **III** K Hurst Farm L M

K5 1 Hambrook Cl

A B C

D E F

Nickle
Farm

North Downs Way

1 Cremer Cl
E4

New

Hat
ne

E3
1 Old School Ms

I

North Downs Way

LC

Cemetery
†

ASHFORD   ROAD
A28

A28

Riverside

LC

Chartham
Station

2

A
Road

Shalmsford Street

Chartham
Surgery

The Green

Chartham
Station

Stour Valley Walk

Shalmsford

Stour Valley Walk

Shalmsford   Street
The Hyde

†

1 Old School
Surgery

Parish Road

River
Court

†

River Court
School

Stour Ro

3

Lane

PO

†

Bolts

Hill

PO

Rathmo

Rentain Road

Baker's

Lane

Great Stour

Pilgrims

ROAD

Thruxted

Bobbin Lodge Hill

Shalmsford Ct

Chartham
CP School

Shalmsford Street

Brice Avenue

Highland Road

Pomfret
Road

Bowerland
Farm

CANTERBURY

Bowerland Lane

Lane

Stour Valley Walk

The Crescent

Chartham Downs
Road

Cockering

4

93

Meadow Close

Pickelden Lane

Mystole   Road

Mystole Lane

Chilham
Station

Stile
Farm

Stour Valley Walk

Mystole
House

Pot Lane

Thruxted

5

Penny

6

Stour Valley Walk

Upper
Mystole Park
Farm

7

Down
Wood

8

Denge
Wood

A B C

D E F

Penny Pot Lane

e Stre

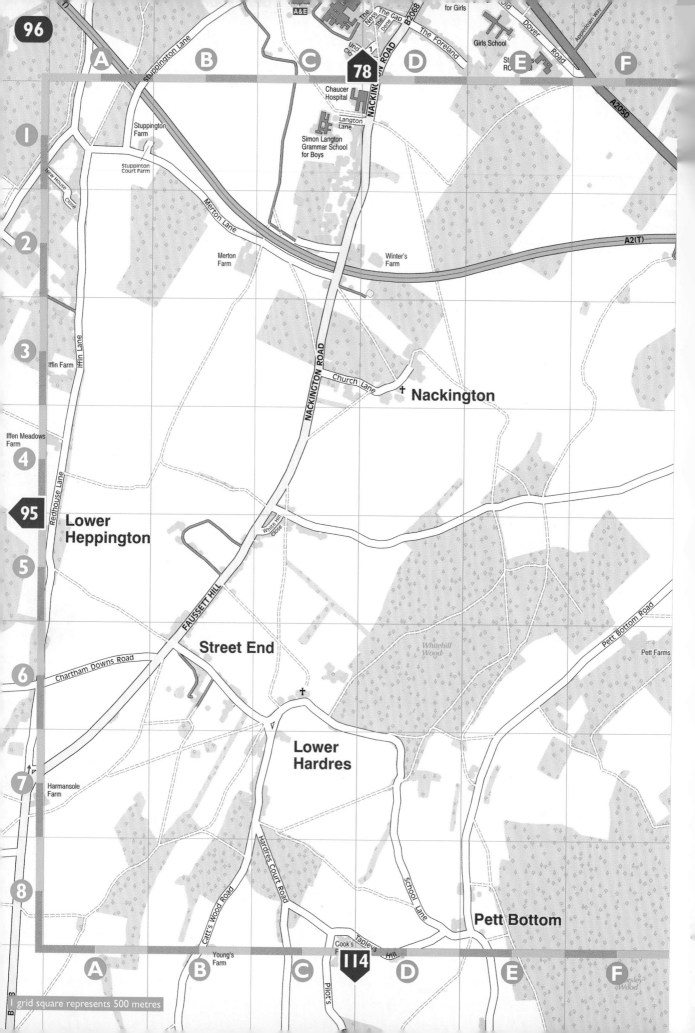

A   B   C   D   E   F

78

I
2
3
95
5
6
7
8

New House Close

Stuppington Lane

Stuppington Farm

Stuppinton Court Farm

Iffin Lane

Iffin Farm

Merton Lane

Merton Farm

Redhouse Lane

Iffen Meadows Farm

Chaucer Hospital

A&E

Langton Lane

Simon Langton Grammar School for Boys

NACKINGTON ROAD

The Ness

The Gap

The Dene

B2068

The Foreland

for Girls

Girls School

St RO...

A2050

Dover Road

Appledown Way

A2(T)

Winter's Farm

Church Lane

† **Nackington**

Lower Heppington

White's Hill Close

FAUSSETT HILL

Street End

Chartham Downs Road

Whitehill Wood

Pett Bottom Road

Pett Farms

†

Lower Hardres

Harmansole Farm

Catt's Wood Road

Hardres Court Road

School Lane

Pett Bottom

Cook's

Young's Farm

Tapleys Hill

Pilot's

114

A   B   C   D   E   F

nsley Wood

Bekesbourne Hill

G   H   J   79   K   L   M

Bekesbourne

Oakleigh Lane
Bekesbourne
Bekesbourne Hill
School Lane
Bekesbourne Station
I

Milestone

Hode Farm

North Downs Way

Bifrons Road
Station Road
School Lane

Bekesbourne

2

Birrons Hill

Patrixbourne

The Street
St. Mary's Road

Chalkpit Hill
Hop Farm
Adisham Road
Aerodrome
De Hal

Bekesbourne Road

Elham Valley Way

Patrixbourne Road

Keeper's Hill

3

Station Road

Conyngham Lane

High Street

Bridge & Patrixbourne Primary School

Bridge

Dering Close
Dering Road
Filmer Road
PO
Churchill Close
Union Road
Western Avenue
Windmill Road
Riverside Close
3
Saxon Road
2
1
Brewery Lane
Mill Lane

North Downs Way

4
Shepard's Close

98

Pett Hill

Bridge Road

Meadow Close
Bridge Hill
Beech Hill

Bridge Down
Higham Lane

A2(T)

Highland Court Farm

5

Bridge Place Country Club

Elham Valley Way

Pippin Avenue

Coldharbour Lane
Cold Harbo
6
Cold Harbour Farm

Bourne Park

Barham Downs

Lenhall Farm

Bourne Park Road

Frog Lane

Coldharbour Lane

7

Bishopsbourne

Dover Road

The Street

Park Lane
Rose Lane

Bonny Bush Hill

8
A2(T)

G   H   J   115   K   L   M

Crows Camp Road
Charlton Park
Elham Valley Way

A B C **80** D E F

I

Bramling
Downs

1 Lysander Cl

Bramling Road

Aerodrome Rd

De
Havilands

2 Adisham Rd

Adisham Road

Bramling Road

Adisham Downs Road

3

Pond Hill

Boss

Church
Lane

4 Shepard's
Close

Shepherd's Close

97

The Street

5

PO
Adisham

Woodlands

Woodlands Road

Donkey
Lane

Cooting Lane

Coldharbour Lane

6 Cold Harbour
Farm

Cooting
Farm

Pit
Wood

7

Cooting
Downs

8

A21(T)

Ileden
Farm

Ash

Cox Close

A B C **116** D E F

Barham
Downs

Ileden
Wood

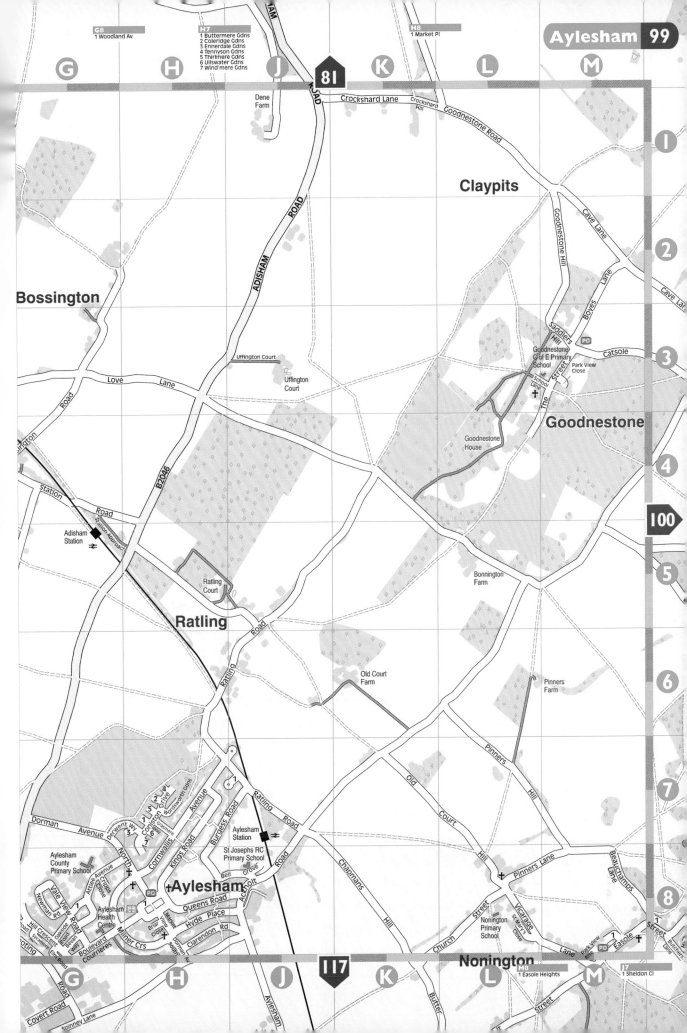

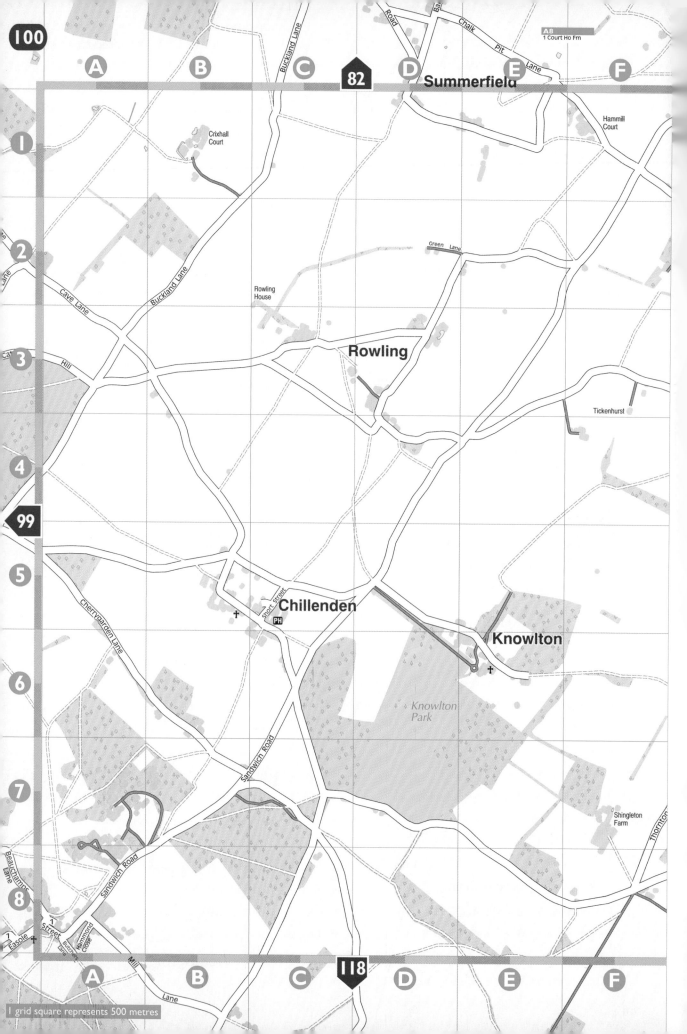

G **H** **J** 83 **K** **L** **M** SANDWICH

Denne
Court

I

Felderland Lane

White Cliffs Country Trail

Hammill

Statenborough

2

Selson Road

Selson

Orchard Rd

Hill Drive

Woodnesborough Lane

Peak Drive

Sandwich

Walton

White Cliffs Country Trail

Gore

Gore Road

Boystown Pl

Long Drive

Lane

Place

Wilm

3

Hal Farm

Albion Road

Cook's

Eastry Medical Surgery

St Mary's

Hay

Hill

Hotel

Primary School

Eastry

PO Street

Swaynes Wy

Church St

Centenary Gdns

High

Street

White Cliffs Country Trail

Gore

Mill Gn

Wheelwrights Way

Brook

4

Heronden Rd

Lane

Mill

Lane

White Wood Road

Holly Close

Lower

The Lynch

Heronden

Thornton

Liss Road

Buttsole

102

Heronden Road

Street

Updown Farm

5

A256

Thornton Lane

Dover

Road

Updown House

6

7

Venson Farm

Betteshanger

Northbourne Park School

DOVER ROAD

8

Thornton Farm

G **H** 119 **J** **K** **L** **M**

North Court

Dane Court

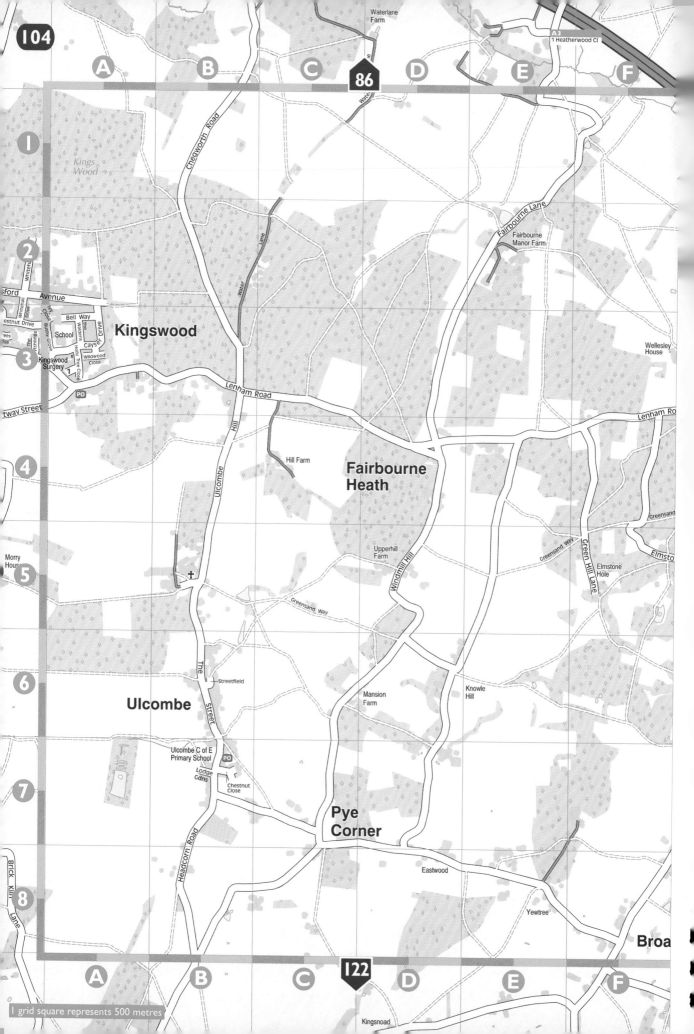

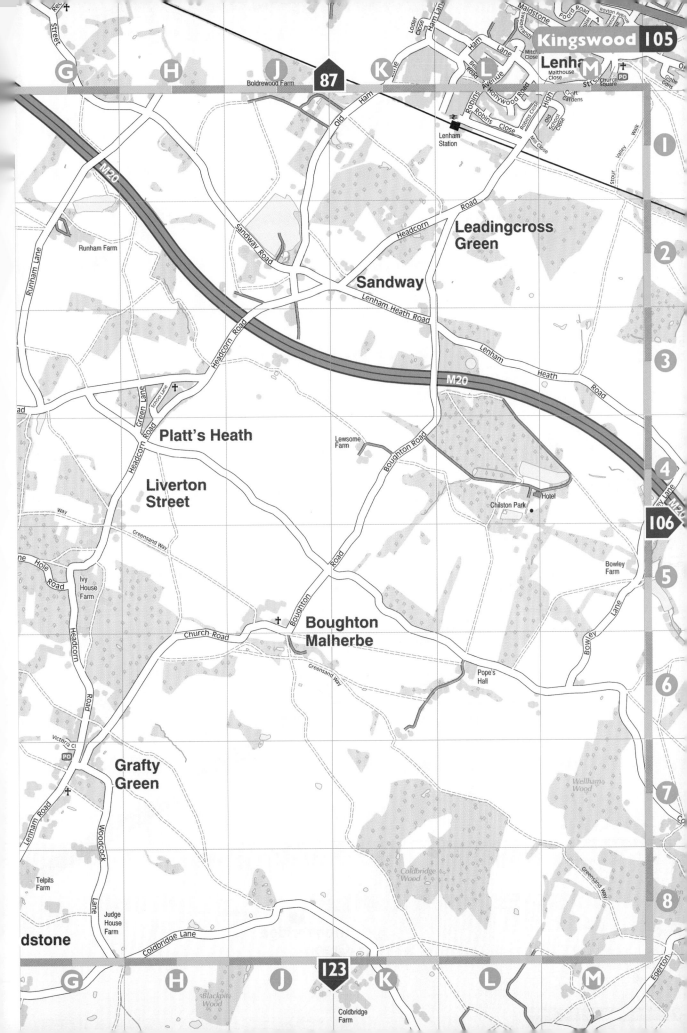

G　H　J　[87]　K　L　M

I
2
3
4
[106]
5
6
7
8

Kingswood
Lenham
Malthouse
Close
Church
Square
PO

Maidstone
Ford
Road
Royton Avenue
Netherlands
Loder
Close
Ham
Lane
Mitch...
Close
Ham
Lane
Robins
Avenue
Honeywood Road
Robins
Close
Mill
Close
Old
School
Close
High
Croft
Gardens
Old
School
Close
Glebe
Gdns

Lenham
Station

Boldrewood Farm

M20

Leadingcross
Green

Headcorn
Road

Lenham
Road

Sandway

Lenham Heath Road

Lenham
Heath
Road

M20

Chilston Park
Hotel

Bowley
Farm

Runham Farm

Runham Lane

Sandway Road

Green Lane

School Lane

Headcorn Road

Platt's Heath

Lewsome
Farm

Boughton Road

Liverton
Street

Way

Greensand Way

...ne Hole Road

Ivy
House
Farm

Headcorn Road

Boughton
Road

Church Road

Boughton
Malherbe

Greensand Way

Pope's
Hall

Bowley Lane

Wellham
Wood

Greensand Way

Victoria Cl
PO

Grafty
Green

Lenham Road

Woodcock Lane

Coldbridge
Wood

Telpits
Farm

Judge
House
Farm

...dstone

Coldbridge Lane

Blackpit
Wood

Coldbridge
Farm

Egerton

Waterditch Farm

L5
1 Clearmount Dr
2 Wheler Rd

Waterditch Lane

G   H   J   89   K   L   M

Cobham
Farm

Vent
House

Warren   Street

Stonestile

Stonestile Farm Road

Hart Hill

Bowl Road

Cornhill
Farm

Kenylon
Farm

Hawk's
Nest

Dormestone
Farm

North Downs Way

Acton
Farm

Hart
Hill   Hart Hill

Crows Hole
Farm

**Charing
Hill**

A20(T) MAIDSTONE ROAD

Charing Heath Road

Tile Lodge

Great
Hook

Lodge   Road

Cherry
Tree Road

**Charing
Heath**

Whild
Hill

Swan
Street

Little Hook
Farm

Hook Lane

Charing   Heath   Road

Newlands Road

Hurst Lane

Hurst
Wood

Newlands
Stud

Raywood
Farm

Pluckley Road

**Coppins
Corner**

A252   NORTHERN BY-PASS

Saver Road
2   New Downs Close   1
School Road
Cemetery
School   Monks
Charing   The High St
Surgery   Market Pl
Doctors Surgery   PO

Station Rd
Hither Fld   St Burleigh
Charing   Road
Station

Old Ashford

The Moat

The Wynd

Bowl

Charing

Pett Lane
Woodbrook

Pett Lane

The Hill

Kennelling   Road

Pilgrims

Tol

G   H   J   125   K   L   M

Hunger
Hatch   Hunger

Summerlands
Special School

I
2
3
4
108
5
6
7
8
A20(T)

Wicken

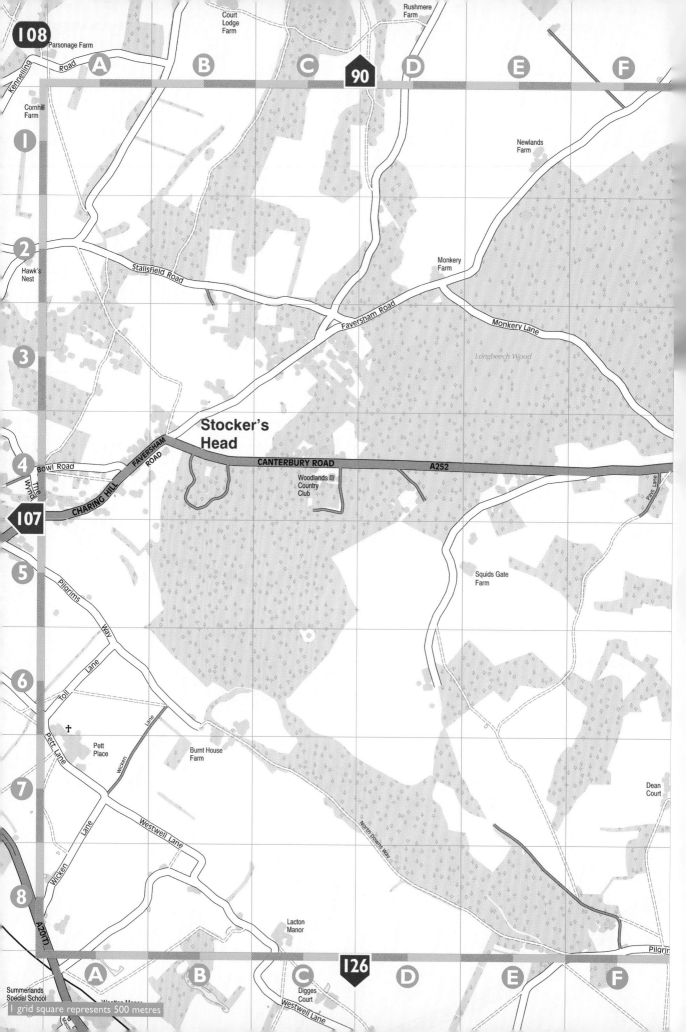

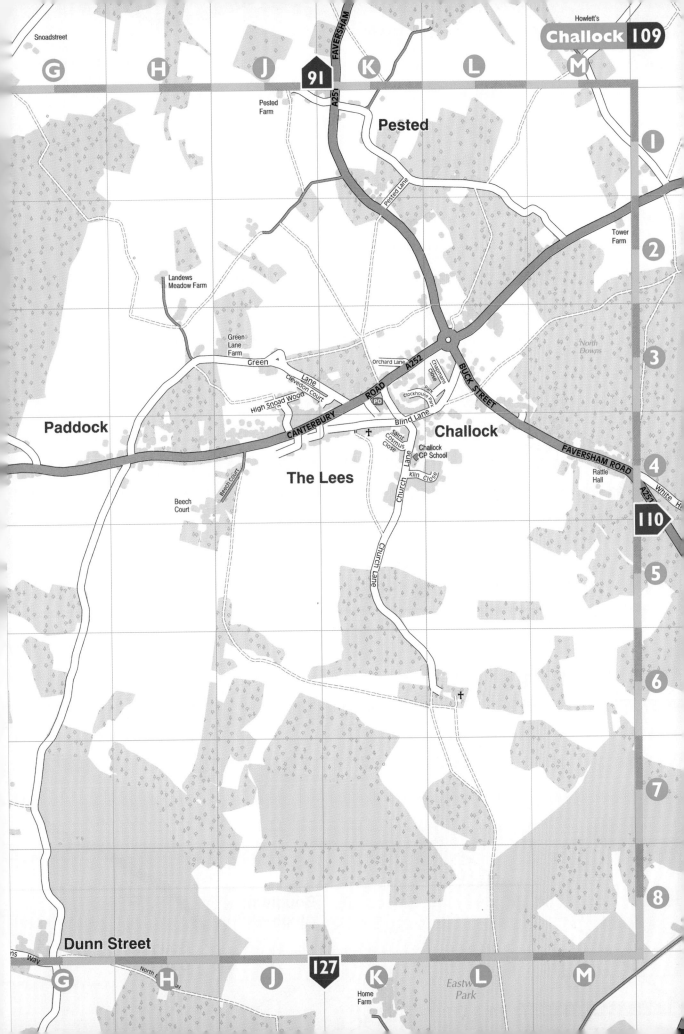

Howlett's

Snoadstreet

G **H** **J** **91** **K** **L** **M**

FAVERSHAM

A251

Pested Farm

Pested

I

Tower Farm

2

Landews Meadow Farm

Pested Lane

North Downs

3

Green Lane Farm

Green Lane

Orchard Lane

A252

Chapmans Close

Clockhouse Park

BUCK STREET

Clevedon Court

High Snoad Wood

Paddock

CANTERBURY ROAD

PO

Blind Lane

Saint Cosmus Close

Challock

FAVERSHAM ROAD

Rattle Hall

4

A257

White Hi

110

Beech Court

The Lees

Church Lane

Challock CP School

Kiln Close

5

Beech Court

Church Lane

†

†

6

7

8

Dunn Street

ns Way

North

G **H** **J** **127** **K** **L** **M**

Home Farm

Eastw Park

A B C 92 D E F

Cutlers

✝

Church Road

Coppins Farm

Molash

A252 Pound Lane

I

Tower Farm

2

Oathill Farm

North Downs

King's Wood

3

SHA
RA
Hall

4 AD

A251 White Hill

109

White Hill

North Downs Way

5

Soakham Downs

FAVERSHAM ROAD

6

North Downs Way

A251

Warren Farm

Soakham Farm

7

White Hill

Buckwell Farm

8

CANTERBURY ROAD A28

Boughton Aluph

✝

Boughton Corner

A A251 B C 128 Church Lane D E F

1 grid square represents 500 metres

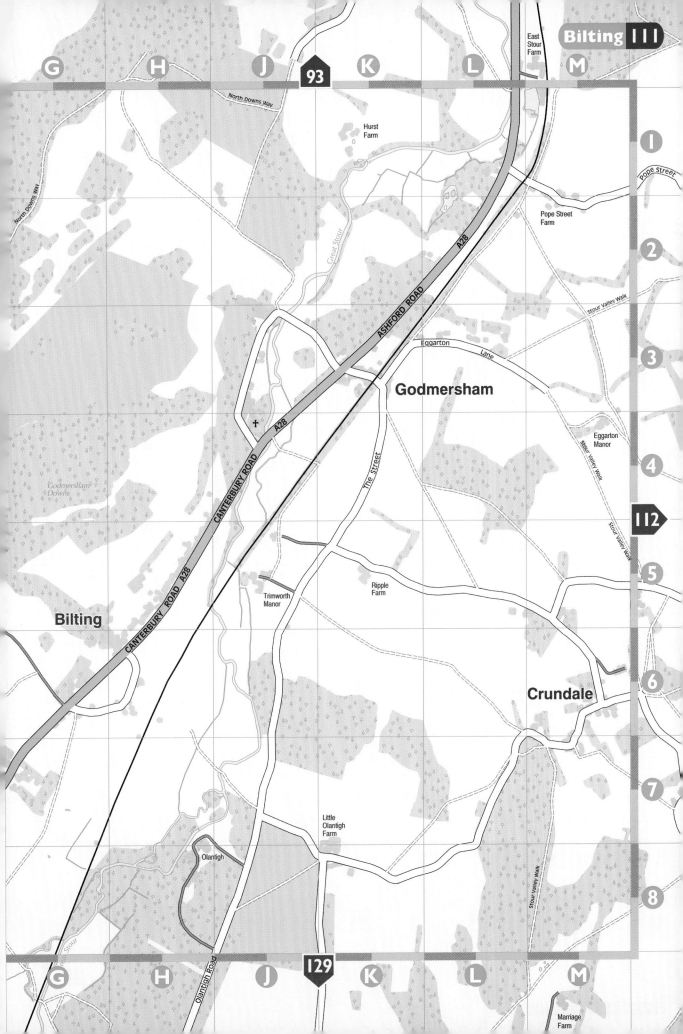

G   H   J   **93**   K   L   M

I

North Downs Way

East Stour Farm

Pope Street

Hurst Farm

Pope Street Farm

2

North Downs Way

A28

ASHFORD ROAD

Stour Valley Walk

3

Eggarton   Lane

Godmersham

Great Stour

Eggarton Manor

Stour Valley Walk

4

A28

†

112

Godmersham Downs

The Street

Stour Valley Walk

5

CANTERBURY ROAD

Ripple Farm

Bilting

Trimworth Manor

6

CANTERBURY ROAD A28

Crundale

7

Little Olantigh Farm

Olantigh

Stour Valley Walk

8

Stour

Olantigh Road

Marriage Farm

A B C D E F

94

1
2
3
4

111

5
6
7
8

A B C 130 D E F

Pope Street

Stour Valley Walk

Woodsdale Farm

Denge Wood

Upper Thruxted Farm

Penny Pot Lane

Stour Valley Walk

Eggarton Manor

Stour Valley Walk

Eggringe Wood

Penny Pot Lane

Buckholt Farm

Sole Street

Anvil Green

Winchcombe Farm

Richdore Road

Waltham

Kake Street

PO

Crundale House

Huntstreet

Woods Hill

Crundaley Downs

1 grid square represents 500 metres

G H J K L M

95

Watery Lane

Town Road

†

Debden Court

I

Wootton Farm

Vicarage Hill

Capel Road

Capel Farm

The Street

Petham

Church Lane

Tillard Close

Petham CP School

†

2

Broadway Green Farm

Petham House

Chequers Hill

Stone Street

B2068

Hogg Lane

3

Broadway

Earley Wood

Duckpit Road

CT4

4

Waltham Road

Waltham Court

Hault Farm

New Barn Farm

Dane Chantry

114

5

Waddenhall Wood

M

6

Ansdore

Sarness Farm

Little Wadden Hall

7

Waddenhal Farm

†

Little London

Duckpit Road

Gogway

8

Yockletts Banks

Stone Street

G H J K L M

131

Church Lane

Yockletts Farm

Whiteacre Lane

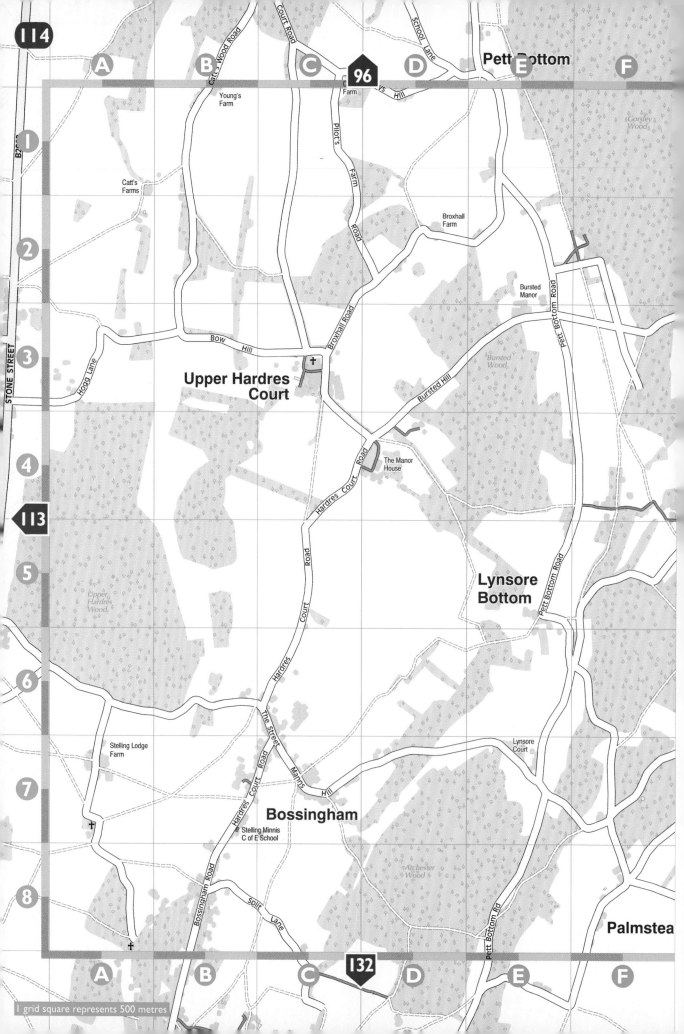

I

Charlton Park

Elham Valley Way

Nailbourne Close

Bonny Bush Hill

Kingston

Church Lane

2

Covet Lane

Greenacre

Whitelocks Close

Woodgate

Langham Park Farm

Pheasants' Hall Road

Croys Camp Road

Charlton Wood

The Street

3

Covet Lane

Reed Farm

Jesse's Hill

Marley Lane

Marley

4

Bar

116

Heart's Delight

Green

Westwood

Marley Lane

Covet Lane

Duskin Farm

Elham Valley Way

5

Rai

Derri

6

Ham Farm

Elham Valley Way

Covet Wood

7

Covet Wood

South Barham

8

d

Dane Farm

Wood Road

field

Breach

A   B   C   98   D   E   F

Cooting
Do...
F3
1 Church La
B6
1 Farmhouse Cl
2 Old Valley Rd

I

2

3

4

115

5

6

7

8

A   B   C   134   D   E   F

Wallbourne
Close

Bonny Bush Hill

Covet Lane

Black Robin Lane

Farm

Ileden
Farm

Barham
Downs

Ileden
Wood

North Downs Way

North Downs Way

Wom

Aylesham
Cemetery

ADISHAM

ROAD

Pond
Lane

The Street

Wo

Denne Hill
Farm

Denne
Hill

Out Elmstead

Out   Elmstead   Lane

Valley   Road

Rectory   Lane

Lane

Dover Road

DOVER ROAD

A2(T)

OLD DOVER RD

A260

A260

A2(T)

DOVER ROAD

DOVER RD

Barham

Green Hills

Barham C of E
Primary School

PO

The Yard

The Street

Heathfield Way

Fox
Way

The Grove

Valley

Road

Kitchener
Close

Birch Court

1   2

Crookenden
Place

Oxenden Way

Cemetery

Gravel Castle Road

Gravel
Castle

Castle   Road

Hole

Railway

Hill

Derringstone
Street

Brickfield Road

Gravel

Rabbit

Wick Lane

Derringstone

South Barham

Road

Derringstone   Hill

Broome
Parke

7

Waldershain
Wood

Broome
Park
Hotel

Clints Lane

Breach
Downs

TERBURY   ROAD

Shelvin L

DOVER RD

South Barham

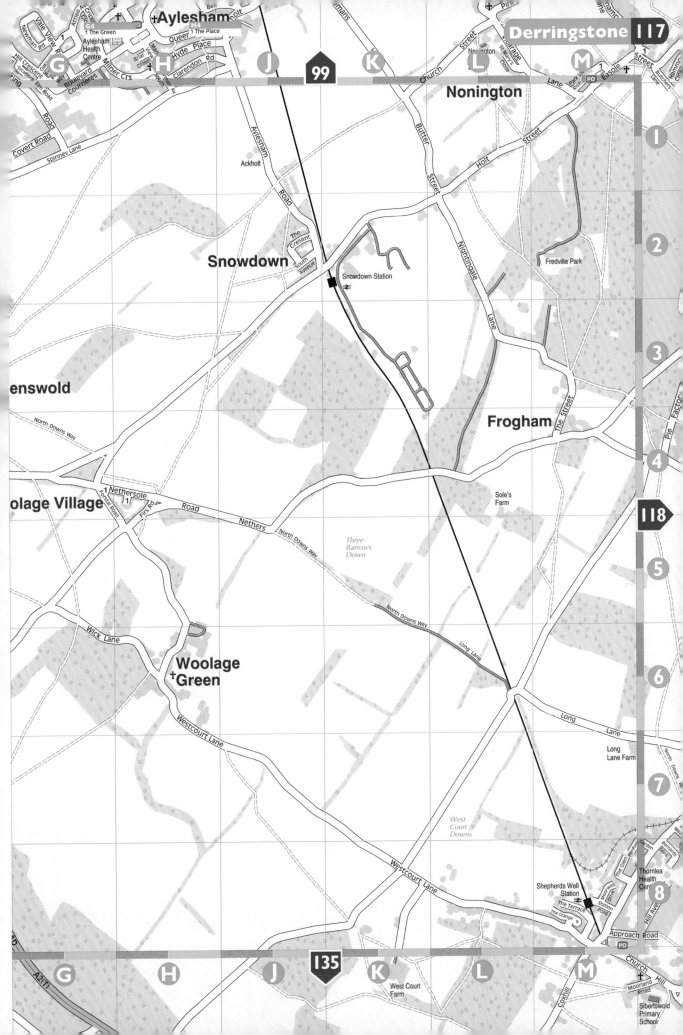

G

H

J

99

K

L

M

I

2

3

4

118

5

6

7

8

+Aylesham

G4
1 The Green
Aylesham
Health
Centre

Courrieres

Boulevard

Hill Crescent

Newman Rd

Vale View Rd

Cav Rd

Well

Milner Crs

Sycamore Rd

Elm Road

Arthur Ave

Chipp

Bell

Queer 1 The Place

Hyde Place

Clarendon Rd

Briar
Close

Marl
Close

West
South Av

H4

O

Covert Road

Spinney Lane

Road

enswold

North Downs Way

olage Village

Nethersole

Foxhall Road

Firs Rd

1

1

Wick Lane

Woolage
+Green

Westcourt Lane

Snowdown

Ackholt

Aylesham Road

The Crescent

South Avenue

Snowdown Station

Nonington

Church

Street

Holt

Street

Butter

Street

Nightingale Lane

Leafield

Nonington

St Mary's
Close

Pinn

Church Street

M
PO
Easole

7

Park View Rd

Fredville Park

Frogham

The Street

Sole's
Farm

Nethers

Road

North Downs Way

Three
Barrows
Down

North Downs Way

Long Lane

Long
Lane

Long
Lane Farm

North

West
Court
Downs

Westcourt Lane

West Court
Farm

Shepherds Well
Station

The Terrace

The Grange

Moorwell
Station
Road

Coxhill

Church
Hill

Approach Road

PO

The Glen

Penbrook Garden

Bernards

Thornlea
Health
Cent

Hill Ave

Siberswold
Primary
School

Moorland
Road

G

H

J

135

K

L

M

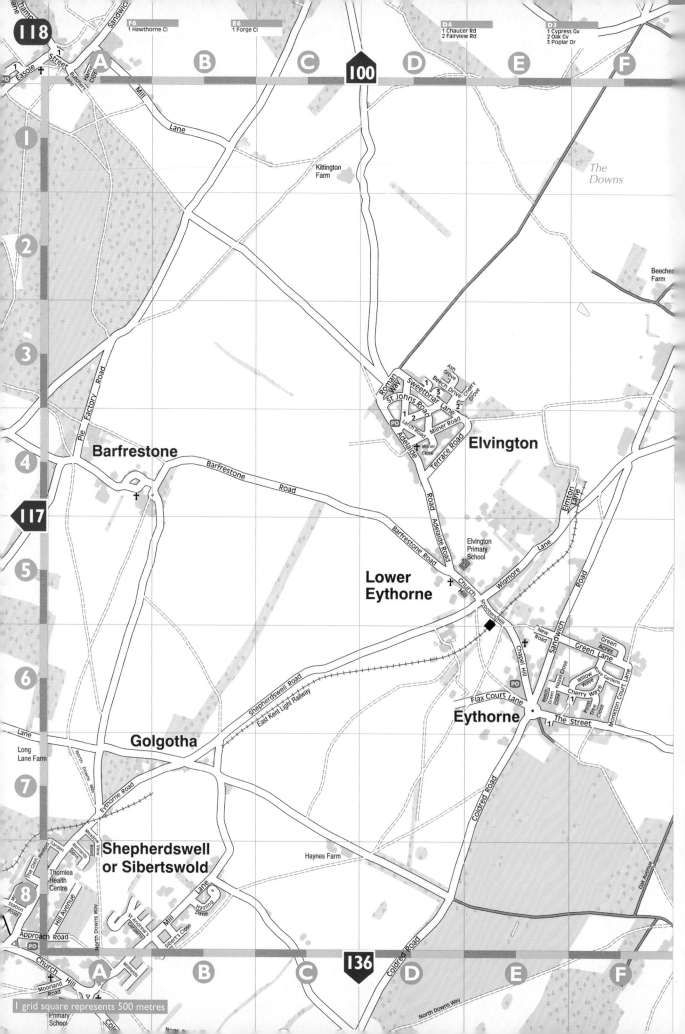

K2
1 Chapel Rd

G Thornton Farm H J 101 K L M

I

Dane Court

North Court

North Court Lane

Dover Road

St Mary's Gv

School Road

School Road

Upper Street

St Andrews Way

Pike Road

Vicarage Lane

Chapel Road

Tilmanstone

1

Lower Street

Whites Hill

A256

DOVER ROAD

Telegraph Farm

2

3

Barville Road

Barville Farm

arville Road

4

West Studdal Farm

120

East

Stonehean Road

Downs Rd

5

Strakers Hill

Downs Close

A256

Studdal

Homestead Lane

6 De

Malmains Farm

Kennel Hill

Sandwich Road

Chapel Lane

7

Ashley

Minacre Farm

Waldershare Road

Northdowns Close

North Downs Way

North Downs Way

Roman Road

Maydensole Farm

8

A256

Sandwich Road

Eastling

G H 137 J K L M

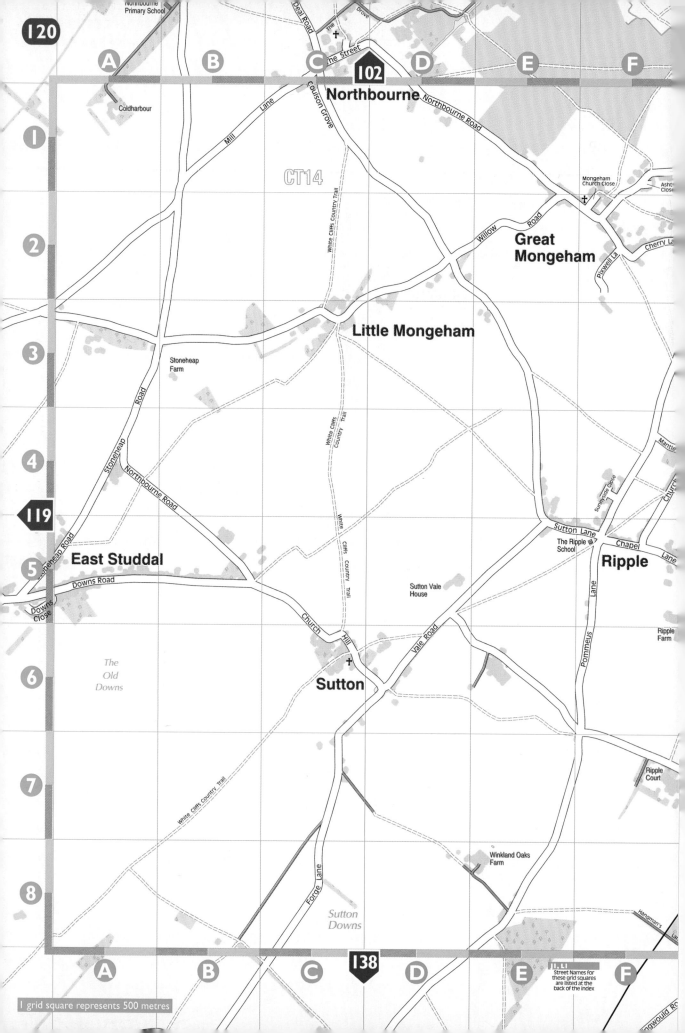

120

A   B   C   **102**   D   E   F

Northbourne Primary School

The Drove

The Street

Deal Road

Coulson Grove

Coldharbour

Mill Lane

Northbourne

Northbourne Road

CT14

Mongeham Church Close

Asht Close

White Cliffs Country Trail

Willow Road

Great Mongeham

Cherry La

Pixwell La

Little Mongeham

1

2

3

Stoneheap Farm

Stoneheap Road

Northbourne Road

White Cliffs Country Trail

119

Stoneheap Road

4

Sunnyside Close

Church

Mantle

Sutton Lane

East Studdal

The Ripple School

Chapel Lane

Ripple

Downs Road

Downs Close

White Cliffs Country Trail

Sutton Vale House

Pommeus Lane

Ripple Farm

5

The Old Downs

Church Hill

Vale Road

6

Ripple Court

Sutton

7

White Cliffs Country Trail

Forge Lane

Winkland Oaks Farm

8

Sutton Downs

Hangman's

A   B   C   **138**   D   E   F

ngwould R

1 grid square represents 500 metres

Street Names for these grid squares are listed at the back of the index

G H J 105 K L M

Telpits Farm

Judge House Farm

dston G

Coldbrid ne Lane

Blackpit Wood

Coldbridge Farm

Hazeldene Farm

I

Park House

Pembles Cross

Barham's Mill Road

Link House

2

Barham's Mill Road

Barham's Mill Farm

Chapel Lane

Crocken Hill

Link Hill Lane

Southernden Road

Potter's Forstal

Road

3

Coldharbour Farm

†

Forstal Road

Forge Lane

Egerton Forstal

Rock Hill Road

4

124

Newland Green

Bedlam Lane

Wanden Lane

Heronsdale

Newland Green Lane

5

Clark Hill Farm

Wanden

6

Kingsden Farm

Frith Wood

Bedlam Lane

Burnt House

7

Park Farm

Swift's Green

Rosemary Lane

The Quarter

Oaklands

Dening Wood

8

G H J 141 K L M

Lewd Lane

A B C D E F

106

Foxden Wood

Road

Egerton House

Greensand way

Court Lodge Farm

Stonebridge Green Road

Stonebridge Cn

Mill Rd

Southfield

Stonebridge Green

Iden Road

stour valley Wk

Iden Lane

Iden

Barnfield

1

Glebeland

The St

Stisted Wy

Egerton CP School

PO

Stevens Cl

Egerton

Old School Court

Harmer's Way

Elm Cl

Hill Road

Lin House

2

Rock Hill

Stone Hill

Stone Hill

New Road

Greenhill Farm

Pivington Lane

Pivington Mill

stour valley walk

Greensand Way

3

Rock Hill Road

Little Houses

Greenhill La

Egerton Road

4

Ragged Farm House

Kingsland Lane

Britcher Farm

123

Munday

Newland Green Lane

Bois Road

Greensand Way

Elvey Farm

Egerton Road

Munday Farm

5

Mundy Bois

PH

Westfields

Pluckley

PO

The St

6

Greenhill Lane

Smarden Road

Pluckley C of E Primary School

Pluckley Thorne

Station Road

7

Giles Farm

The Pinnock

The Thorn Estate

Lambden Road

Fir Toll

8

Dering Wood

Rose Farm

Smarden Road

Rushbrook Farm

Coop Farm

A B C D E F

142

G   H   J   107   K   L   M

Wickel

A20(T)

Summerlands
Special School

I

Westw
Leacor

2

M20

3

4

126

5

6

West Street

7

Stour

8

Newlands
Stud

Raywood
Farm

Pluckley Road

Hunger

Hunger
Hatch

Hatch   Lane

M20

Leacon
Farm

Swallow Mill
Farm

Calehill
House

Hurstford Lane

Chart
Court

Stour Valley Walk

Nettlepole
Lane

**Little
Chart**

†

**Little Chart
Forstal**

Greensand Way

Ram Lane

Rooting
Street

Sheerland

Greensand Way

Surrenden

Rooting
Manor

Malmains

Saracens

Pluckley Road

G   H   J   143   K   L   M

Dowle
Street
Farm

Pluckley Road

109

G   H   J   K   L   M

Dunn Street

H8
1 Wyndy La

K8
1 Bradfield Rd
2 Thomson Rd

L6
1 Kenbrook
2 Tile Kiln Rd
3 Towers Vw

Westwell

North Downs Way

Eastwell Park

Home Farm

North Downs Way

Hotel

Eastwell Park

I

2

North Downs Way

Lenacre Street

Shottenden Manor

Dignash

3

Eastwell Court

4

Lenacre Street

128

Castle Farm

Lenacre Hall Farm

5

Sandyhurst Lane

Watsons

Technical Procurement Sports Club

Sandyhurst Lane Close

Kingsland Lane

Kingsland

Trinity Road

Friesian Way

Coat Leeds Lane

Jeffery Close

Cowley Close

The Towers School

Kennington Cricket Club

Downs View County Infant School

6

Towers View

Grosvenor Road

Broadhurst Drive

Rookery

Ulley

Kennington C of E Junior School

Upr Vicarage Rd

Kennington

PO

M20

Ashford Golf Club

Rothbrook

Bloomsbury Way

Portland

Dale Dr

Walk

Hurst Road

Lower Vicarage Road

Glebe Way

Walnut Close

Stone Close

FAVERSHAM ROAD

Church Road

Ker

Nicholas Road

Westwell Lane

Sandyhurst Lane

Hoads Wd Gdns

Potters Cl

Potters Corner

Grasmere Close

Larch Walk

Crofton Close

Bracken Close

Thirlmere Close

Ashborne Close

Meadowbrook

The Pasture

Park Vale

Tabret Close

Park Road

Greenbank

Tudor Road

Tudor End

7

A20(T)

The Warren

Almond Close

Lodge Wood Drive

MAIDSTONE

Farrer Cl

Landbury

Trinity Road

Rutherford Road

Bockhanger

Bybrook Road

Belmont Road

PO

Bybrook County Junior School

Bybrook County Primary Infants School

Mardol Road

Beecholme

Nine Acres

Tadworth Road

Rectory Way

Bybrook

Northumberland Avenue

York Road

Nettlefield

Pudley Cl

Carden Place

8

Junction 9

M20

145

Hotel

FOUGERES WAY

Warren Lane

CANTERBURY

New Hayesbank Surgery

Hotel

A28

A251

G   H   J   K   L   M

M8
1 Eythorne Cl
2 Kingswood
3 Shaw Cross

M7
1 Meadowbrook Cl
2 Midsummer Hl
3 Tudor Byway
4 Underwood Cl

M6
1 Kennington Pl
2 Sherwood Cl

L8
1 Old Ash Cl

L7
1 Riding Hl
2 Woodstock Wy

SIMONE WEIL AVENUE A20(T)

B7
1 Canon Woods Wy

B6
1 East Mountain La
2 Okehampton Cl

A8
1 George Wms Wy
2 North Pends
3 Randolph Gdns
4 The Ridge

A6
1 Kings Meadow
2 St Marys Gn
3 Tritton Flds

A7
1 Billington Gdns

Boughton Aluph

Boughton Corner

A
B
C
110
D
E
F

I

stwell rk

2

FAVERSHAM ROAD A251

Malthouse Lane

Breakhouse Lane

Boughton Lees

Wye Road

Bramble Lane

Perry Court Farm

North Downs Way

Wye Station

LC

3

Wye Road

CANTERBURY ROAD A28

Kempe's Corner

Spring Grove School

Harville Road

127

4

Park Barn Farm

5

Wilmington Farm

Great Stour

Stour Valley Walk

Kennington Hall

6

Kennington Cricket Club

Downs View County Infant School

Ball Lane

Over Field

7

Upr Vicarage Rd
PO
Kennington C of E Junior School

Church Road

Studio Close

The Ridge

The Street

Tritton Fields

Marlborough Way

Tritton Close

CANTERBURY ROAD A28

Orchard Lane

Stour Valley Walk

Kennington

Hillcrest Close

Hotel

Stour Valley Walk

8

FAVERSHAM ROAD

A251

Greenbank

Tudor Road

Nettlefield

Warwick Road

Beauchamp Close

Dudley Road

A28

WILLESBOROUGH ROAD

Blackwall Farm

ckwall Road

George Williams Way

Clarke Crescent

Raymond Fuller Way
Vincent Place

A
B

B5
1 Atkinson Wk
2 James Haney Dr
3 Jn Newington Cl

C
146
D

F2
1 Bramble Cl

E

F7
1 Heron's Brook

F

F3
1 Dennes Mill Cl

G2
1 Abbots Wk

G3
1 The Close
2 The Forstal
3 The Green
4 Old Vic'ge Gdns
5 St Ambrose Gn

H3
1 Cherry Gdn Crs

G   H   J   **111**   K   L   M

1
2
3
130
4
5
6
7
8

I
2
3
4
5
6
7
8

Marriage
Farm

Coombe
Manor

Wye
Court

Wye
Business
Park

Abbots Walk
1
2
Churchfield Way
High Street
Wye College
Scotton Street
PO
3
4
Upper Bridge Street
Coldharbour
Lane
Witchersdane
Hall
Coldharbour
Farm
Wye
Downs

Lady Joanna
Thornhill Primary
School
Little Chequers
Stonegate
Church Street
5
Cherry Garden Lane
Jarman's Field
1
1
1

Chequers
Park
Orchard Dr
Wye
Wye Surgery
Oxenturn Road

Silks
Farm
Amage Road
Amage
Farm

North Downs Way

Witchersdane

Broad
Downs
North Downs Way

Oxenturn Road

Brabourne Road

The Street

Naccolt

Troy Town Lane
Brook

**Troy
Town**

Nat's Lane
Nat's Lane
7

Spelders
Hill
Hampton

Hampton Lane

G   H   J   **147**   K   L   M

J8
1 Stonebridge

Brook CP
School

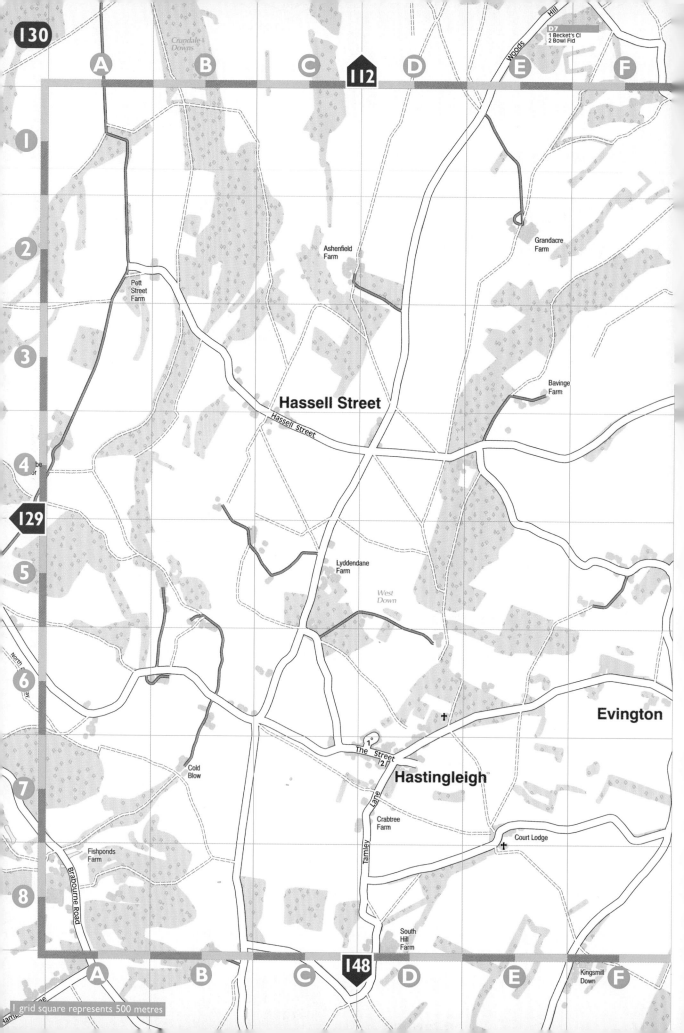

A   B   C   **112**   D   E   F

Hill

D7
1 Becket's Cl
2 Bowl Fld

Woods

1

*Crundale
Downs*

2

Ashenfield
Farm

Grandacre
Farm

Pett
Street
Farm

3

Bavinge
Farm

Hassell Street

Hassell Street

4

5

Lyddendane
Farm

*West
Down*

North D... W

6

Evington

The   Street
1
2

Cold
Blow

Hastingleigh

7

Crabtree
Farm

Court Lodge

Tamley Lane

Fishponds
Farm

Brabourne Road

8

South
Hill
Farm

A   B   C   **148**   D   E   Kingsmill   F
Down

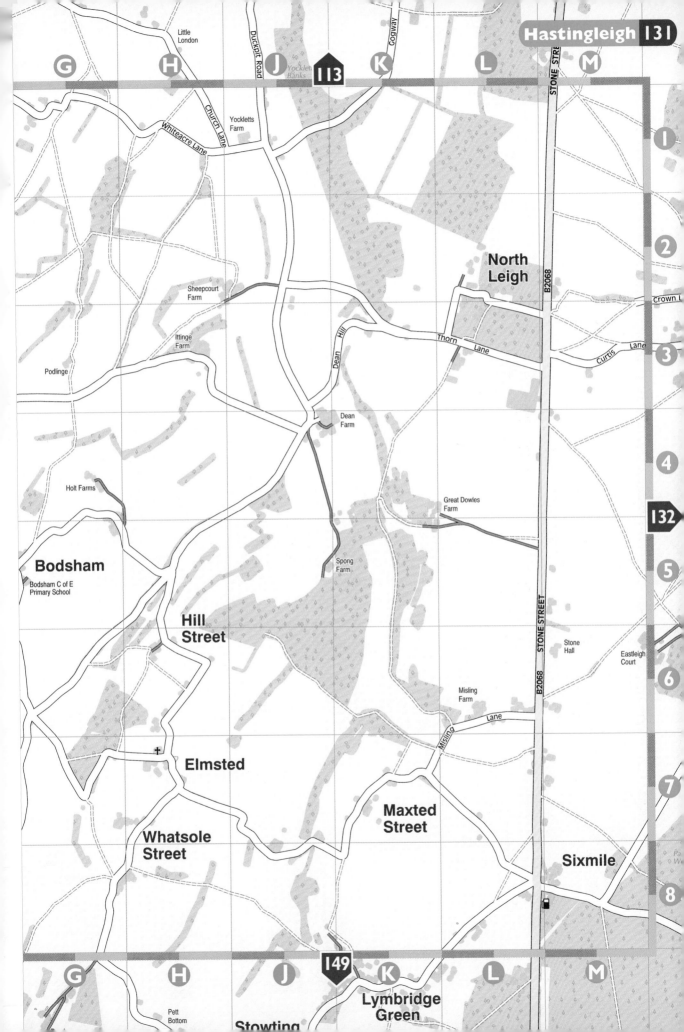

G H J **113** K L M

Little London

Duckpit Road

Yocklets Banks

Cogway

Whiteacre Lane

Church Lane

Yockletts Farm

Sheepcourt Farm

Ittinge Farm

Podlinge

North Leigh

B2068

Crown L

Thorn Lane

Curtis Lane

Dean Hill

Dean Farm

Holt Farms

Great Dowles Farm

132

Bodsham

Bodsham C of E Primary School

Spong Farm

Stone Hall

Eastleigh Court

Hill Street

Elmsted

Misling Farm

Misling Lane

STONE STREET

B2068

Maxted Street

Whatsole Street

Sixmile

G H J **149** K L M

Pett Bottom

Lymbridge Green

Stowting

1 2 3 4 5 6 7 8

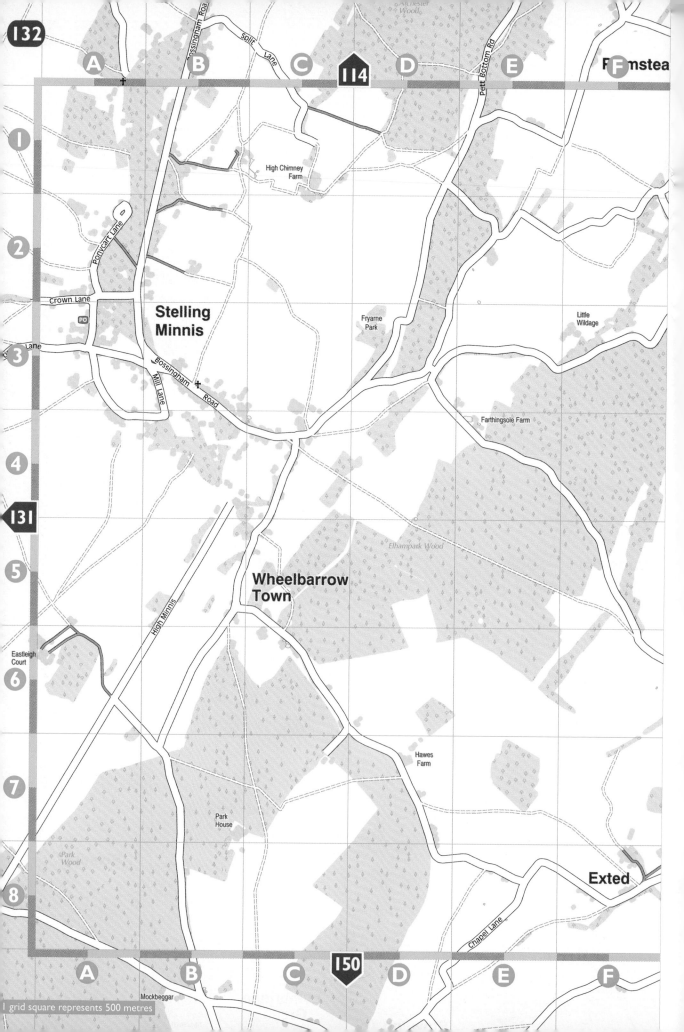

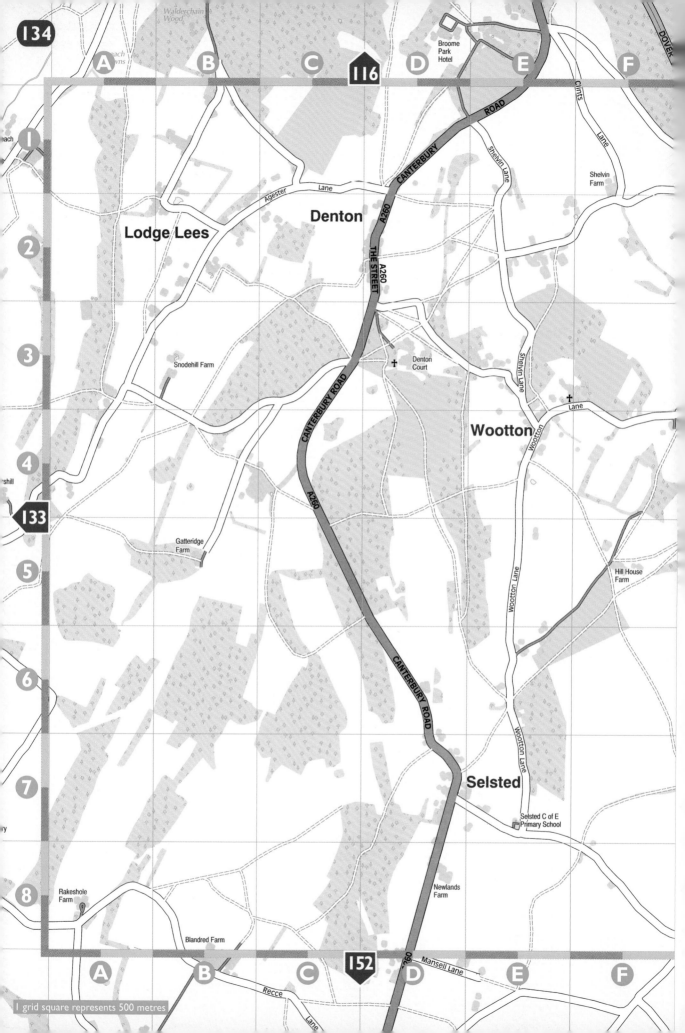

116

133

152

A B C 116 D E F

Walderchain Wood

DOVER

Broome Park Hotel

CANTERBURY ROAD

Clints Lane

Shelvin Lane

Shelvin Farm

Agester Lane

Denton

Lodge Lees

A260

THE STREET

A260

Snodehill Farm

CANTERBURY ROAD

† Denton Court

Shelvin Lane

† Lane

Wootton

Wootton

Gatteridge Farm

A260

Wootton Lane

Hill House Farm

CANTERBURY ROAD

Wootton Lane

Selsted

Selsted C of E Primary School

Rakeshole Farm

Newlands Farm

Blandred Farm

A B C 152 D E F

Recce Lane

A260

Mansell Lane

1
2
3
4
5
6
7
8

G H J `117` K L M

Westcourt Lane

The Grange

Thornlea Health

Approach Road

PO

Church Hill

Moorland Road

Sibe Primary School

West Court Farm

Coxhill

Coxhill Farm

Coxhill

Halfway Street

A2(T)

DOVER ROAD

A2(T)

Coxhill

Upton Wood

Geddinge Farm

A2(T)

`136`

Wickham Bushes

Lydden Hill

Swanton Lane

Warren Lane

Swanton Lane

Swanton Court Farm

Little London

St Johns Farm

North Court

G H J `153` K L M

I

2

3

4

5

6

7

8

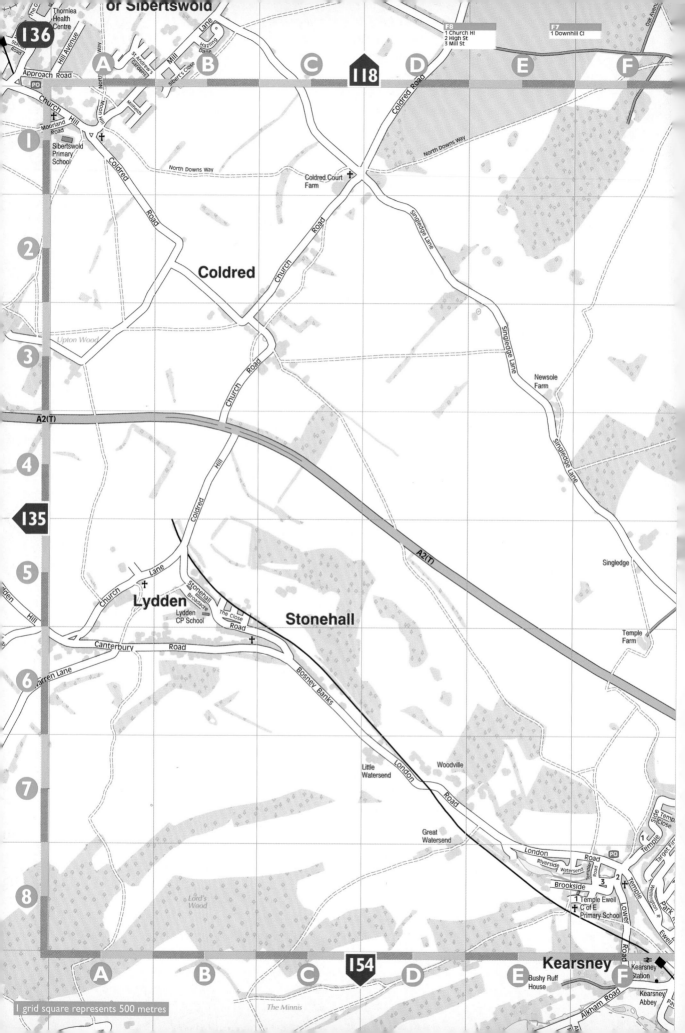

or Sibertswold

Thornlea
Health
Centre

A   B   C   118   D   E   F

Hill Avenue
Station
Road
Approach Road
PO

St Andrew's
Gardens
Sibert's Close
Mill
Lane
Hazling
Dane
North
Moor
Way
Minniefield
North Downs Way

Moorland
Road
Church
Hill
Sibertswold
Primary
School

1

Coldred
Road
North Downs Way

Coldred Court
Farm

Singledge Lane

North Downs Way

2

Coldred

Church
Road

Upton Wood

3

Newsole
Farm

Singledge Lane

A2(T)

135

4

5

Church
Lane

Lydden

Coldred
Hill

Stonehall
Broadacre
The Close

Lydden
CP School

Stonehall
Road

Stonehall

A2(T)

Singledge

Temple
Farm

6

Warren Lane
Canterbury
Road
den
Hill

Bosney Banks

Little
Watersend

Woodville

London
Road

7

Great
Watersend

London
Road
PO
Riverside
Watersend
Brookside

1 Temple Ewell
C of E
Primary
School

Temple
Side
Close

Target Fm

Temple
Park

Wellington R

8

Lord's
Wood

Kearsney
Kearsney
Station

A   B   C   154   D   E   F
Bushy Ruff
House
Alkham Road
Lower
Ewell
Road
Kearsney
Abbey

The Minnis

1 grid square represents 500 metres

J5
1 Chapel Rd
2 Chestnut Cl
3 Forge La
4 Orchard Cl

J6
1 Joyes Rd
2 Manley Cl

J7
1 Alison Cl

G   **H**   **J**   **119**   **K**   **L**   **M**

1

Eastling
Wood

Napchester

Maydensole
Farm

CT15

2

Eastling Down
Farm

West
Langdon

3

Holly
Lodge

4

Beechwood Cl

**Church
Whitfield**

138

5

Whitfield

Pineham

Whitfield
CP School

6

Whitfield
Surgery

Whitfield
CP School

PO

Hotel

7

Enterprise
Business
Centre

Council
Offices

White
Cliffs
Business Park

White Cliffs
Business Park

Honeywood Parkway

Gu

A2(T)

**Temple
Ewell**

Honeywood
Road

Archers Court
Secondary
School

8

The Abbey
Practice

Woodside
Close
Laburnum Close

Melbourne
CP School

K6
1 Joyes Cl
2 Loxwood Cl

Frith
Farm

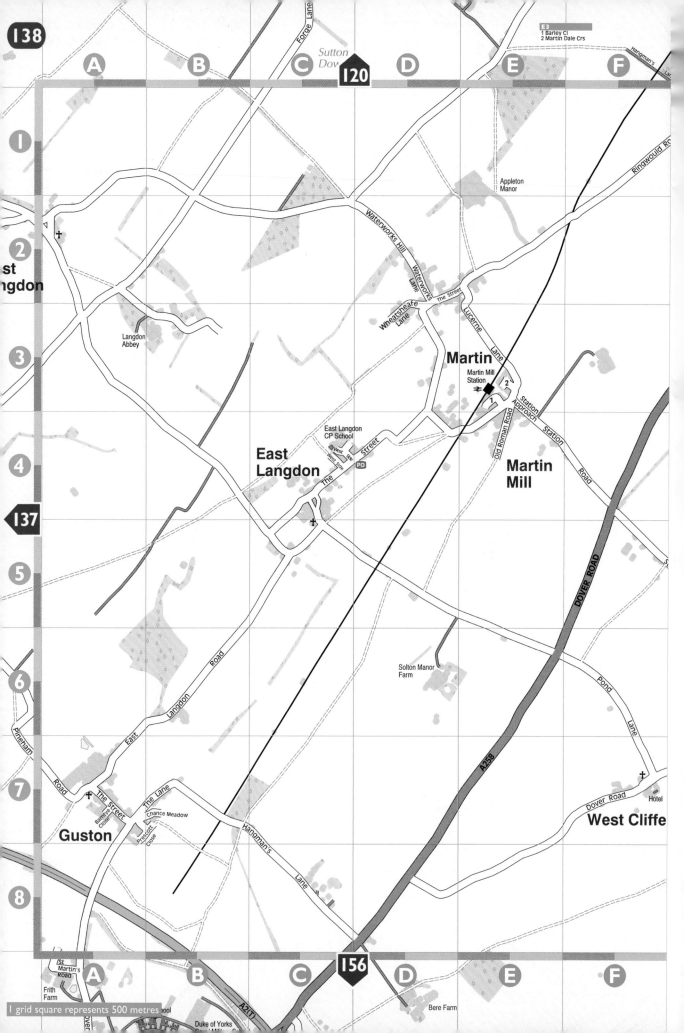

A **B** **C** **D** **E** **F**

Sutton Dow

120

E3
1 Barley Cl
2 Martin Dale Crs

Ringwould Rd

Hangman's La

1

Appleton
Manor

2
st
ngdon

Waterworks Hill

Langdon
Abbey

Waterworks Lane

The Street

Lucerne Lane

Wheatsheafe
Lane

3

Martin

Martin Mill
Station

2

7

4

East Langdon
CP School

West Side

The Street

PO

**East
Langdon**

The

Station Approach

Old Roman Road

Station Road

**Martin
Mill**

137

5

6

East Langdon Road

Solton Manor
Farm

Pond Lane

DOVER ROAD

Pineham Road

A258

7

The Street

The Lane

Barnsye Close

Chance Meadow

Prescott Close

Hangman's Lane

Dover Road

Hotel

West Cliffe

Guston

8

1st
Martin's
Road

Frith
Farm

A **B** **C** **D** **E** **F**

156

A2(T)

Bere Farm

Duke of Yorks

1 grid square represents 500 metres

G   H   J   K   L   M

Ringwould

`121`

Kingsdown

DOVER ROAD

Ringwould Road

The Avenue

Victoria Road
Hillcrest Road
Kingsdown Hill
Queensdown
Bayview Road
Northcote Road
Oldstairs Road
Waln
Kingsdown
Golf Club

The Leas

Hill Farm

The Lynch

Oldstairs Road

Granville Road

Free Down

Otty Bottom

Hope Point

Green Lane

Curling Road

Margarets Road

Nelson Park Road

Collingwood Road East

East Valley Farm

Boyne Road

Norway Road

Fleet Road

Drove

Saxon Shore Way

Seymour Road

Collingwood Road

Nelson Park Road

Hardy Road

St Vincent Road

Kingsdown Road

Hog's Bush

Bockhill Farm

The Droveway

The Freedown

The Avenue

St Margaret's at Cliffe

Wallett's Court

Townsend Farm Road

Chapel Lane

High Street

Well Lane

Sea Street

Vicarage Lane

St Georges Place

Glebe Close

Linden Close

Reach Close

Reach Road

Roman Way

Churchill Close

St Margarets Hotel & Country Club

St Margarets at Cliffe CP School

Portal House School

Medical Centre

Kenilworth Close

Convent Close

Chittenden Road

Norman Road

The Rise

Salisbury Road

Granville Road

Hotel Road

Victoria

Granville Road

Saxon Shore Way

St Margaret's Bay

Bay Hill

The Droveway

St Margaret's Road

Bay Hill

Reach Court Farm

The Crescent

Forelands Way

Beach Road

The Pines Garden

The Bay Museum

Lighthouse Road

Sea View Road

Goodwin

Front

Shore

`157`

G   H   J   K   L   M

1
2
3
4
5
6
7
8

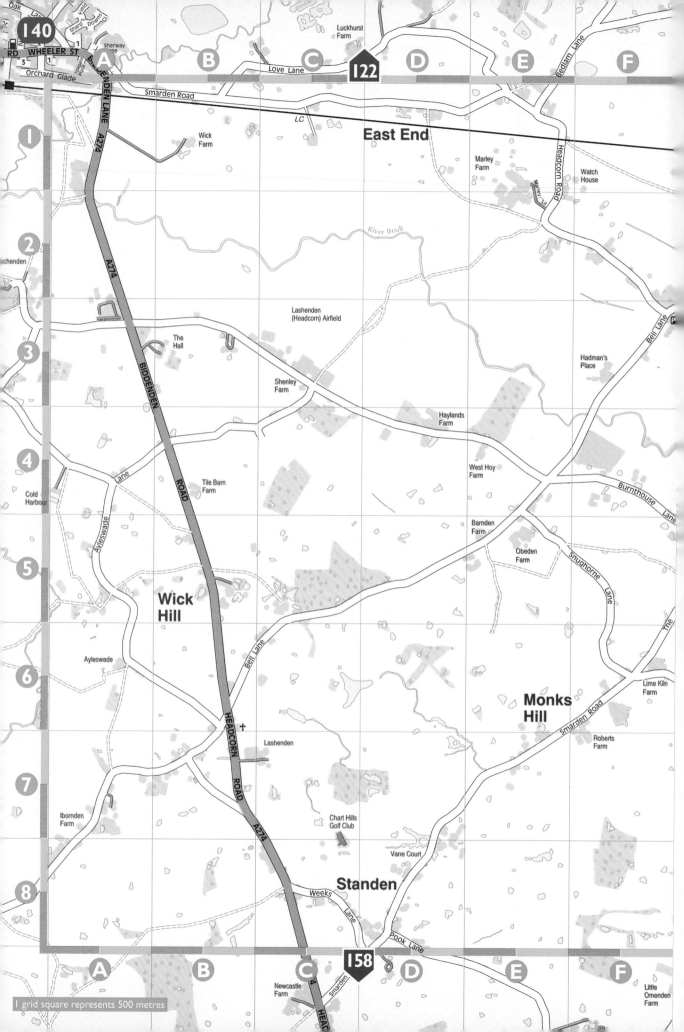

140

RD WHEELER ST

Oak Lane
Sharp Field Downs Cl
Sherway House
Tongate Place
Orchard Glade

A274 BIDDENDEN LANE

A

Smarden Road

Love Lane

B

122

C

D

E

Bedlam Lane

F

Luckhurst Farm

1

Wick Farm

East End

Marley Farm

Watch House

Headcorn Road

Marley La

2

chenden

River Beult

A274

BIDDENDEN ROAD

The Hall

Lashenden (Headcorn) Airfield

Hadman's Place

Bell Lane

3

Shenley Farm

Haylands Farm

4

Cold Harbour

Ayleswade Lane

Tile Barn Farm

West Hoy Farm

Burnthouse Lane

Barnden Farm

Obeden Farm

Snughorne Lane

5

Wick Hill

Bell Lane

Monks Hill

Lime Kiln Farm

6

Ayleswade

Smarden Road

The

Roberts Farm

HEADCORN ROAD

†

Lashenden

7

Iborden Farm

A274

Chart Hills Golf Club

Vane Court

8

Weeks Lane

Standen

Pook Lane

A

B

Newcastle Farm

C

Smarden

158

HEAD

D

E

F

Little Omenden Farm

1 grid square represents 500 metres

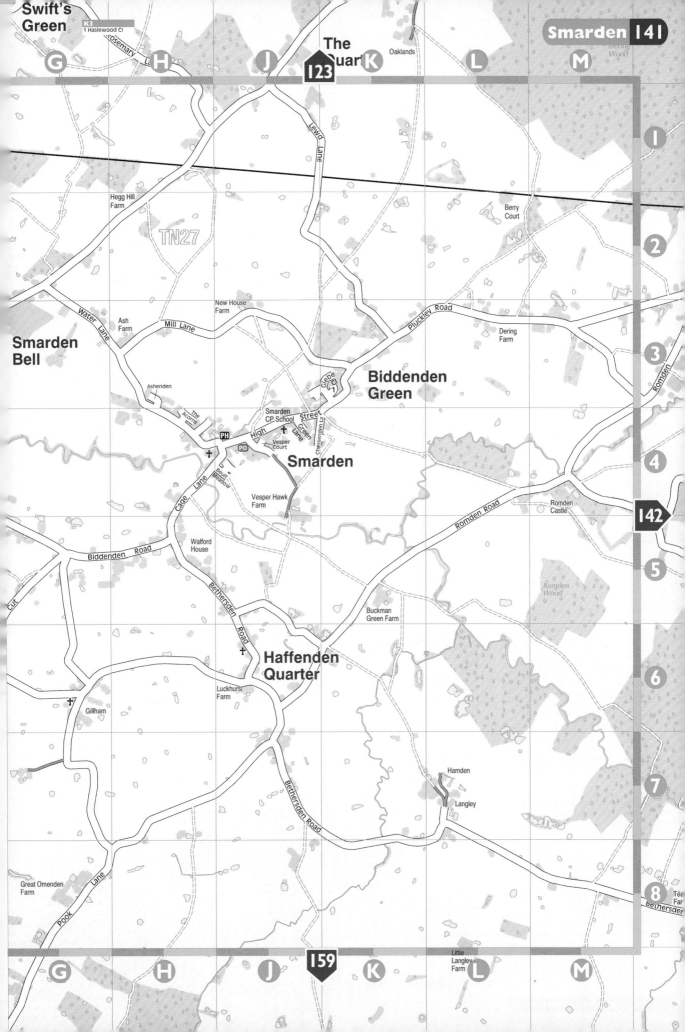

Swift's Green

K3
1 Haslewood Cl

G H J **123** The Quar K Oaklands L M

I

2

Dering Wood

Berry Court

Hegg Hill Farm

TN27

New House Farm

Pluckley Road

Dering Farm

3

Romden

Water Lane

Ash Farm

Mill Lane

Smarden Bell

Ashenden

The Acorns

Glebe Ct

Biddenden Green

Smarden CP School

High Street

Green Lane

Chessenden

PH

Vesper Court

Smarden

4

142

Romden Castle

PO

Beult Meadow

Vesper Hawk Farm

Romden Road

5

Cage Lane

Walford House

Biddenden Road

Romden Wood

Cut

Bethersden Road

Buckman Green Farm

6

Haffenden Quarter

Luckhurst Farm

Gillham

Hamden

7

Langley

Bethersden Road

Great Omenden Farm

Pook Lane

8

Tea Far

Bethersden

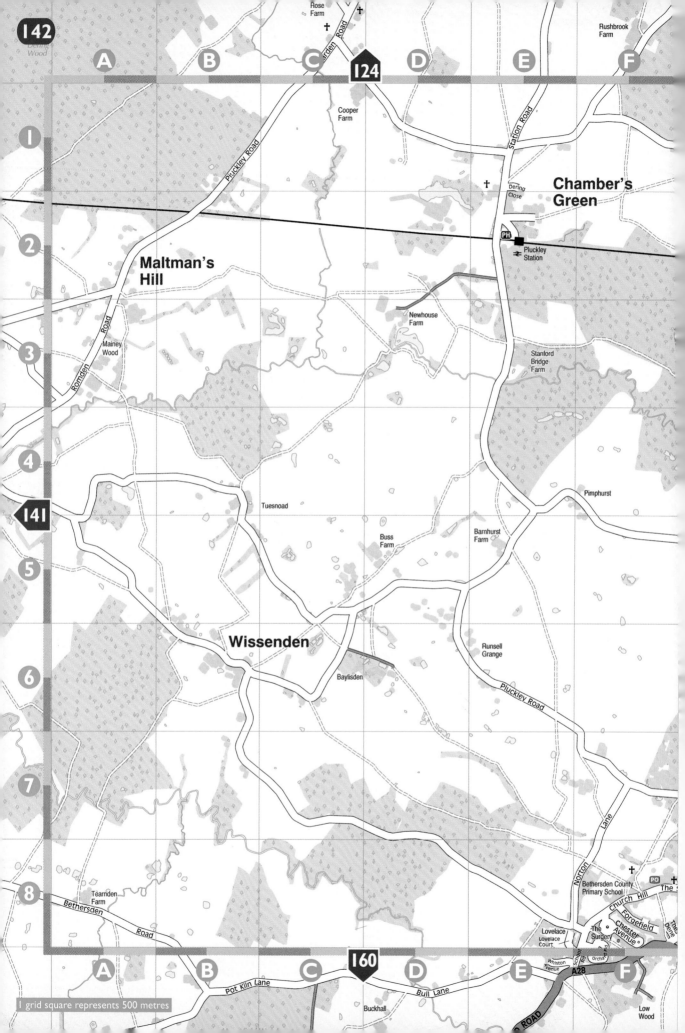

G   H   J   **125**   K   L   M

1

Saracens

Pluckley Road

Dowle
Street
Farm

Bethersden Road

**Ripper's
Cross**

Bear's Lane

Pluckley Road

2

Stour Valley Walk

The
Forest

3

Hoad's
Wood

Dynes
Farm

Belmont Farm

4

Belmont Farm
Business Centre

144

Snoadhill
Farm

Etchden Road

Etchden
Farm

5

**Daniel's
Water**

Oakdene
Farm

Purcha

Frid
Farm

Longberry
Farm

Park Lane

6

Sandy Lane

Yardhurst

Etchden Road

7

Vitters
Oak

Old Surrenden Manor Road

Mill
Farm

Winters Farm

8

Street

Mill Road

Old Surrenden
Manor

Forge Hill

Bethersden

Kiln Lane

161

G   A28   H   J   **161**   K   L   M

ASHFORD ROAD   A28

A B C **126** D E F

1

ipper's
ross

Bethersden Road

Bear's Lane

Stour Valley Walk

Worten

Swinford Old Manor
Residential School

Greensland Way

Godinto
CP Schoo

Springw

2

Etchden Road

Ninn Lane

Ninn
Lodge
Farm

Stour Valley Walk

Bucksfo
Manor

3

Goldwell Lane

Goldwell

Ninn Lane

Greensland Way

Great Chart
Cricket
Club

Chart Road

A28

4

**Great
Chart**

Street

Singleton Road

The Paddocks Dr

Coronation Dr

Bean
Close

Stour valley
Walk

Hopper's
Way

Millfield

Haymakers
Lane

Bucksford

Friars
School

The Paddock Lane

Hillcrest

Singleton Medical
Centre

Grey Willow Gdns

The Bulrushes

PO

Barn

Tithe

Hoxton
Cl

Great
Chart C
School

5

Ashford Road

A28

Singleton

Bradbridge Gn

Strouts
Road

Quarry
View

Bis

Purchase Lane

Purchase
Farm

Goldwell Lane

Little Moat
Farm

Greensland Way

Singleton

Buckford Lane

Longacre

Harvest

Hedgerows

6

Sandy Lane

Chart Road

Cuckoo Lane

New Rd

7

New
Street
Farm

ASHFORD ROAD

Mock Lane

Greensland Way

The Surgery

8

A28

**Chilmington
Green**

Greensland Way

A
B
C **162** D
E
F

Barnett
Farm

Greensland Way

1 grid square represents 500 metres

A28

Godinton Lane

B4
1 Hewitts Pl
2 Holmlea Cl
3 Taywood Cl
4 Willow Tree Cl

B3
1 Foxglove Gn

B1
1 James Allchin Gdns

A5
1 Breadlands Cl
2 Eastern Gdns
3 Hunter Cl

A3
1 Ashburton Cl

A4
1 Clive Dennis Ct

A   B   C   D   E   F

CANTERBURY ROAD
George Williams Way
A28
WILLESBOROUGH ROAD A2070

128

1

2

Sewage Works

Factory

Conningbrook Manor

TN24

Great Stour

M20

Henwood
Henwood Business Centre
Wyvern Way

3

HYTHE
The Norton Knatchbull School
Sandilands
Cradle Bridge Drive
Birch Close
Woodlands Road
Harvey Road
House Field
Foxglove Road
Earls Avenue
Stour Valley Walk
Blackwall Road
Vincent Close
Abbey Way
Silver Hill Road
KENNINGTON ROAD

Willesborough Lees

Hinxhill

4

Essella Park
Essella Road
ROAD
Romney Road
Glover Road
Albemarle Road
Spratlands Av
Stanhope Surgery
Oast Meadow
Special School
Mill Lane
Cornes Close
Lees Road
A2070
William Harvey Hospital
A&E
Ouseley Farm
Hinxhill Road

145

Wellesborough
Osborne Road
Hunter Rd
Onion Way
Wharton Gdns
Mill View
Osborne Cres
Milne Road
A292
Lees Road
The Street
Lacton Oast

5

Western Gdns
Summer Gdns
Breadlands Road
Park Place
Church Road CP School
Wickenden Crescent
Highfield Road
Harward Close
Ripley Road
Hill Park

6

Hunter Avenue
Twelve Acres
Blake
Bentley
Willesborough Health Centre
Sevington Lane
Evans Rd
Drake Road
Kingfisher Rd
Junction 10
A20(T)
HYTHE ROAD

7

Cudworth
Curtis Road
Gladstone Road
Mead Rd
Canterbury Road
Bath Road
Crowbridge Road
Hall
Boys
Church Road
Foster Road
Barrey Road
MUNSTEREIFEL ROAD
Church Road
Sevington
Court Lodge
Highfield Lane

8

BAD MUNSTEREIFEL ROAD
The Long Barrow
The Boulevard
Hall Avenue
Monument Way
The Parade
A2070
Waterbrook Avenue
Waterbrook

164

C3
1 Romsey Cl

B5, C5
Street Names for these grid squares are listed at the back of the index

C4
1 Field End
2 Fountains Cl
3 Queen's Rd
4 Silver Hill Gdns

C6
1 Knott Crs
2 Troubridge Cl

D5
1 Nelson Cl
2 Yeoman Gdns

D4
1 Longbridge

D6
1 Cornwallis Cl
2 Duckworth Cl
3 Nightingale Cl

1 grid square represents 500 metres

G   H   J   **129**   K   Troy Town   L   M

M8
1 Chestnuts

Nat's Lane

Nat's Lane

Hampton

Hampton Lane

Beddlestone Farm

I

Spelders Hill

Brook CP School

Spelders Hill

Cadman's Wood

2

Elmtree Farm

Hampton Lane

3

Plumpton Farm

Hampton Lane

4

148

Naccolt Farm

Fords Water

5

Quarrington Lane

Seeley Farm

Bircholt Forstal

6

Brockham Lane

Quarrington Lane

Quarrington Farm

Bircholt Court

Lees Road

7

Mountgarten W.

Prospect Way

Flatch Park

The Lees Close

Brockham Farm

The Warren

M20

8

Woolpack Hill

Ridgeway

Smeeth CP School

The Orchids

Old Rectory Cl

The Ridgeway

Church Road

Caroland

Oaklands

Kingsford

165

A20(T)

Home Farm

G   PO   **Mersham**   H   J   K   L   M   **Smeeth**

The Street

A   B   C 130 D   E   F

Hamden Lane

Kingsmill Down

1

Beddlestone Farm

Bulltown Farm

North Downs Way

2

Cadman's Wood

North Downs Way

3

The Hall

Brabourne Coomb

North Downs Way

4

TN25

Fords Water

Penstock Hall

PH Brabourne

Canterbury Road

Scot's Lane

5

Brabourne C of E Primary School

Canterbury Road

Bircholt Forstal

Manor Pound Lane

Lees Road

6

Pound Lane

7

Park Farm

Mountmarten Way

Prospect Way

The Lees Close

Water Farm

The Warren

Bridge Rd

Manse Field

Canterbury Road

knatchbull way

Brabourne Lees

The Pound House

Southenay Lane

Heminge Farm

8

Woolr

Sandy Pl

Cilland

Plain Road

Ranstone Close

Manor Leaze

Pound Lane

Granary Court Rd

neeth School

Lodge House

A   B   C 166 D   E   F

Southenay Farm

Priory

1 grid square represents 500 metres

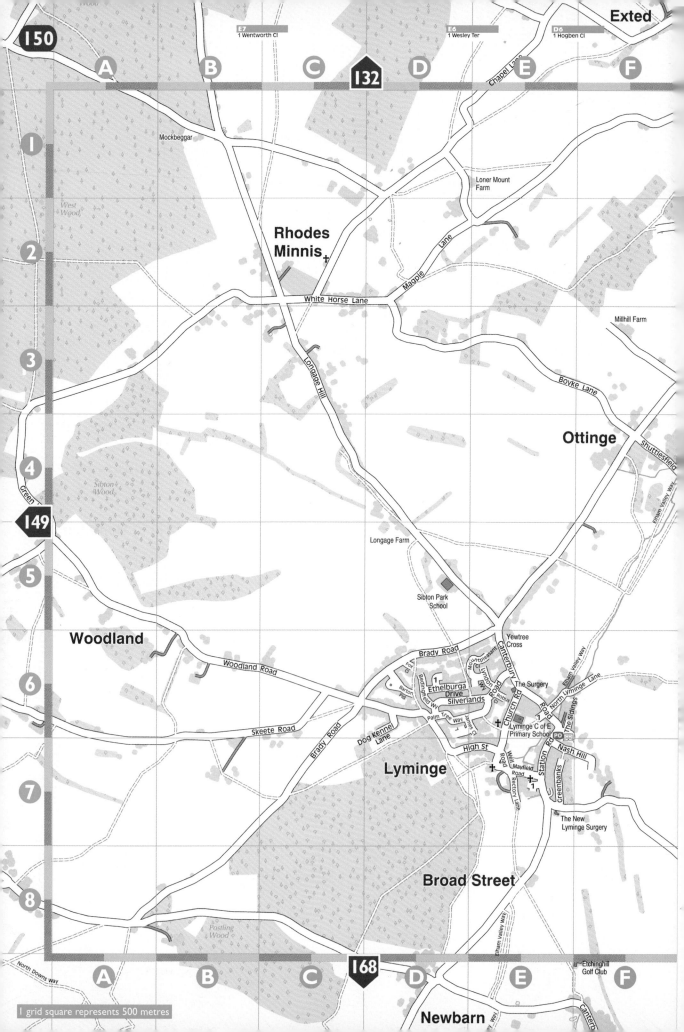

Exted

A   B   C   132   D   E   F

1   Mockbeggar

E7
1 Wentworth Cl

E6
1 Wesley Ter

D6
1 Hogben Cl

Chapel Lane

I

West Wood

Loner Mount Farm

2   Rhodes Minnis †

White Horse Lane

Magpie Lane

Millhill Farm

3   Longage Hill

Boyke Lane

Ottinge

Shuttlesfield

4   Sibton Wood

Green Lane

149

Longage Farm

Elham Valley Way

5   Sibton Park School

Woodland   Yewtree Cross

Brady Road

Canterbury Road

North Lyminge Lane

6   Woodland Road   Fox   Mount pleasant   Lyndon Cl   Robus Cl   The Surgery   Elham Valley Way   The Sidings

Bedingfield Way   Ethelburga Drive   Silverlands   Barton Fld   Palm Tree Way   James Cl

Skeete Road   †   Lyminge C of E Primary School   PO   Nash Hill

Dog Kennel Lane   High St   Well Road   Greenbanks

7   Brady Road   Lyminge   Mayfield Road   Rectory Lane   †   Station Rd

†   The New Lyminge Surgery

Broad Street

Postling Wood

Etchinghill Golf Club

8   North Downs Way   A   B   C   168   D   E   F   Canterb

Newbarn

G H J K L M

133

H1
1 Hunters Bank
2 The Orchards
3 Pound La
4 The Square

Elham

Old
Hospital

Cock La

Duck Street

Elham Surgery

Elham C of E
Primary School

Cemetery

Hog Gn

Canterbury Road

Elham Valley Way

Bereforstal
Farm

Standardhill
Farm

The Old
Rectory

Ladwood

Wick Farm

Mounts Court
Farm

Acrise
Place

152

White
Gate

Great Shuttlesfield
Farm

Lower
Winterage Farm

Winterage Lane

Shuttlesfield

CT18

Paddlesworth Court
Farm

Paddlesworth

Leas Road

I
2
3
4
5
6
7
8

G H J 135 K L M

Ⅰ

St Johns
Farm

North
Court

Belsey
Lane

Chalksole

Ewell
Minni

2

Ferne   Lane

Green   Lane

Green   Lane

Lane

Ellinge

Beard's Hall
Farm

3

Chalksole

Slip Lane

Slip Lane

Alkham Valley

4

Alkham

Short Lane

Glebelands

Gt Everden
Farm

Newlyn's
Meadow

154

Alkham Valley Road

Lane

Hill

5

**South
Alkham**

Meggett

Meggett
Farm

Hogbrook

6

Drellingore

7

Lower
Standen
Farm

8

Upper Standen
Farm

Alkham Valley Road

Capel Church
Farm

Hockley
Sole

G H J 171 K L M

Satmore Lane

A   B   C   136   D   E   F

Kearsney

Bushy Ruff
House

Kearsney
Station

Kearsney
Abbey

1

Ewell
Minnis

The Minnis

Alkham Road

Abbey
Road

Chilton Avenue

Coxhill
Crescent

Coxhill
Gardens

Minnis

Sanctuary
Close

2

RIVER

Alkham Valley Road

Chilton
Farm

Badgers
Rise

3

Wolverton

Alkham Valley Road

Minnis Lane

River
Bottom
Wood

4

153

St Radegund's
Abbey

Abbey Road

5

Mount Ararat

6

Poulton
Farm

Copt Hill
Farm

7

Elms Hill

Chilverton
Elms

Elms Vale Road

Lowslip   Hill

8

Broadsole Lane

PO

Lady
Road

Garne
Road

The Street

Young's Place

West
Hougham

Church
Hougham

Church Lane

Forge Field

Crook's Court

A   B   172   C   D   E   F

Temple Ewell
C of E
Primary School

Brookside

1 grid square represents 500 metres

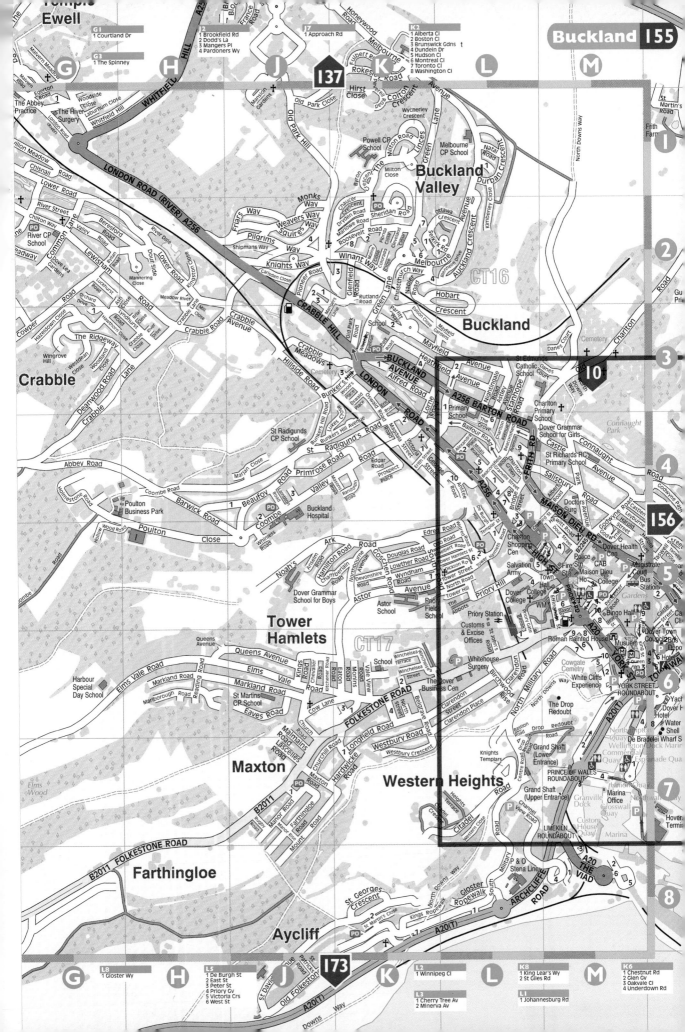

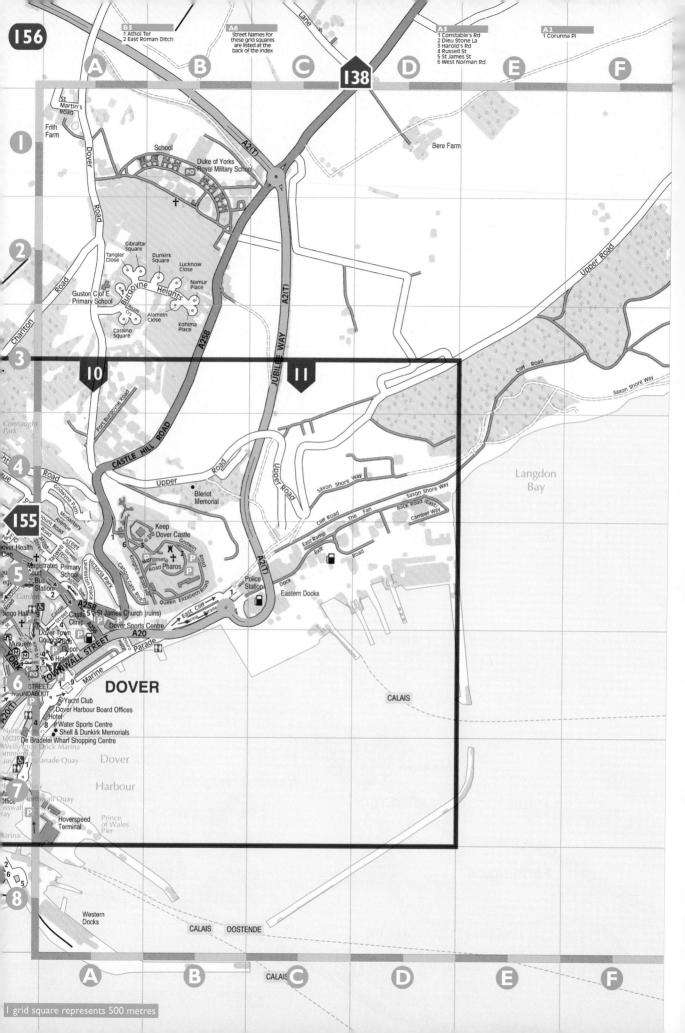

138

A   B   C   D   E   F

St
Martin's
Road

Frith
Farm

Bere Farm

School

Dover

Duke of Yorks
Royal Military School

PO

A2(T)

Road

Upper Road

Gibraltar
Square

Tangier
Close

Dunkirk
Square

Lucknow
Close

Namur
Place

Guston C of E
Primary School

Burgoyne Heights

Anzio
Crs

Alamein
Close

Kohima
Place

Cassino
Square

Chariton

Road

JUBILEE WAY

A2(T)

A258

Cliff Road

Saxon Shore Way

10

11

Connaught
Park

Fort Burgoyne Road

CASTLE HILL ROAD

Upper Road

Upper

Road

Cliff Road

Saxon Shore Way

Saxon Shore Way

Langdon
Bay

Godwyne Path

Road

Bleriot
Memorial

The Fan

Back Road (East)

Camber Way

155

Monastery

Avenue

Mount Road

Keep
Dover Castle

Godwin
Road

Knight's Road

East Ramp

Exit

Dock

Road

Dover Health
Cen

Magistrates
Court
Bus
Station

Primary School

Victoria Park

Laureston Place

Canons Gate Road

Mortimer
Road

Pharos

P

P

P

Police
Station

Eastern Docks

Garden

A258

Castle

Castle
Clinic

A256

St James Church (ruins)

Dover Sports Centre

Queen Elizabeth Road

East Cliff

Marine

Parade

A2(T)

Bingo Hall

YORK

Museum

M

A20

Dover Town
Council

Bus
Depot

A20

TOWNWALL STREET

Parade

Marine

DOVER

CALAIS

STREET

ROUNDABOUT

A20(T)

Yacht Club

Dover Harbour Board Offices

Hotel

Water Sports Centre

Shell & Dunkirk Memorials

De Bradelei Wharf Shopping Centre

Northampton
Quay

Wellington Dock Marina

Commercial
Quay

Esplanade Quay

Dover

Harbour

Prince
of Wales
Pier

7

Northwall Quay

Crosswall
Quay

Office

Hoverspeed
Terminal

Marina

8

Western
Docks

CALAIS   OOSTENDE

CALAIS

A   B   C   D   E   F

St Margaret's Hotel & Country Club

Read Farm

Roman Way

Churchill Close

St Margaret's Road

Lighthouse Road

Sea View Road

Goodwin Road

Foreland Crescent

Beach Road

The Bay Museum

The Pines Garden

139

The Front

Saxon Shore Way

Wanstone Farm

South Foreland Lighthouse (NT)

South Foreland

Fan Bay

Saxon shore way

G H J K L M

1 2 3 4 5 6 7 8

G H J K L M

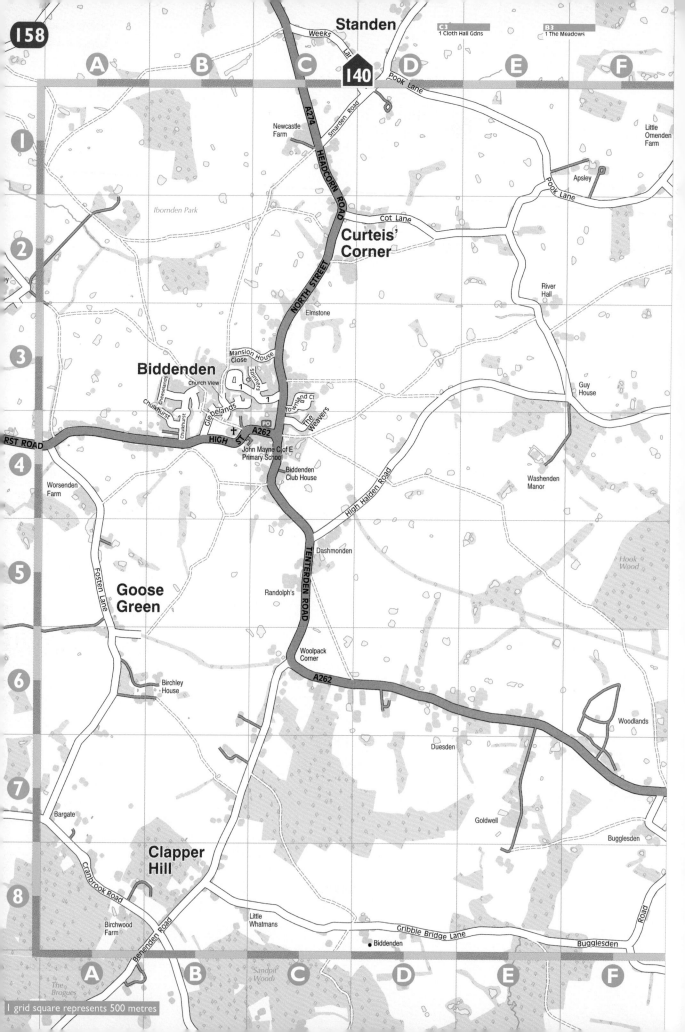

Standen

Weeks Lane

C3 1 Cloth Hall Gdns   B3 1 The Meadows

A   **B**   **C**   **D**   **E**   **F**

140

Pook Lane

Newcastle Farm

Smarden Road

Little Omenden Farm

1

Iborんden Park

Apsley

Pook Lane

A274

HEADCORN ROAD

Cot Lane

Curteis' Corner

River Hall

2

NORTH STREET

Elmstone

3

Mansion House Close

Biddenden

Guy House

Church View

Spinners

1

Cheeselands

Chulkhurst

Glebelands

1

Townland Cl

Chulkhurst

The Weavers

RST ROAD   HIGH   ST   A262

Washenden Manor

PO

4

John Mayne C of E Primary School

Worsenden Farm

Biddenden Club House

High Halden Road

Fosten Lane

Dashmonden

Hook Wood

5

Goose Green

Randolph's

TENTERDEN ROAD

6

Birchley House

Woolpack Corner

A262

Woodlands

Duesden

7

Bargate

Goldwell

Bugglesden

8

Clapper Hill

Cranbrook Road

Benenden Road

Little Whatmans

Gribble Bridge Lane

Bugglesden

Birchwood Farm

Biddenden

Road

A   **B**   **C**   **D**   **E**   **F**

The Brogues

Sandpit Wood

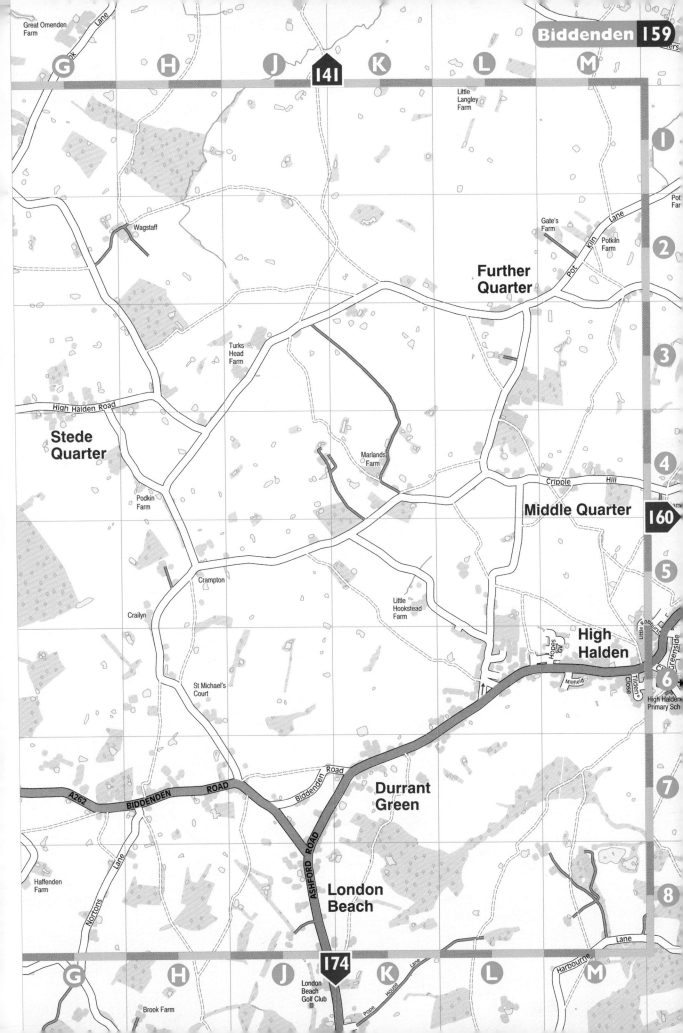

Great Omenden Farm

141

G H J K L M

Little Langley Farm

I

Pot Far

Wagstaff

Gate's Farm
Potkiln Farm

Kiln Lane

Pot

2

Further Quarter

Turks Head Farm

3

High Halden Road

Marlands Farm

Stede Quarter

Cripple Hill

4

Middle Quarter

Podkin Farm

160

Crampton

5

Little Hookstead Farm

Crailyn

Little Robhurst

Hopes Gv

High Halden

St Michael's Court

Millfield

Tilden Close

Greenside

6

High Halden Primary Sch

Road

Biddenden

Durrant Green

7

A262   BIDDENDEN   ROAD

ASHFORD   ROAD

Haffenden Farm

Nortons Lane

London Beach

8

Harbourne Lane

174

G H J K L M

London Beach Golf Club

Pope House Lane

Brook Farm

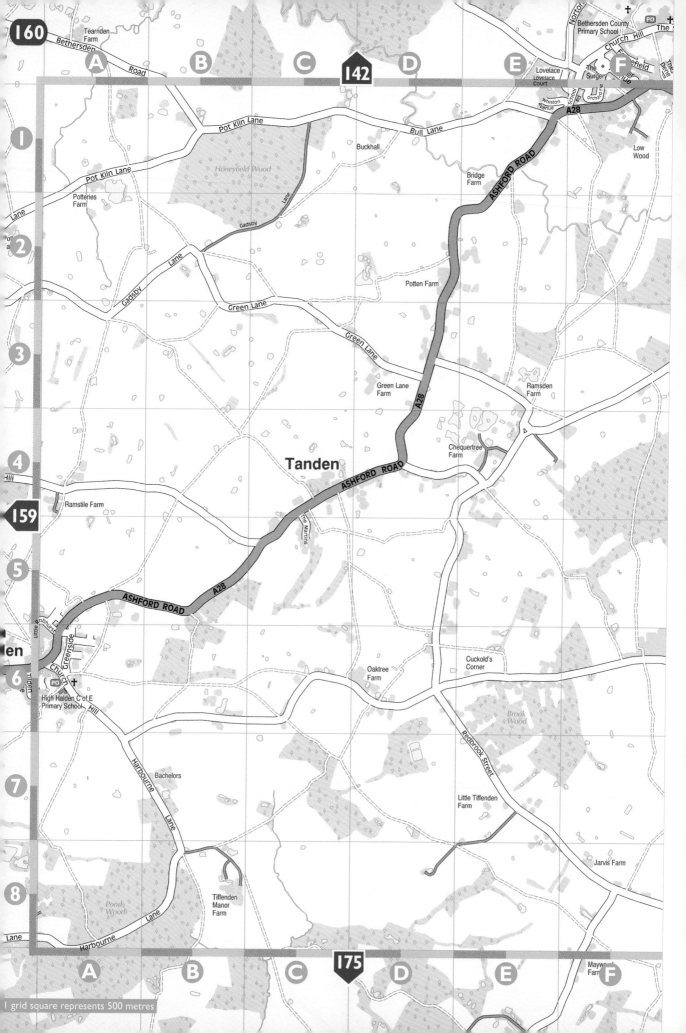

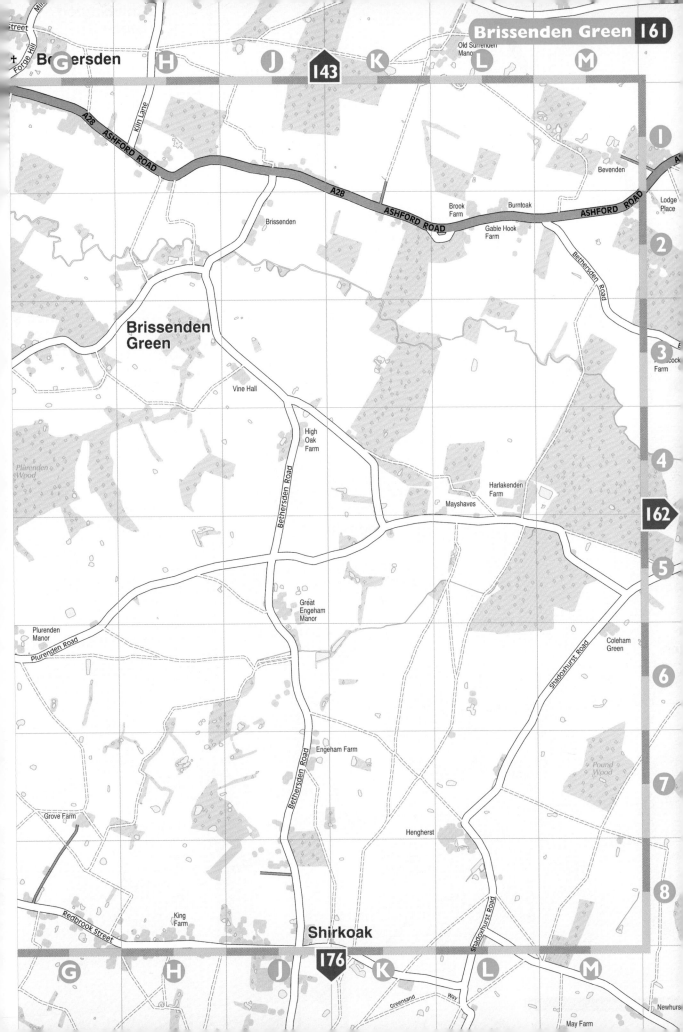

G Betgersden H J 143 K L M

Forge Hill

Kiln Lane

A28

ASHFORD ROAD

I
1

Old Surrenden Manor

Bevenden

Lodge Place

ASHFORD ROAD

A28

Brissenden

Brook Farm

Burntoak

Gable Hook Farm

Bethersden Road

2

Brissenden Green

3
Peacock Farm

Vine Hall

High Oak Farm

4

Plurenden Wood

Bethersden Road

Harlakenden Farm

Mayshaves

162

5

Great Engeham Manor

Plurenden Manor

Plurenden Road

Coleham Green

Shadoxhurst Road

6

Engeham Farm

Pound Wood

7

Grove Farm

Hengherst

8

Redbrook Street

King Farm

Shirkoak

Shadoxhurst Road

G H J 176 K L M

Greensand Way Newhurst

May Farm

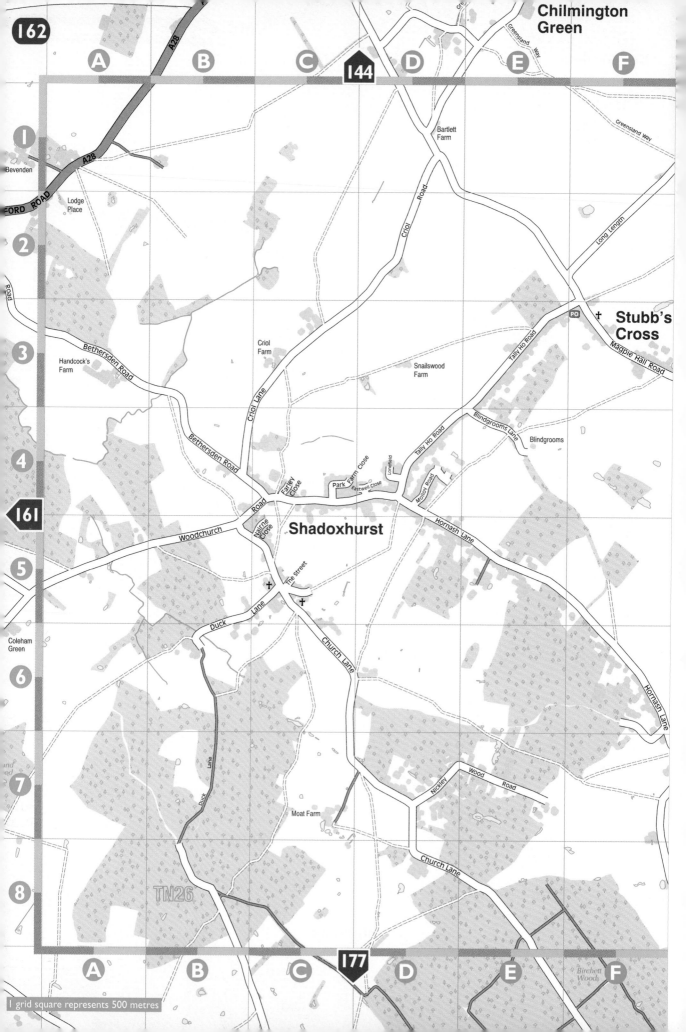

BAD-MUNSTEREIFEL-ROAD A2042

G   H   J   145   K   L   M

Washf...
Chart Road
Brisley Farm
K1
1 Bluebell Cl
Bensted
Millbank Rd
Ellingham Industrial Centre
Bluebell C.

Willowbed Farm

Long Length

Court Lodge Farm

Pound Lane
Greensland Way

River Cre Cl

Ashford Road

Pound Court
South Lea
PO

Forestall Meadow
Park Farm Recreation Centre
Field View

† **Kingsnorth**

Church Hill

Kingsnorth C of E Primary School
†

Roman Way
Centurion Walk
Moorfield Meadow
Newborn Road
Silver Birch
Farrers Way
WK
The Rectory
Primrose Dr
Primrose Drive
Bluebell Road
SnoWell Road
Shipley Ml
Shipley Rd
Bell Chapel Cl
Smithy Drive
Sheepfold Lane
Battendge Rd
Saw Lodge Field
Conker Cl
Acorn Close
Dove Cl
Mnr House Drive
A2070

I

2

Bond Lane
Greensland Way
Steeds Cl
Steeds Lane
Stumble Lane
Church Hill
Finn Farm
Finn Farm Co.

3

4

Wix's Farm
Ashford Road

Ashford Town Football Club

Braeside Farm

Greensland Way

Steeds Lane

164

5

Bishop's Wood

Lone Barn Farm

6

Hamstreet Road
Bromley Green
Bromley
Green
Road

Golden Wood

Greensland Way

Brisley Lane

7

Row...
Stree...

8

G   H   J   178   K   L   M

Capel Road

Gorse Green Farm

A2070

Pound...

Woodreeve Farm

Capel

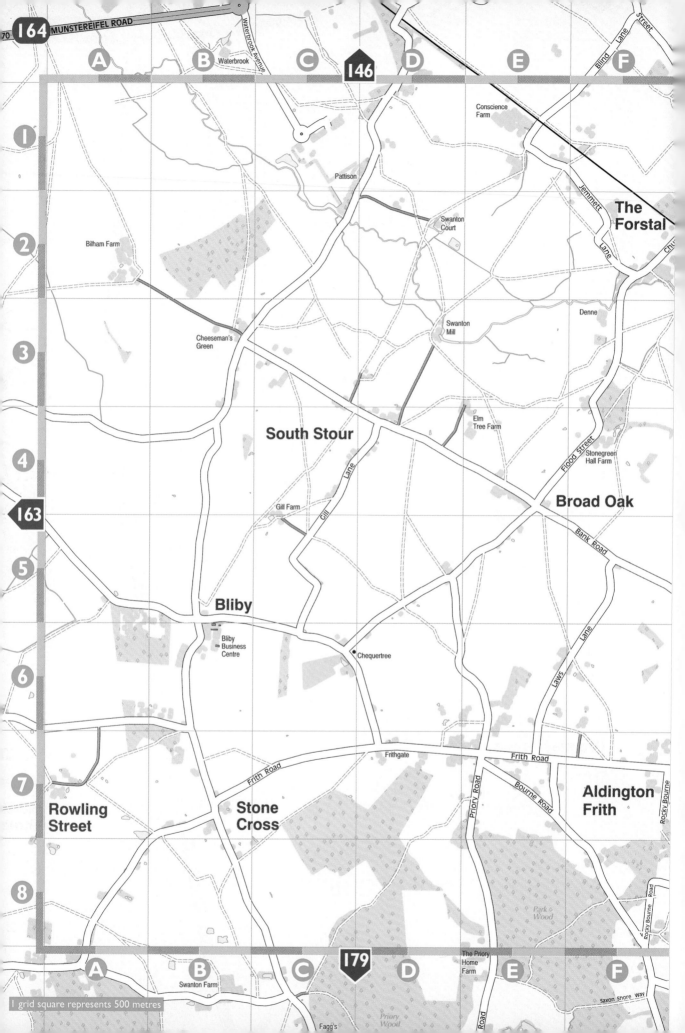

G
H
J
147
K
L
M

1 Flanders Fld

The Orchid

Kingsford street

PO

Mersham

Oaklands

The Street

Road

Church

Orchard Cl

Cherry

Glebe

Bower Road

Mersham CP School

Home Farm

The Paddocks

Stock Lane

A20(T)

HYTHE ROAD

Station Rd

Smeeth

M20

A20(T)

Bower Road

Evegate Manor Farm

Evegate Business Centre

Little Stock Farm

Apple Barn

East Stour River

Evegate Mill

166

Blackhouse Wood

Handen Farm

Bank Farm

Clap Hill

Calleywell Lane

Symnell

Stonestreet Green

Goldwell Lane

Hogben Farm

Lower Park F

Frith Road

Longfield

Quarry Wood

Bagstone Hollow

Coldwell Cl

The Surgery

Church Vw

Church Lane

Road

Dicksons

Bourne

Mill Lane

Mill Lane

Earlsfield

Forge Hill

Aldington CP School

Saxon Shore Way

Aldington

Court Lodge Farm

Middle Park Farm

New Road Hill

1 2

Pattison's Farm

G
H
1 2
J
180
K
L
M

Cherry

Orchard

Lane

Saxon Shore Way

I

2

3

4

5

6

7

8

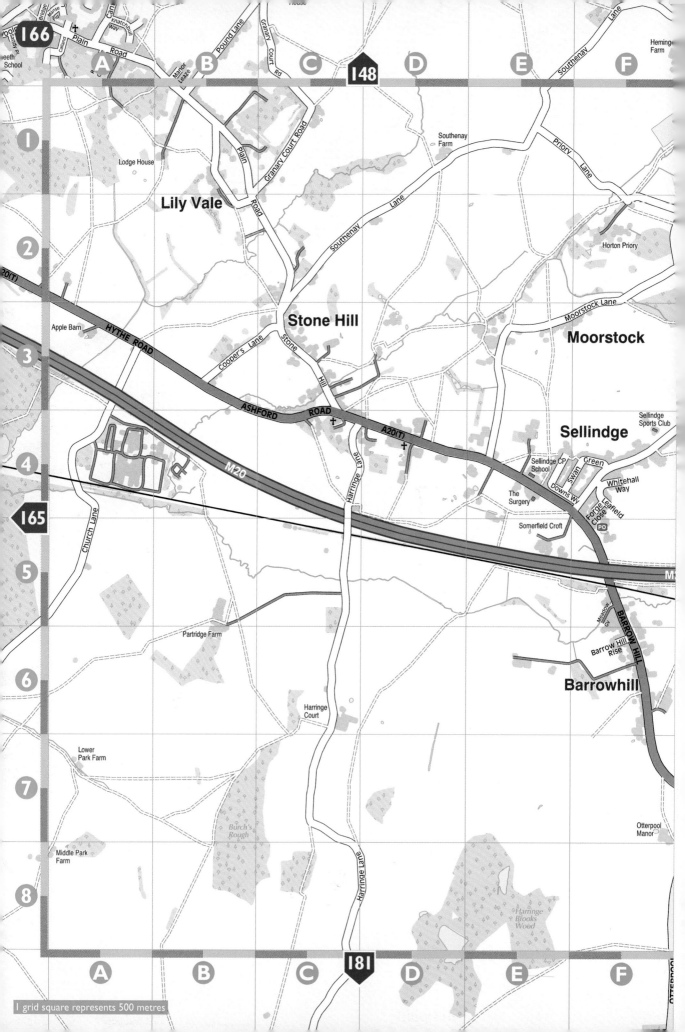

G5
1 Creteway Cl
2 Dallas-brett Crs
3 Kitchener Sq

G6
1 Browning Pl
2 Holly Cl
3 Tennyson Pl

G7
1 Arthur St
2 Ash Tree Rd
3 Elm Rd
4 Myrtle Rd
5 Ormonde Rd
6 Rossendale Gdns
7 The Tram Rd

G

H

J

153

K

L

M

I

Alkham Valley Road

Hockley Sol

A20(T)

Cauldham Lane

Hurst Lane

Capel Street

Satmore Lane

A20(T)

Capel Church Farm

Lane

Swinge Hill

Winehouse Lane

Satmar

Satmar

2

PO

Capel-le-Ferne CP School

3

Green La

Capel Street

Elizabeth

Lancaster Av

Beatrice Road

Helena Road

Capel-le-Ferne

Cauldham

Doctors Surgery

Victoria Road

Clarence Road

Albert Road

Alexandra Rd

Avondale

Helena Rd

NEW DOVER ROAD

Capel Court

Old Dover Road

3

Hope Farm

Cauldham Lane

NEW DOVER ROAD

Capel St

Albany Road

Old Dover Road

North Downs Way

4

B2011

172

The Warren

Crete Road East

Dover Hill

B2011

East Wear Bay

5

Montgomery

Brabner Close

DOVER HILL

Dover Road

Stanbury Crs

Hollands Avenue

6

Calgary Crs

HILL ROAD

Tyson Road

DOVER ROAD

Wear Bay Road

Bowles Well Gdns

A260

Greenfield Road

Sidney Street

Alexandra St

George Spurgen CP School

Green

Stuart Rd

Bowles Wls Gdns

Channel Cl

Lawrence Cl

Martello Industrial Estate

Warren Way

Warren Cl

Whitecliff Way

13

Princess St

Denmark

Highfield Ind Estate

Bradley Rd

Foreland Avenue

7

Doctors Surgery

Folly Rd

Warren Road

Burrow Rd

Pentold Road

Segrave Rd

Segrave Crs

St Marys (C of E (aided) Primary School

Hasborough Rd

Varne Pl

Wear Bay Rd

Varne Rd

Doctors Surgery

DOVER ROAD

Martello

MORRISON RD

Dudley Road

East Cliff

Wear

THE TRAM ROAD

Radnor Br Road

PO

Copt Point

8

The Burrock

The Stade

Radnor

Folkestone Yacht & Motor Boat Club

Marine Ter

MARINE PARADE

SUR ROAD

The Pde

Old High St

F7, F8, G8
Street Names for these grid squares are listed at the back of the index

Harbour Station

H

K4
1 Sea View Cl

J

K

L

M

H8
1 East Cliff Pas
2 Southbourne Rd

H7
1 Neason Wy
2 Thanet Gdns

A   **B**   **C**   **D**   **E**   **F**

Lowslip   Hill

Broadsole Lane

PO

The Street

Forge Field

Lady Road

Young's Pla

W B t
Hougham

Church
Hou D am

154

Church Lane

Crook's Court Lane

Gravel

Lane

Gravel Lane

Plough

Hill

I

Satmar

atmar

2

Great Hougham
Court Farm

Hougham Court La

B2011

A20(T)

Samphire Hoe
Country Park

3

ER   ROAD

B2011

A20(T)

over Road

North Downs Way

Abbot's
Cliff

Lydden
Spout

4

◀ **171**

5

6

7

8

A   **B**   **C**   **D**   **E**   **F**

Farthingloe

B201

St Georges
Crescent

St Martin's Close

Aycliff

St Davids Avenue

Old Folkestone Road

A20(T)

North Downs Way

North Downs Way

Aycliff
CP
School

Shakespeare
Cliff

Kings Ropewalk

Gloster
Ropewalk

Stena Line

155

A20(T)

G H J K L M

1
2
3
4
5
6
7
8

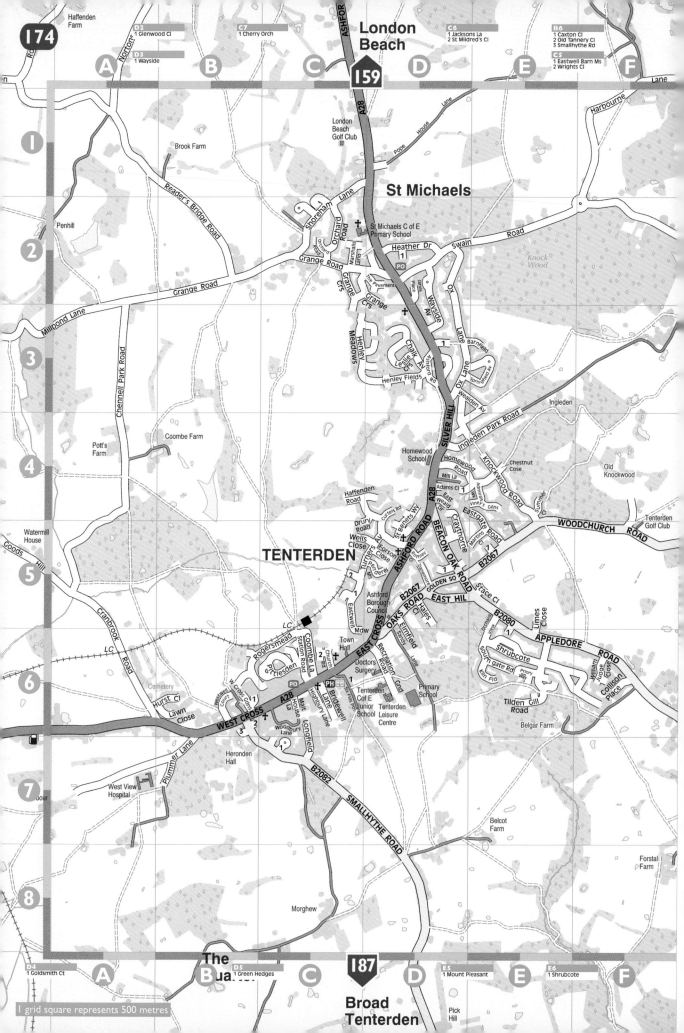

London
Beach

St Michaels

D2
1 Glenwood Cl
D3
1 Wayside
C7
1 Cherry Orch
C6
1 Jacksons La
2 St Mildred's Cl
B6
1 Caxton Cl
2 Old Tannery Cl
3 Smallhythe Rd
C5
1 Eastwell Barn Ms
2 Wrights Cl

A   B   C   D   E   F

I
2
3
4
5
6
7
8

Haffenden
Farm

Brook Farm

Penhill

Reader's Bridge Road

Millpond Lane

Chennell Park Road

Pott's
Farm

Coombe Farm

Watermill
House

Goods Hill

Cranbrook Road

Hurst Cl

Lawn
Close

Cemetery

West View
Hospital

Plummer Lane

Heronden
Hall

Morghew

London
Beach
Golf Club

Shoreham Lane

Orchard Road

Grange Road

Grange Road

Grange Crs

Grange Crs

Henley
Meadows

Henley Fields

Chalk Av

Leslie Crs

The Pavement

Heather Dr

PO

St Michaels C of E
Primary School

Swain   Road

Ashford Rd

Wayside

Ox Lane

Ox Lane

Silver Hill

Wealden Av

Springfield Av

Barnfield

Ingleden Park Road

Knock
Wood

Ingleden

Chestnut Cose

Old
Knockwood

Knockwood Road

Homewood
School

Homewood
Road

Mill La

Adams Cl

East
Weald

Eastgate Road

Vine Gdns

Summer

Woodchurch Golf Club

WOODCHURCH   ROAD

Haffenden
Road

Drury
Road

Wells
Close

Curteis Rd

St Beners Wy

Forson Close

Turden Derel

Eastwell
Mdw

TENTERDEN

Ashford Borough
Council

ASHFORD ROAD

BEACON OAK ROAD

Craythorne

Martins

GOLDEN SQ

B2067

Stace Cl

EAST HIL

B2080

Limes
Close

APPLEDORE   ROAD

Shrubcote

Southgate Rd

Priory
Way

Collison
Place

Tilden Gill
Road

Belgar Farm

LC

Rogersmead

Coombe La

Station Road

Artlesden

Church Rd

Town
Hall

PO

Doctors
Surgery

Tenterden
C of E
Junior
School

Bridewell

PH

Highbury Lane

West Cross Gdns

Westwell Court

Malt House La

WEST CROSS

Woodbury Lane

A28

Longfield

B2082

SMALLHYTHE ROAD

Belcot
Farm

Forstal
Farm

Recreation Gnd

Primary
School

Tenterden
Leisure
Centre

OAKS ROAD

Elmfield

Hales

Kiln Fld

Pick
Hill

A   B   C   D   E   F

1 grid square represents 500 metres

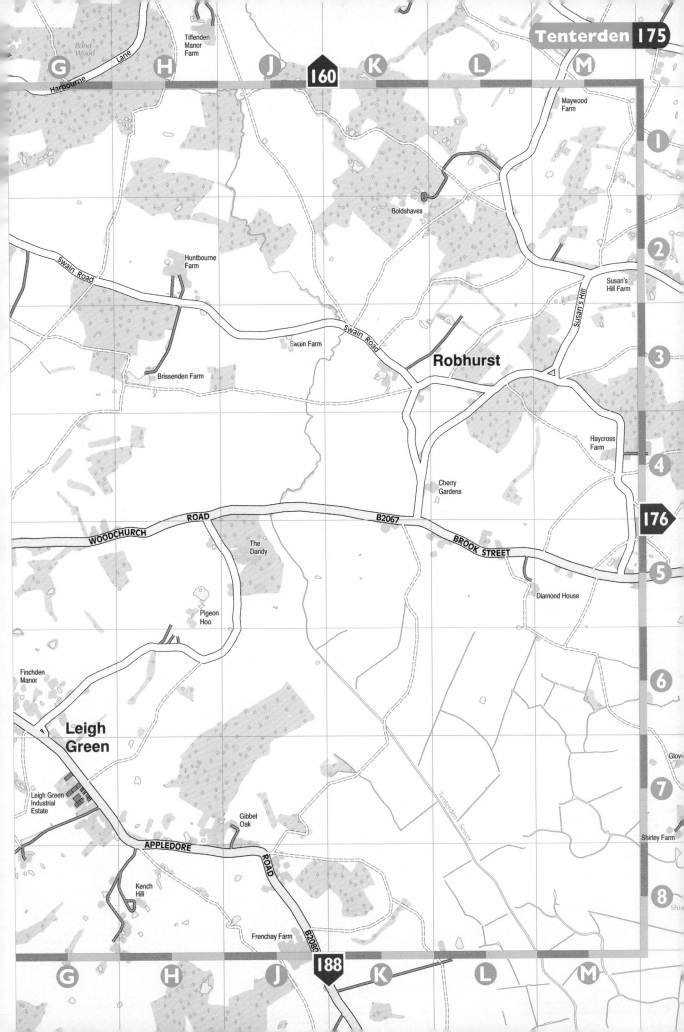

160

G
H
J
K
L
M

Pond Wood
Harbourne Lane
Tiffenden Manor Farm

Maywood Farm

1

Boldshaves

2

Swain Road

Huntbourne Farm

Susan's Hill Farm

Swain Road

3

Swain Farm

Robhurst

Susan's Hill

Brissenden Farm

Haycross Farm

4

Cherry Gardens

176

WOODCHURCH ROAD
B2067
BROOK STREET

5

The Dandy

Diamond House

Pigeon Hoo

6

Finchden Manor

Leigh Green

Glov

7

Leigh Green Industrial Estate

Tenterden Sewer

Shirley Farm

Gibbet Oak

APPLEDORE ROAD

8

Kench Hill

B2080

Shi

Frenchay Farm

188

G
H
J
K
L
M

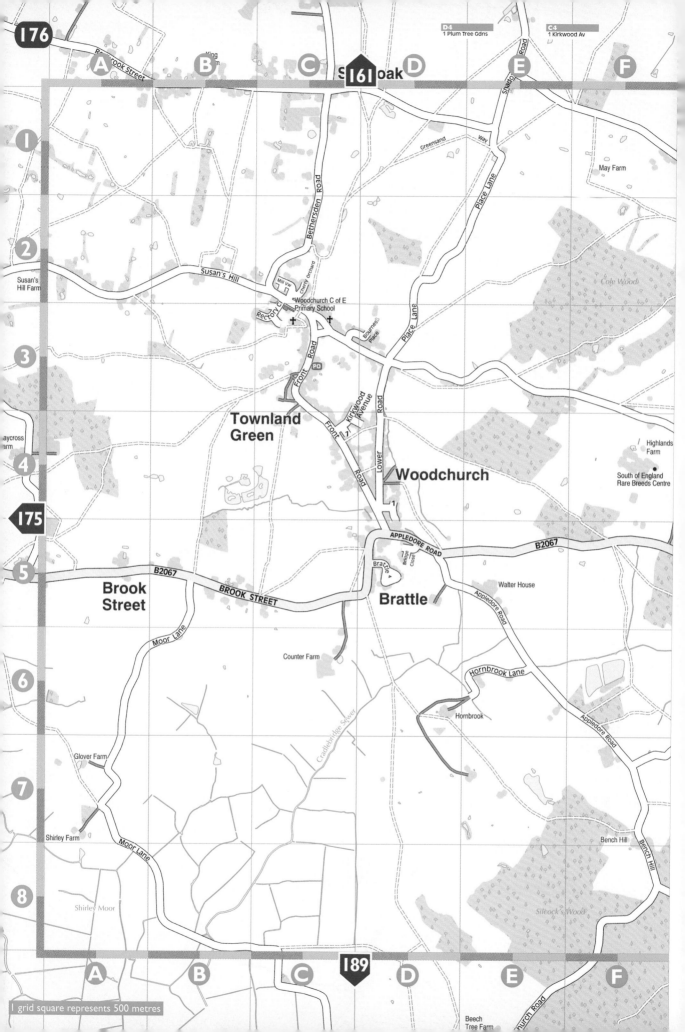

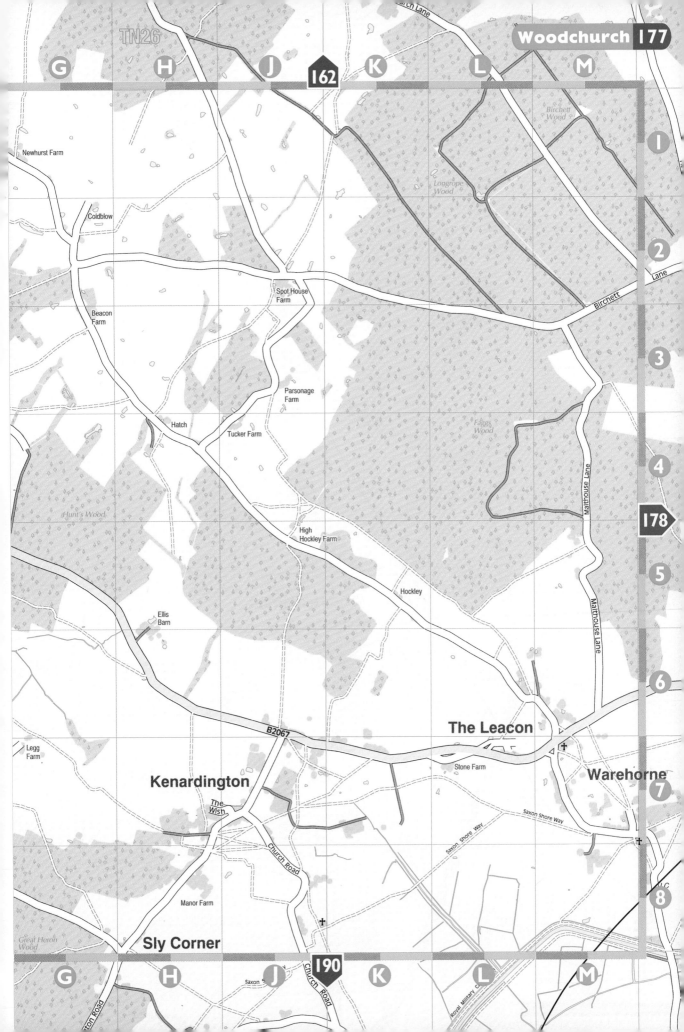

TN26

G   H   J   162   K   L   M

1

2

3

4

178

5

6

7

8

Newhurst Farm

Coldblow

Beacon
Farm

Spot House
Farm

Longrope
Wood

Birchett
Wood

Birchett Lane

Parsonage
Farm

Hatch

Tucker Farm

Faggs
Wood

Malthouse Lane

Hunt's Wood

High
Hockley Farm

Hockley

Malthouse Lane

Ellis
Barn

The Leacon

Legg
Farm

Kenardington

Stone Farm

Warehorne

The
Wish

Saxon shore way

Saxon Shore Way

B2067

Church Road

Manor Farm

Sly Corner

Great Heron
Wood

Royal Military C

G   H   J   190   K   L   M

Church Road

Saxon S

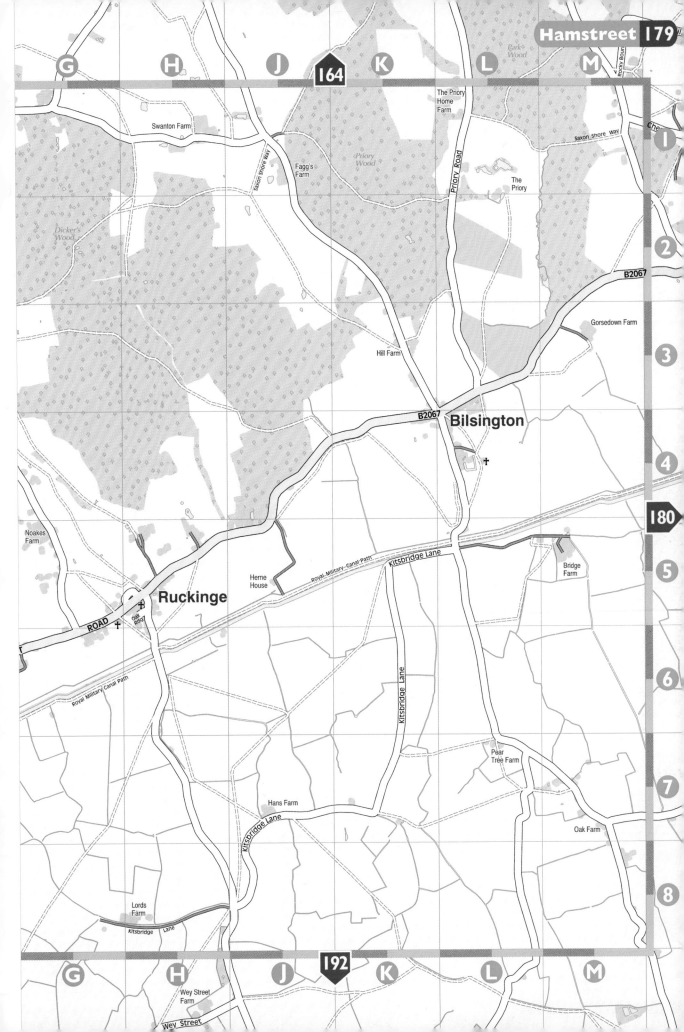

G H J **164** K L M

Swanton Farm

The Priory Home Farm

Saxon Shore Way

Fagg's Farm

Priory Wood

The Priory

I

Saxon Shore Way

Dicker's Wood

2

B2067

Gorsedown Farm

3

Hill Farm

B2067 **Bilsington**

† **4**

180

Noakes Farm

Royal Military Canal Path

Kitsbridge Lane

Bridge Farm

5

Herne House

Ruckinge

ROAD † Oak Road

Royal Military Canal Path

Kitsbridge Lane

6

Pear Tree Farm

7

Hans Farm

Kitsbridge Lane

Oak Farm

8

Lords Farm

Kitsbridge Lane

G H J **192** K L M

Wey Street Farm

Wey Street

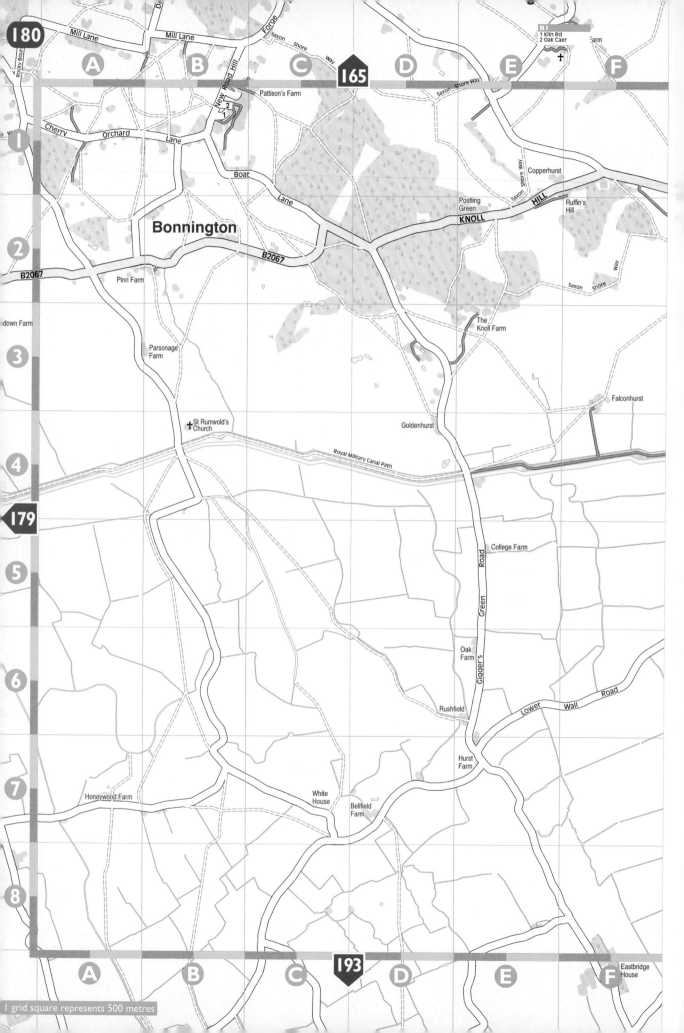

166

G   H   J   K   L   M

I

2

3

4

182

5

6

7

8

G   H   J   K   L   M

194

Upper Park Farm

Court-at-Street

B2067

Saxon Shore Way

Honeypot

Marwood Farm

Saxon Shore Way

ALDINGTON ROAD

B2067

Aldin

Saxon S

Reach Road

Port Lympne

Aldergate Wood

Saxon Shore Way

Royal Military Road

Royal Military Canal

Aldergate Lane

Tontine Farm

Selby Farm

Lower Wall

Lower Wall Road

Lower Wall Road

Dale

Tame Lane

Abbott's Court

Latne Barn

Donkey Street

Tame Lane Cottage

Shear Way

Donkey Street

Church Road

Forty Acre Cottage

The Green

PO

Tame Pike Road

Burmarsh

Harringe L

Harringe Brooks Wood

OTTERPOOL LAN

A   B   C   D   E   F

167

Upper Otterpool

F5 1 Cornbrook Rd   E5 1 The Haven

1

OTTERPOOL

HYTHE ROAD

Berwick

Honeywood Close

Pedlinge

Folks Wood

Saxon Shore Way

B2067

2

Lympne

Belcaire Cl

Berwick Lane

Harman Avenue

Isis

Octavian Dr

Tourney Cl

Lympne C of E Primary School

Beacon Way

Ridgeway

Aldington Road

Shepway Cross

Reach

Road

Saxon Shore Way

The Street

3

Castle Close

Lympne Hill

Stutfall Castle

West Hythe

4

Royal Military Road

St Mary's Road

Royal Military Road

The Roughs

al Military Canal

181

West Hythe Road

Riverside Industrial Estate

The Haven

Burmarsh Rd

Burmar

Grebe Crs

Dove Cl

Kingfisher

1

Meadow Way

Robin's Cl

Martin's Wy

Nightingale Ln

Finch

Palmarsh

Heron's Wy

Selby Farm

5

St George's Pl

School

Palmbeach Avenue

Keddow's Close

Marsh View

Studfall Close

DYMCH

Jubilee Close

LC

Oaks View

PO

Lower

Wall

Road

6

Botolph's Bridge

Botolph's Bridge

Burmarsh Road

LC

Daleacres

Botolph's Bridge Road

LC

7

The Little Piece

DYMCHURCH ROAD A259(T)

Barn

8

onkey treet

LC

195

Woodland Way

Brockman Crescent

Denham

mond

Beverlee Gdns

Way

7

A   B   C   D   E   F

1 grid square represents 500 metres

168
Saltwood

CT21

Brockhill Country Park

Brockhill Park School (Upper)

Brockhill Park School (Lower)

Court Farm

LONDON ROAD

Redbrooks Wy

London Road

Old London Road

Sandling Road

Turnpike Hill

Spanton Crs

North Rd West

Britten Cl

Freshfield

High Rise Close

Hartswood Lane

St Johns Rd

Bartholomew La

Barrack Hill

Corunna Cl

Sir John Moore Avenue

A261

Nursery Fields

Mill Fields Road

Green Lane Av

Orchard Va

Green Lane

SCANLONS BR

A2008

MILITARY RD

A261

Lucy's Hill

Hillside

Bartholomew Street

Oak Wk

B.U.P.A.

St

Dental St

High St

Hythe Community Clinic

St

Sun Lane Surgery

William Pitt Av

EAST ST

Twiss Grove

Earlsfield Road

Twiss Avenue

Mill Rd

Station Rd

Cannongate Gardens

Cannongate Avenue

Cannongate Rd

Lower Blackhouse

Sene Park

Farmer Rise

Blackhouse Rise

Cliff Cl

Bassett Close

Bassett Gdns

Blackh

Sene Golf C...

New Road

PO

Rectory La

Rectory Lane

Grange Road

School Road

The Close

Castle Rd

Saltwood Church of English Primary School

Tanner's Hill

Tanner's Hill Gardens

Deedes Close

Lea Close

Lookers La

Seaton

Castle Av

Castle AV

Quarry Rd

Hillcrest Road

North Road

Church Rd

Church St

Town Hall

Chapel St

RAMPART RD

PROSPECT ROAD

Prospect Road

Portland Rd

St Leonards C of E Junior School

The Windsor Gallery

Hythe Town Council

Green Park (Cricket Club)

Sturdy Close

Fisher Close

Hotel

HYTHE

Windmill Street

Napier Gdns

Tower Gardens

South Road

Swimming Pool

Hythe & Saltwood Sailing Club

Theatre

Albert Rd

Albert La

Park Rd

Victoria Rd

Cobden Road

West Parade

Ormonde Rd

St Hilda's

Arthur Rd

Hotel

Range Rd

Range Road Industrial Estate

Wakefield

Cinque Ports Av

St Leonards Rd

Boundary Rd

Lyell Cl

Fort Rd

FORT RD

Frampton Rd

Portland Av

Victoria Av

Red Cl

Chindits

The Green

Hythe County Infants School

Portland

DYMCHURCH ROAD

PO

Romney Hythe & Dymchurch Railway

Royal Military Rd

Kengate Industrial Estate

Pennypot Industrial Estate

A259(T)

Pennypot

Romney Way

Shepherds Walk

Martello

Dymchurch Road

Crofters Cl

Royal Military Road

Wych Elm Wy

URCH ROAD

● Hythe Ranges

184

L3
Street Names for these grid squares are listed at the back of the index

K4
1 Elizabeth Gdns

K3
1 Malthouse Hi
2 Upr Maltho Hi

K1
1 Cylinder Rd
2 The Green

169

183

A B C 169 D E F

I

2

3

4

5

6

7

8

A B C D E F

Blackhouse Hill

Sene Valley Golf Club

Sene Farm

Bassett Gdns

Bassett Close

Cliff Cl

Farmer Sene Park

Cannongate Gardens

Cannongate Avenue

ST

WISS Grove

Earlsf Road

Hotel

P

Cannongate Road

St Augustines R C Primary School

Elm Gdns

Cannongate Cl

Saxon Close

Ferguson Close

SEABROOK

ROAD

Seabrook

Naildown Cl

Naildown Road

Whitenbrook

Ian's Wlk

Highridge

Colin's Cl

Bridle Way

Quarry Walk

Spring

Woodlands Dr

Hampton Va

Everest Rd

Valley Road

Horn Street

Paraker Way

Springfield PW

Seabrook Brook

Seabrook Court

Brook

A259(T)

Seabrook Grove

Sea Rd

Seabrook Gdns

Victoria Gr

PO

Seabrook Primary School

Battery Point

Sandy

Lane

Shorncliffe Military Cemetery

HOSPITAL HILL

Helena Corniche

Temeraire Heights

Temeraire

Castle Bay

The Corniche

Brewer's Hill

Sun inside Rd

Hotel

West Lawn Gdns

Encomb

SANDGATE   **ESPLANADE**

Princes Parade

Hotel

Road

Horn Street

Craythorne Cl

Horn Street

Valestone Close

Seabrook Vale

Shorncliffe Camp

Edgehill Close

Martello

Road

East

B2063

WEST ROAD

B2063

NORTH RD

Underhill Road

School

Valeby Cl

AV

D2 1 Owen's Cl

C1 1 Seadown Cl

F2 1 Prospect Rd 2 Wellington Pl

Military Ave

Alma Rd PO

St Mark's Cl

Royal

Naseby Av

Cromwell Park

Fairfax Cl

Shorncliffe Industrial Estate

North

RISBOROUGH

Crauford

B2063

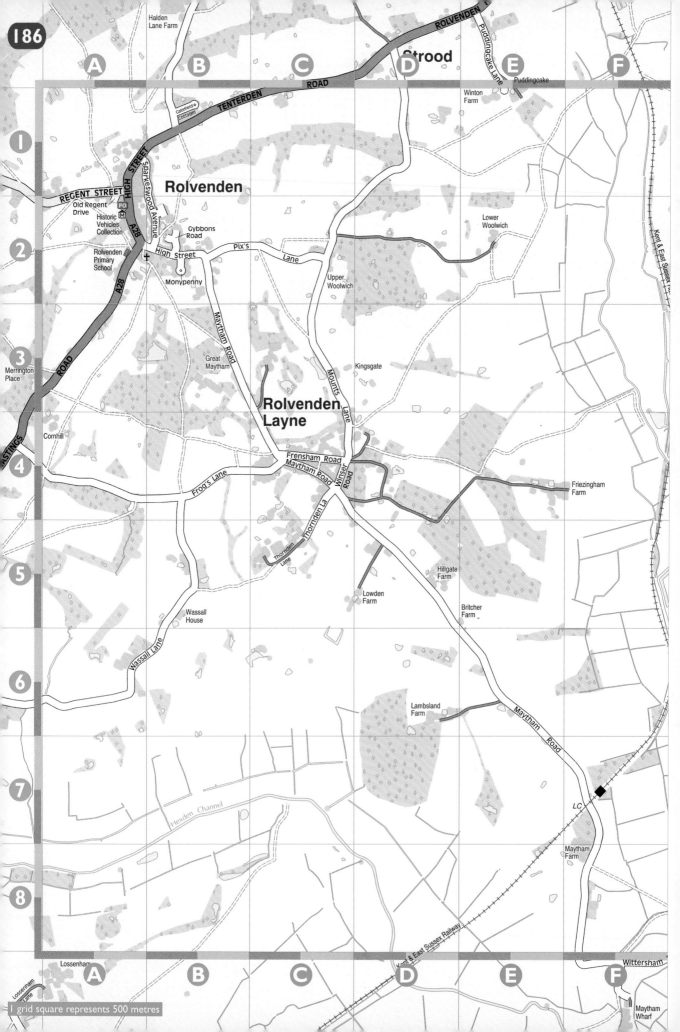

A   B   C   D   E   F

ROLVENDEN

Puddingcake Lane

Strood

Puddingcake

Winton Farm

Kent & East Sussex Rly

TENTERDEN   ROAD

Gatefield Cottages

Rolvenden

Lower Woolwich

HIGH STREET

REGENT STREET

Old Regent Drive

PO

Historic Vehicles Collection

M

Sparkeswood Avenue

A28

Gybbons Road

High Street

Pix's   Lane

Upper Woolwich

Rolvenden Primary School

Monypenny

Mounts   Lane

Kingsgate

Merrington Place

ROAD

HASTINGS

Cornhill

Maytham Road

Great Maytham

Rolvenden Layne

Frensham Road

Maytham Road

Winser Road

Friezingham Farm

Frog's Lane

Thornden La

Thornden Lane

Hillgate Farm

Lowden Farm

Britcher Farm

Wassall Lane

Wassall House

Lambsland Farm

Maytham Road

Hexden Channel

LC

Maytham Farm

Kent & East Sussex Railway

Lossenham

Wittersham

Lossenham Lane

Maytham Wharf

1   2   3   4   5   6   7   8

A   B   C   D   E   F

1 grid square represents 500 metres

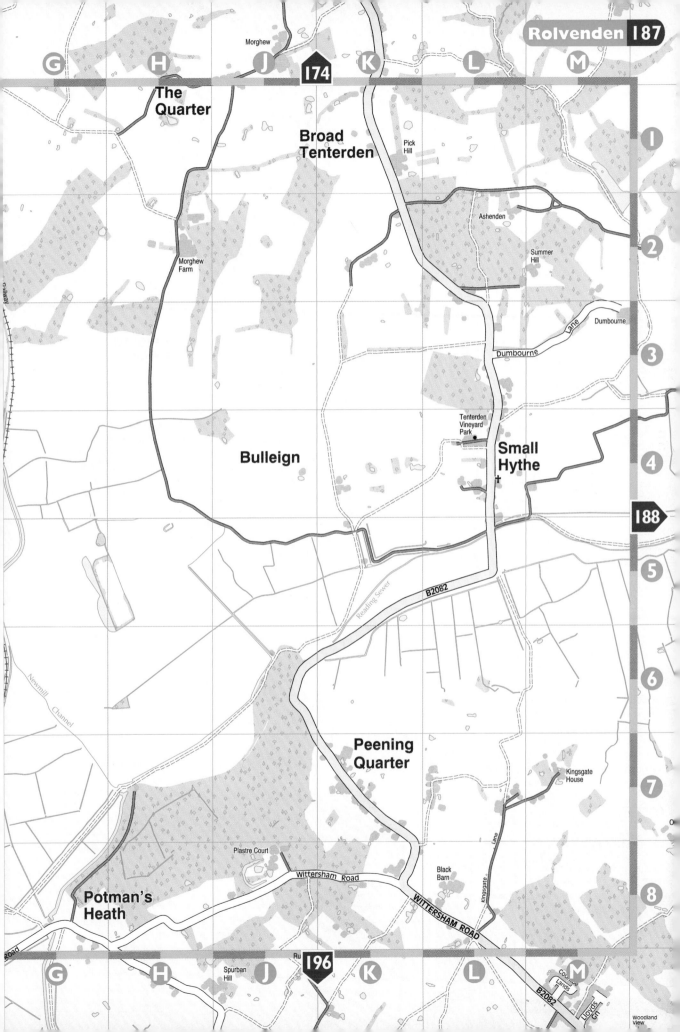

174

G   H   J   K   L   M

The Quarter

Broad Tenterden

Morghew

Pick Hill

Ashenden

Summer Hill

Dumbourne Lane

Dumbourne

Morghew Farm

Tenterden Vineyard Park

Small Hythe

188

Bulleign

Reading Sewer

B2082

Newmill Channel

Peening Quarter

Kingsgate House

Plastre Court

Kingsgate Lane

Wittersham Road

Black Barn

WITTERSHAM ROAD

Potman's Heath

Road

Spurban Hill

196

G   H   J   K   L   M

B2082

Lloyds Gn

Court Lands

Woodland View

I 2 3 4 5 6 7 8

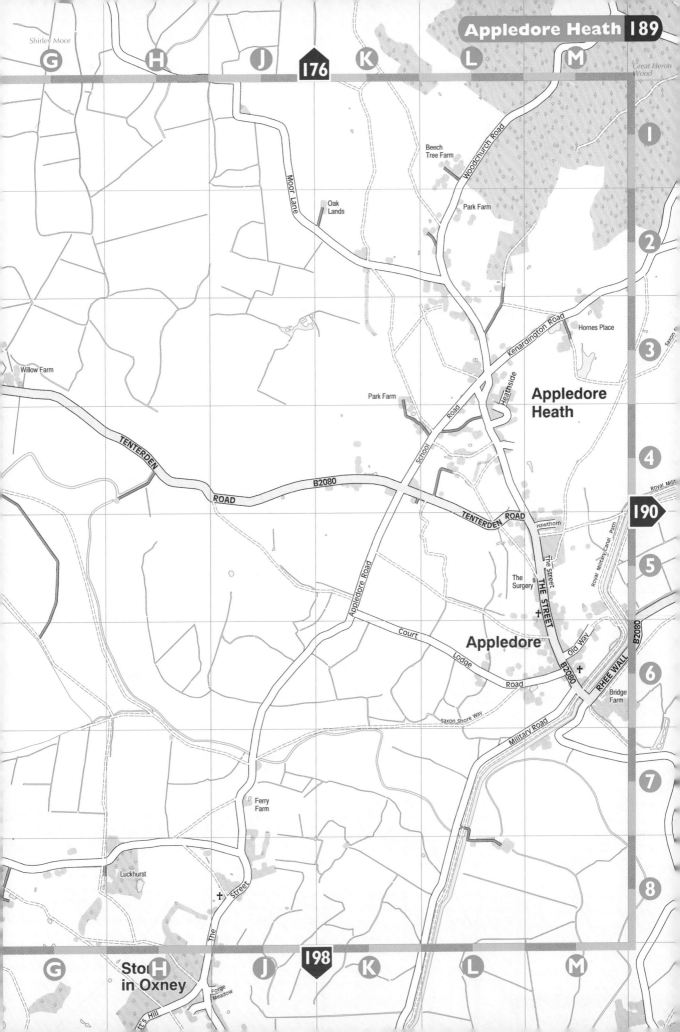

G   H   J   **176**   K   L   M

Shirley Moor

Great Heron Wood

1

2

3

4

190

5

6

7

8

Beech Tree Farm

Woodchurch Road

Park Farm

Kenardington Road

Hornes Place

Heathside

Appledore Heath

Moor Lane

Oak Lands

Park Farm

School Road

Willow Farm

TENTERDEN

ROAD

B2080

TENTERDEN   ROAD

Hawthorn

The Street

The Surgery

THE STREET

B2080

Royal Military Canal Path

Appledore Road

Appledore

Old Way

Court

Lodge   B2080

Road

RHEE WALL

Bridge Farm

Saxon Shore Way

Military Road

Ferry Farm

Luckhurst

The Street

G   H   J   **198**   K   L   M

Stone in Oxney

Forge Meadow

RE'S Hill

190

A   B   Sly Corner   C   177   D   E   F

Manor Farm

Great Heron Wood

1

Saxon Shore Way

Church Road

Kenardington Road

Smith's Farm

Higham Farm

2

The Firs

Thrift Cottage

Royal Military Canal Path

Hornes Place

3

Royal Military Canal

The Dowels

LC

Saxon Shore Way

4

Royal Military Canal Path

189

Royal Military Canal P.

5

B2080

B2080

Appledore Station

Arrowhead Lane

Way

B2080

R

WALL

6

Bridge Farm

7

Snargate Lane

Short

8

A   B   199   C   D   E   F

LC

G H J K L M

178

I

Bridge Farm

Royal Military Canal Path

Ham Lees F-

Ham Mill Farm

A2070

Ham Mill Lane

Kitsbridge Lane

Bainbridge Farm

2

Wev Street

Stockbridge House

3

A2070

Poplar House

4

192

5

Snave

Court-at-Wick

Ham Mill Lane

Mill Lane

Ham Farm

Ham

Whitehall Farm

6

7

Brenzett Green

Snargate

Codhall

Church Lane

Lane

Springfarm Rd

A2070

8

Hope Farm

Lane

Moor Lane

Vdell Lane

B2080

Church Lane

200

New House Farm

Spring Farm

G H J K L M

179

A   B   C   D   E   F

1   Bainbridge Farm

Lords Farm
Kitsbridge

Wey Street Farm
Wey Street

Langdon

Will's Farm

2

Brooker Farm

3   Hill's Farm

Millbank

Norwood Lane

4   Norwood Farm

191

5   Lodgeland Farm

6   Little Appledore

7   Moat House
Newchurch Lane
TN29

Melon Lane

8   Poplar Farm
Moor Lane

Spring Farm

A   Bridge Farm   B   Melon Lane   C   201   D   E   F

Melon Farm

Wenham's Lane

G H J K L M

180

Church Road

1

2

3

4

194

5

6

7

8

Eastbridge House

Newbarn

Newchurch

Patchways

Church View

Manor House

New Barn Farm

Rookelands

Willow Farm

Gammon's Farm Lane

Gammon's Farm

Chapel Lane

Gammon's Farm Lane

Blackmanstone Bridge

Pickney Bush Farm

Pickneybush Lane

Marten Farm

Treloar

North Fording Bungalow

Haffenden Farm

St Mary's Road

Chistenden's Lane

G H J K L M

202

St Mary in the Marsh

182

G3
1 Hythe Rd

K1
1 Livingstone Cl
2 Stanley Cl

G   H   J   K   L   M

1
2
3
4
5
6
7
8

Romney Hythe & Dymchurch Railway

LC

Marine Av

Willop Way

HYTHE ROAD

A259(T)

Woodland

Crimond Gdns

Beach Rd

Beverley

Luden Rd

Redoubt Way

Brockman Crescent

nham lose

Dymchurch Wall

Lower Sands

Lower Sands

Tower Estate

ensway

Crossways Close

Kingsway

Wall

G   H   J   K   L   M

G   H   J   **188**   K   L   M

I

Rosehill

Rose Hill

Isle of
Oxney

Woodland
View

Field

Forge
Meads

PO

Acton

**The
Stocks**

POPLAR ROAD   B2082   STOCKS   ROAD   B2082   Wittersham   Road

2

Tr...ad

Holman's
Farm

Budd's Lane

Tophill
Farm

RYE ROAD

3

Great Prawls
Farm

Budd's
Farm

4

Rother
Levels

198

Newbridge
Farm

Kent County
East Sussex County

5

B2082

Sussex Border Path

WITTERSHAM ROAD

River Rother

Sussex Border Path

6

Thornsdale

Corkwood
Farm

Readers Lane

WITTERSHAM   GARDNER'S HILL

7

Oxenbridge

RD   WITTERSHAM LANE

Baron's
Grange

Bosney
Farm

8

G   H   J   **205**   K   L   M

Grove
Lane

The Elms

Church Lane

PO

Iden

Boonshill

Elmsmead

Luckhurst

The Street

A B C 189 D E F

I

Stone
in Oxney

Forge
Meadow

Catt's Hill

Catt
Farm

2 Top Road

Church Hill

Oxenden

3
Great Prawns
Farm

Saxon Shore Way

Mackley
Farm

Military Road

Royal Military Canal

Knock Hill

Cliff Farm

Stone
Bridge

Stone
Cliff

4

Highknock Channel

5

Cliff Marsh
Farm

Royal Military Canal Path

Five Watering Sewer

6

7

Royal Military Canal

White Kemp Sewer

8

Military Road

Saxon Shore Way

A B C 206 D E F

Boonshill

East Sussex Co
Kent Coun

1 grid square represents 500 metres

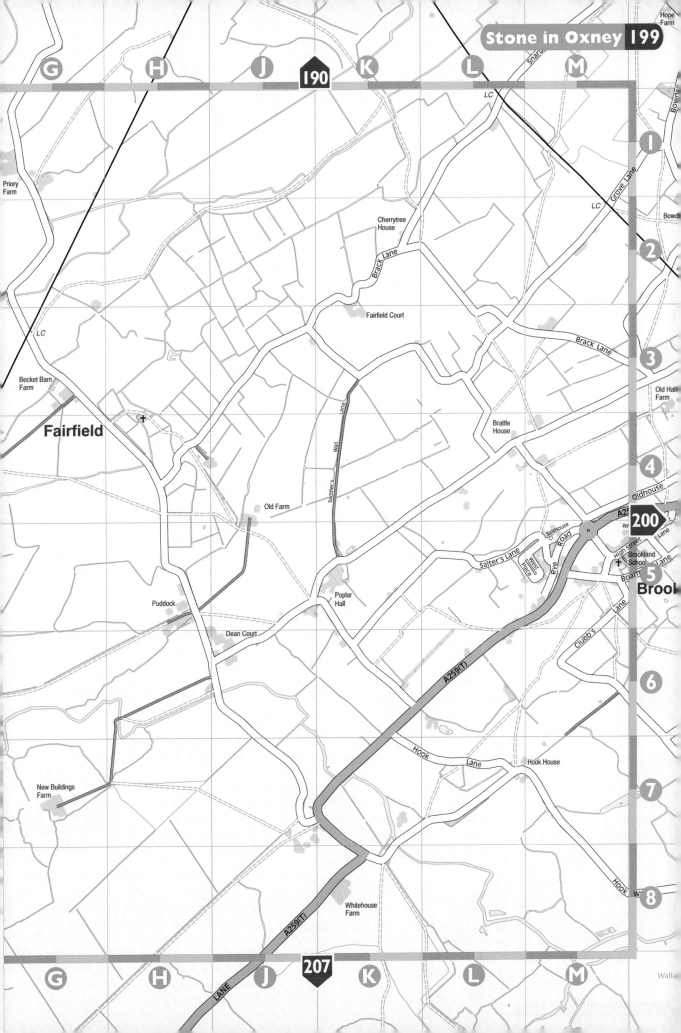

G   H   J   **190**   K   L   M

1

Hope
Farm

Bowr

Snarg

LC

Grove Lane

LC

Bowd

2

Cherrytree
House

Brack Lane

Priory
Farm

LC

Fairfield Court

Brack Lane

3

Old Hall
Farm

LC

Becket Barn
Farm

Fairfield ✝

Brattle
House

4

Oldhouse

Sadlier's

Wall

Lane

Old Farm

Salthouse
Ct.

A2

200

Wr

High Street   Brookland
School

✝

5

Brool

Salter's Lane

West
Place

Rye   Road

Boarn

Puddock

Poplar
Hall

Lane

Clubb's

6

Dean Court

A259(T)

New Buildings
Farm

Hook   Lane

Hook House

7

Hook

W

8

A259(T)

Whitehouse
Farm

G   H   J   **207**   K   L   M

LANE

Walla

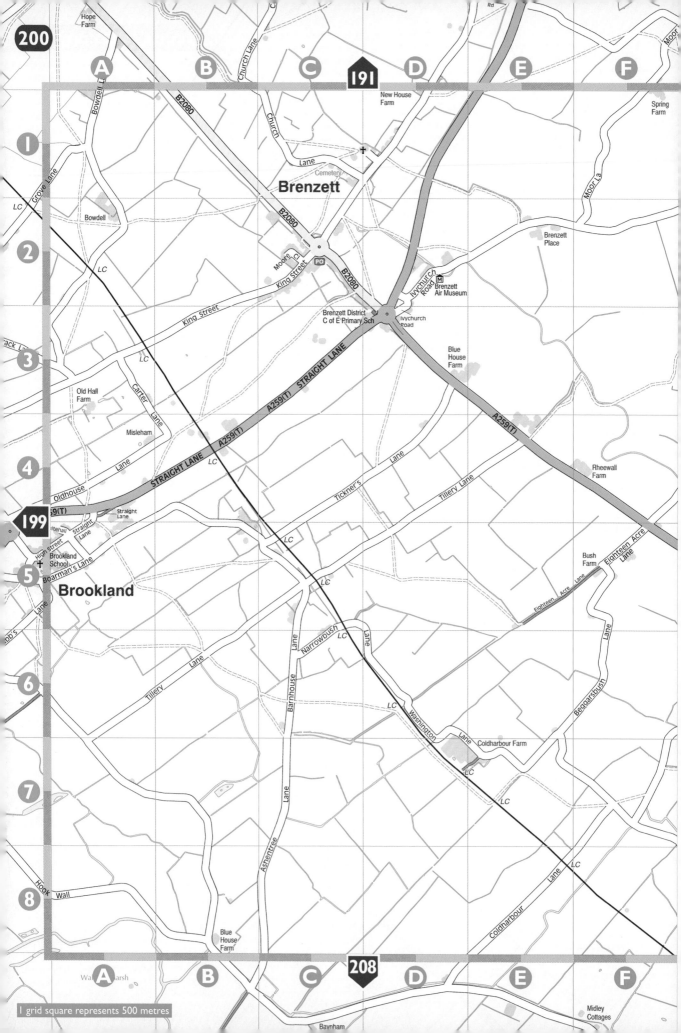

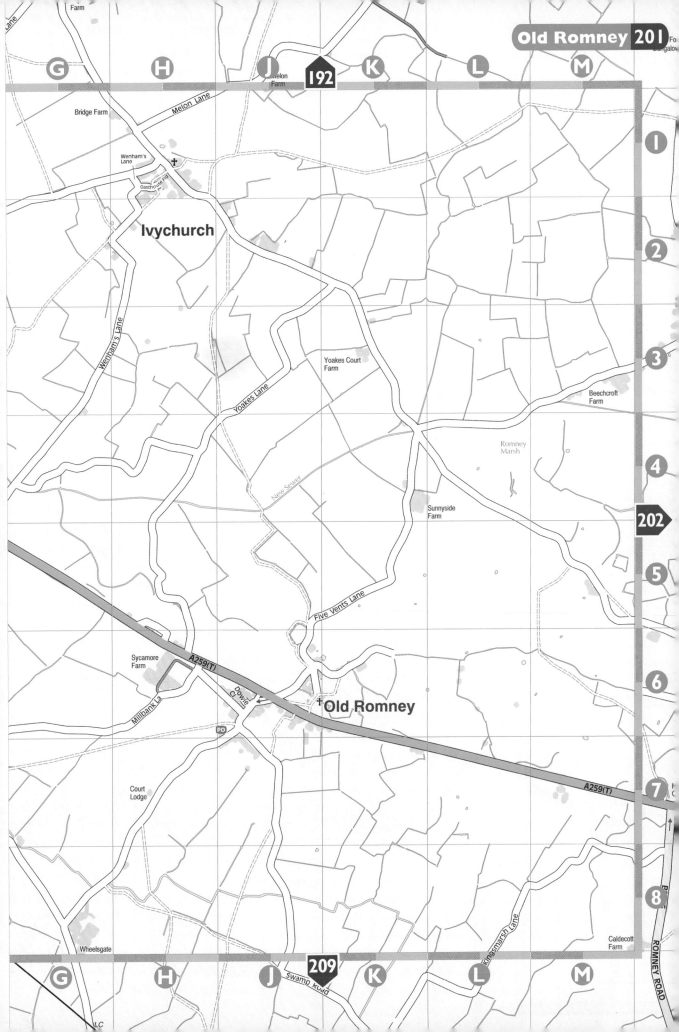

G H J **192** K L M

I

2

3

4

202

5

6

7

8

Farm

Bridge Farm

Melon Lane

Melon Farm

Wenham's Lane

Oasthouse Fld

Ivychurch

Wenham's Lane

Yoakes Lane

Yoakes Court Farm

Beechcroft Farm

Romney Marsh

New Sewer

Sunnyside Farm

Five Vents Lane

Sycamore Farm

A259(T)

Millbank La

Dowle Cl

PO

Old Romney

Court Lodge

A259(T)

ROMNEY ROAD

Caldecott Farm

Wheelsgate

G H J **209** K L M

Swamp Road

Kingsmarsh Lane

LC

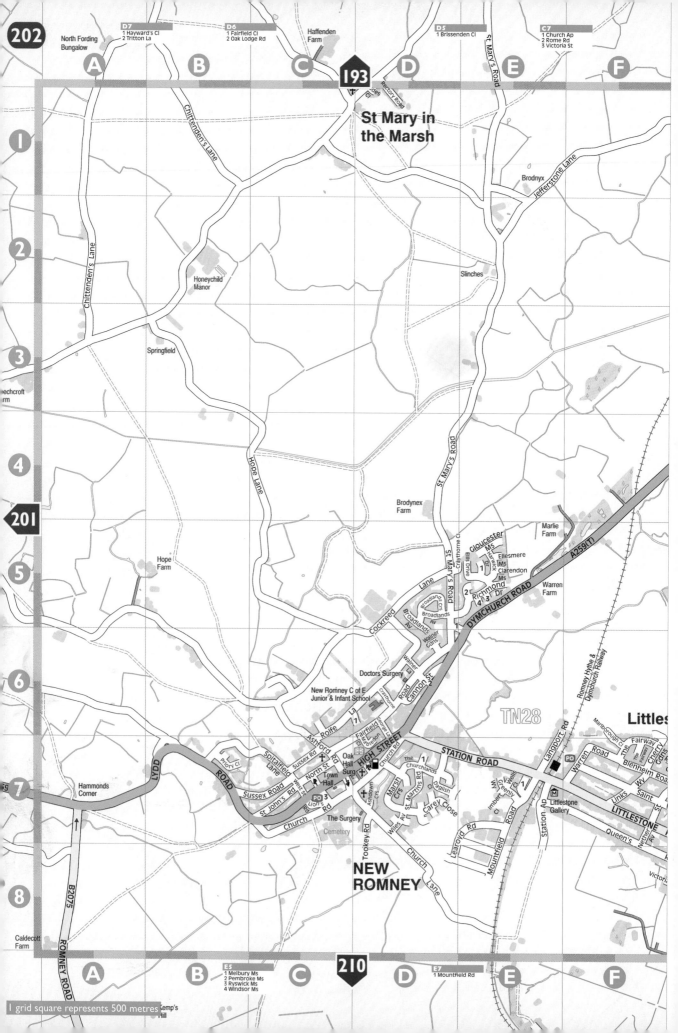

G8
1 The Saltings

H1
1 Old Bakery Cl

J1
1 Cobsden Cl
2 Highlands Crs
3 Kingsland Hollow

G H J 194 K L M

Winton Way
The Fairway
Fairway
The Fairway
Brookside
Dunstall
Dunstall Lane
Dunstall Gdns
Seaway Gdns
Cobsden Road
Spring Hollow
Raymoor
A259(T)
Willowbank
St Mary's Gdns
Seaway Rd
Orchard Cots
Seaway Gdns
Links Crs
Links
Seaway Rd
Cobsden Road
Laurel Avenue
Holly Rd
Jefferstone La
Yew Tree Rd
Maple
Elm Road
Oak Dr
Beechwood
Ash Tree
Aspen Cl
Hawthorn
Cedar Crs
Willow Dr
Taylors
Grassmere
Meads Wy
Grassmere
Jenner's Wy
Old Newlands
Taylors Lane
Brars Rd
Fairway Cl
Cazedown
Coast Drive

St Mary's Bay

I 1
2
3
4
5
6
7
8

Jefferstone Gdns

LC

PO

Coast Road

stone-on-Sea

Romney Warren Golf Club

Andrew's
Anne
Cooper
Orchard Drive
Madeira Road
Blenheim Road
Nicholas Road
ROAD
B2071
Road
Park Rd
Marine Parade
Victoria Road
Road West
Armada
Grand Parade
Meehan Road
Chur...

G H J 211 K L M

Romney Sands

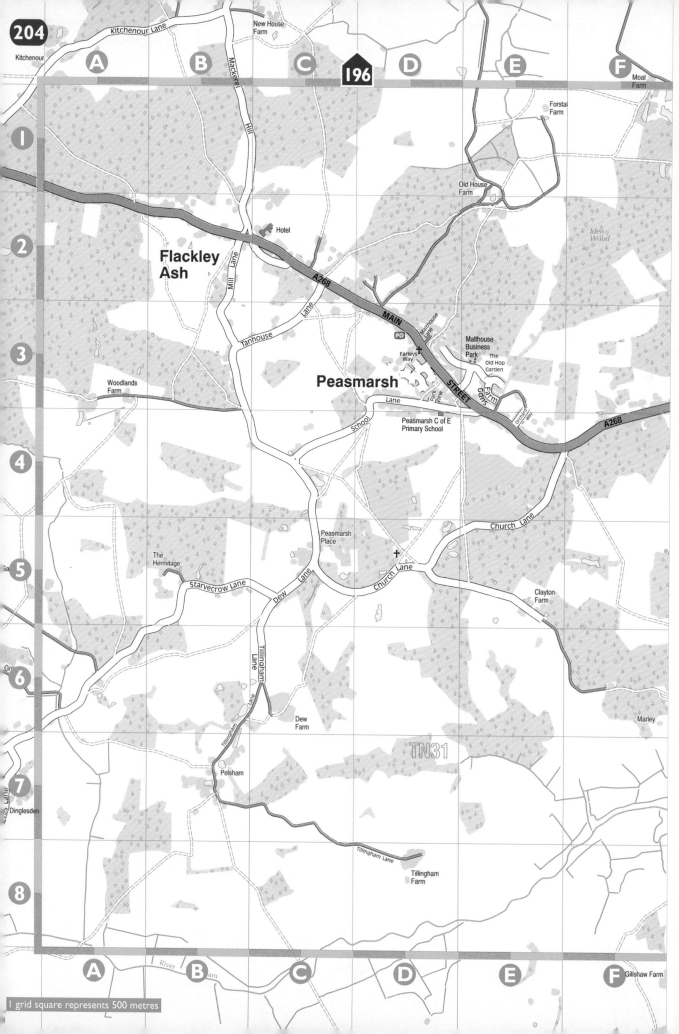

Kitchenour

A   B   C   196   D   E   F   Moat
Farm

Kitchenour Lane

New House
Farm

Mackerel Hill

Forstal
Farm

1

Old House
Farm

Iden
Wood

2

Flackley
Ash

Hotel

A268

MAIN

Mill Lane

Tanhouse

PO

Malthouse Lane

Malthouse
Business
Park

The
Old Hop
Garden

3

Woodlands
Farm

Peasmarsh

Farleys
Way

Lane

School

STREET

Park
View

Farm
Gdns

Orchard Way

Peasmarsh C of E
Primary School

A268

4

Church Lane

Peasmarsh
Place

The Hermitage

Ga

Gro

5

Starvecrow Lane

Dew Lane

Church Lane

Church Lane

Clayton
Farm

6

Tillingham Lane

Dew
Farm

Marley

TN31

7

Dinglesden

Pelsham

Tillingham Lane

8

Tillingham
Farm

River
A   B   am   C   D   E   F   Gillshaw Farm

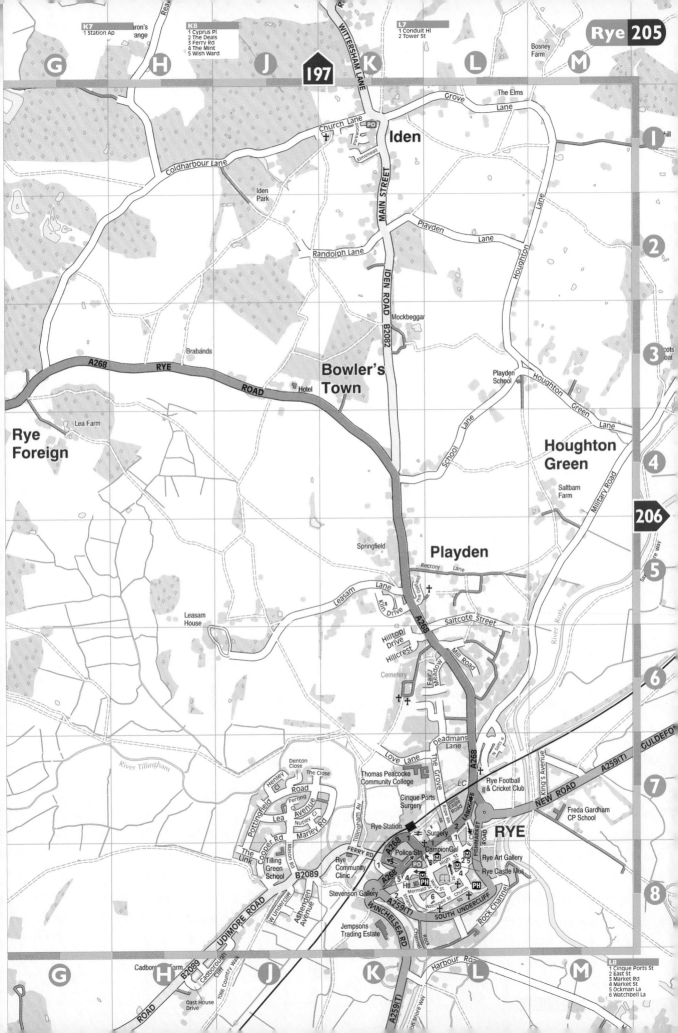

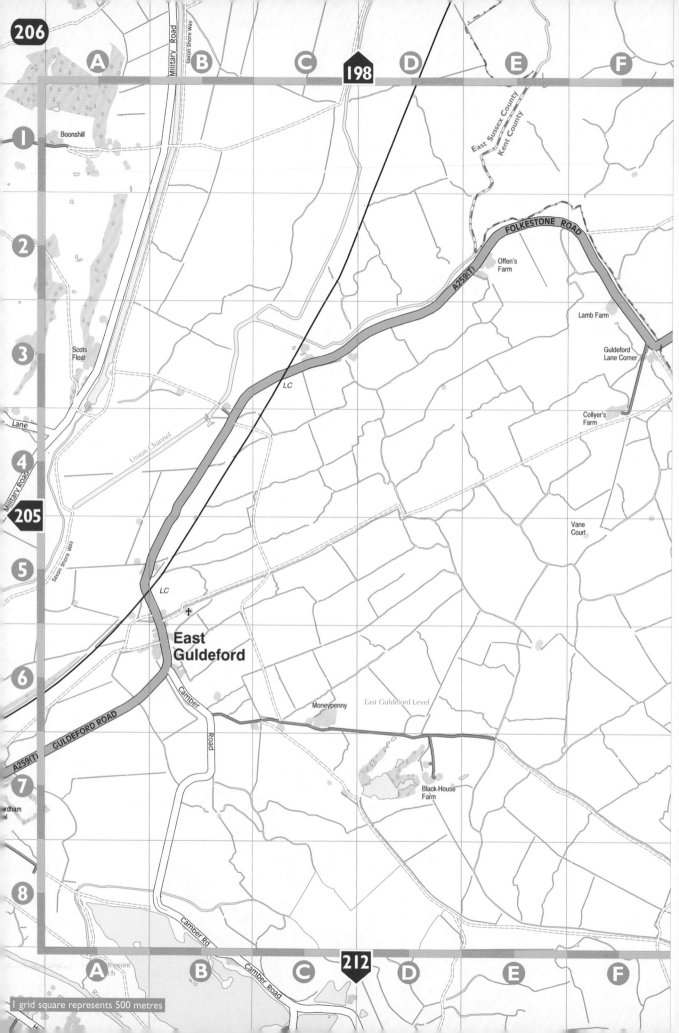

A B C **198** D E F

205

212

A B C **212** D E F

Boonshill

Military Road

Saxon Shore Way

East Sussex County

Kent County

FOLKESTONE ROAD

A259(T)

Offen's Farm

Lamb Farm

Guldeford Lane Corner

Scots Float

Collyer's Farm

LC

Union Channel

Lane

Military Road

Vane Court

Saxon Shore Way

LC

East Guldeford

Camber Road

GULDEFORD ROAD

A259(T)

Moneypenny

East Guldeford Level

Black House Farm

rdham

Camber Rd

thpoint ch

Camber Road

1 grid square represents 500 metres

1
2
3
4
5
6
7
8

G   H   J   K   L   M

A259(T)

199

Whitehouse Farm

GULDEFORD LANE

I

2

3

4

208

5

6

7

8

Wall

Kent Ditch

Little Cheyne Court

Barn Farm

Kent County
East Sussex County

G   H   J   K   L   M

213

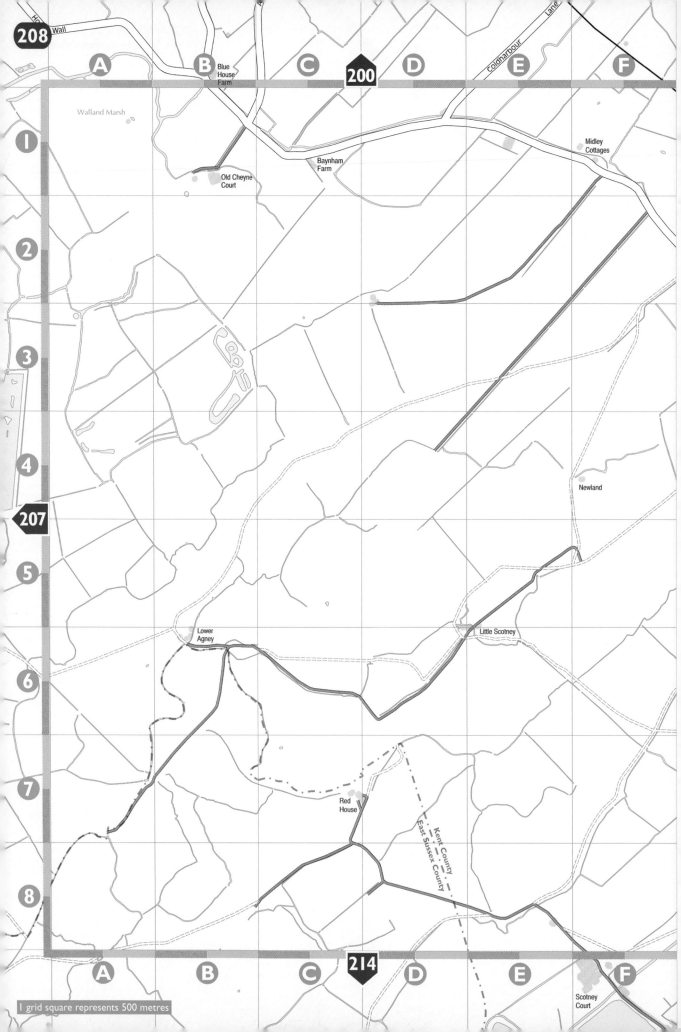

A　B　Blue House Farm　C　200　D　E　Coldharbour Lane　F

Walland Marsh

1

Midley Cottages

Baynham Farm

Old Cheyne Court

2

3

4

Newland

207

5

Lower Agney

Little Scotney

6

7

Red House

Kent County
East Sussex County

8

Scotney Court

A　B　C　214　D　E　F

1 grid square represents 500 metres

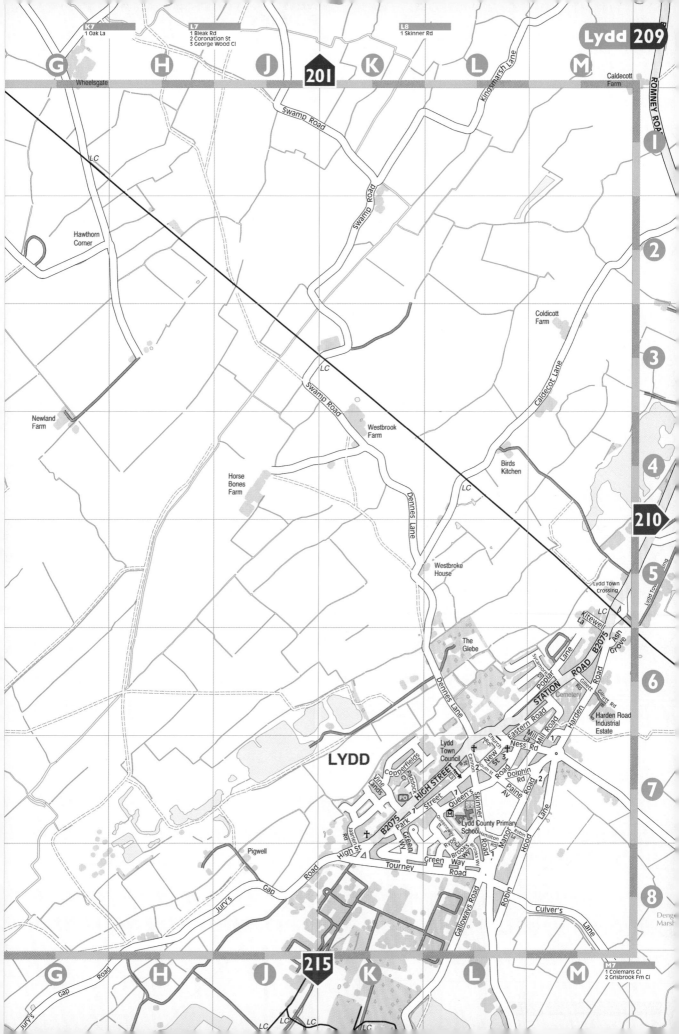

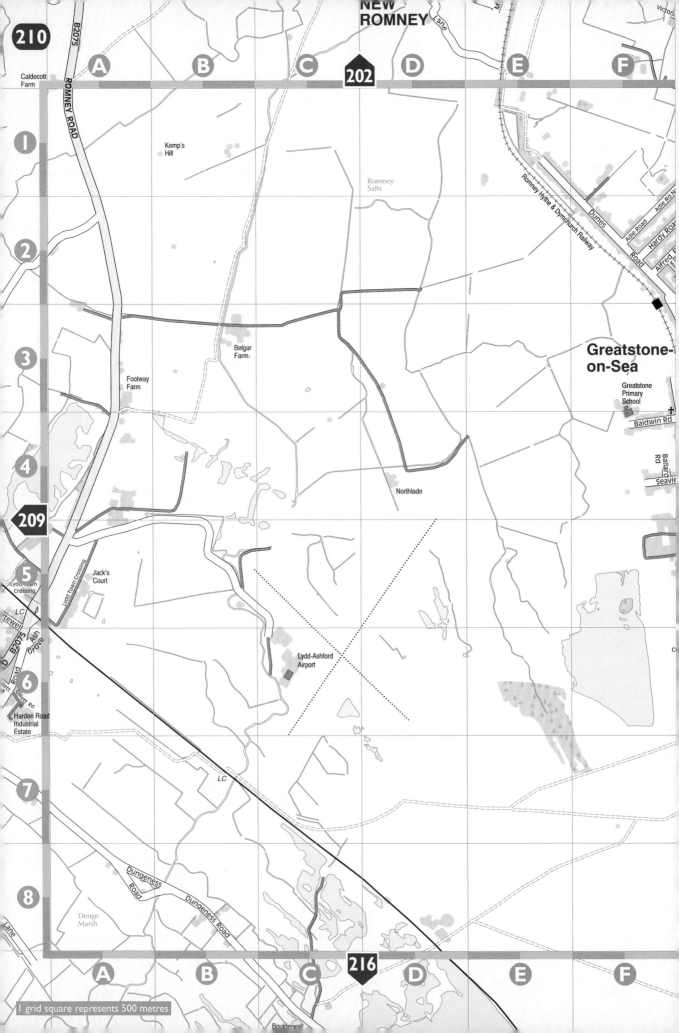

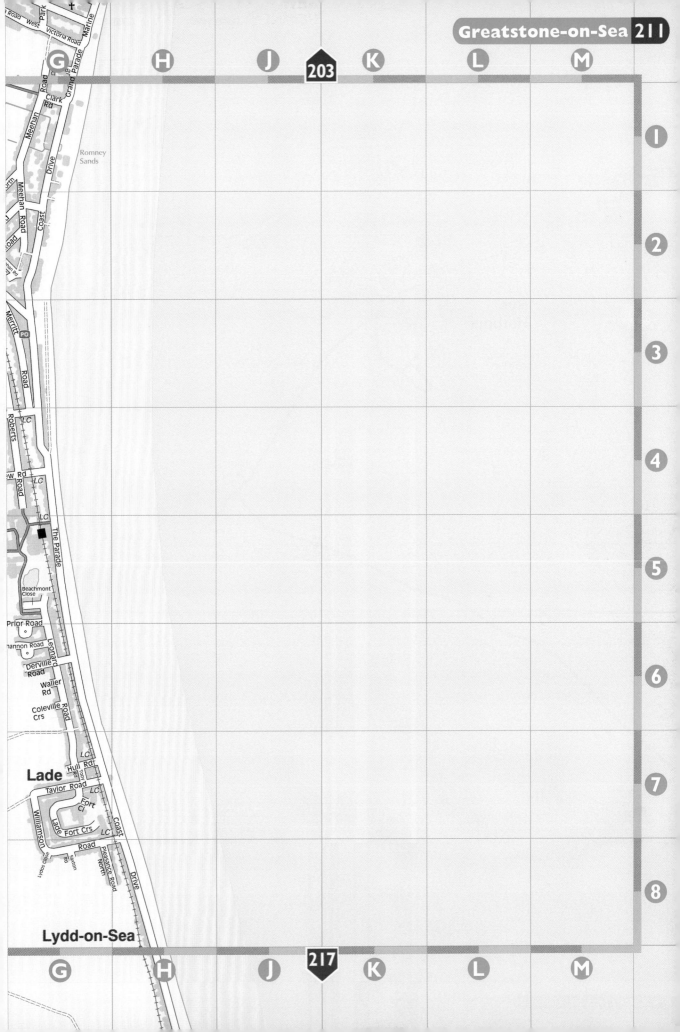

G   H   J   **203**   K   L   M

Romney
Sands

Road
West
Victoria Road
Park
Marine
Grand Parade
Clark
Rd
Meehan
Drive

Meehan
Road
Coast
Road

Merritt
PO

Roberts
Road
LC

Rd
LC

LC
The Parade

Beachmont
Close

Prior Road
Leonard
Shannon Road
Derville
Road
Waller
Rd
Coleville
Crs

LC

Hull Rd
Road
Lade
Taylor Road
LC
Fort
Cl
Williamson
Lade Fort Crs
LC
Coast
Road
Lydos close
Rd
Saxton
Pleasance Road
North
Drive

Lydd-on-Sea

G   H   J   **217**   K   L   M

1
2
3
4
5
6
7
8

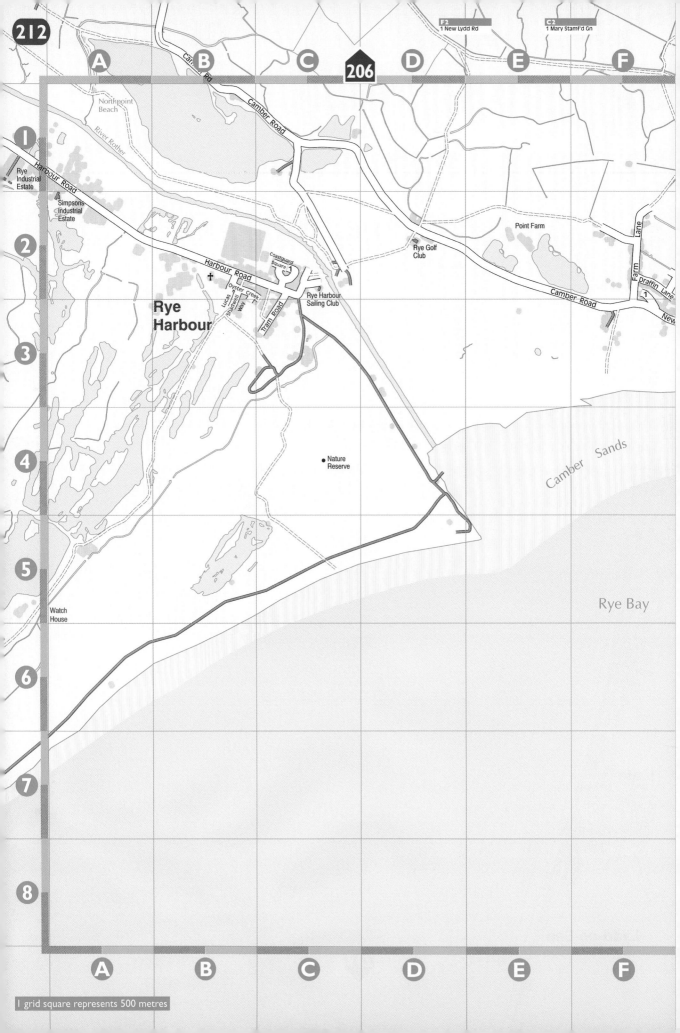

206

A   B   C   D   E   F

Cam... Rd

Camber Road

Northpoint
Beach

River Rother

Harbour Road

Rye
Industrial
Estate

Simpsons
Industrial
Estate

Harbour Road

Coastguard
Square   1

Rye Golf
Club

Point Farm

**Rye
Harbour**

Lucas

Shadwell

Oyster Creek

Way

Tram Road

Rye Harbour
Sailing Club

Camber Road

Farm   Lane

Draffin Lane

New

1

• Nature
Reserve

Camber   Sands

Watch
House

Rye Bay

A   B   C   D   E   F

1 grid square represents 500 metres

G3
1 Peter James Cl
2 Tonbridge Wy

J3
1 Saunders Wy

G   H   J   207   K   L   M

1

2

Broomhill Level

3

Camber

Scotts

Links Way

Acre
Road

Lydd
Road

Dennham Way

Old
Lydd
Road

2 7

Lydd
Road

Marchants

Drive

Dunes Avenue

Sea Road

Daniel Way

PO

First Avenue

Second Avenue

Pelwood
Road

Pelwood Road

Yates Close

1

The Suttons

Lydd Road

Broomhill
Farm

Jury's
Gap

4

Lydd Road

214

Broomhill Sands

5

6

7

8

G   H   J   K   L   M

208

A   B   C   D   E   F

1

2

3

4

213

5

6

7

8

A   B   C   D   E   F

Scotney
Court

The Forelands

Jury's Gut Sewer

Neath Road

Ferguson Road

Neath Road

Neath Road

Jury's
Gap

Lydd Ranges

LC

Midrips

The
Wicks

East Sussex County
Kent County

Lydd R...

Denge Marsh

G H J K L M

209

LC

LC LC LC

LC

West Ripe

LC

LC South Brooks Road

Holmstone

Ferguson Road

LC

LC

LC

South Brooks

Invicta Road

LC

Galloways Road

Brickwall Farm

South Brooks Road

Dengemarsh Road

Galloway's Road

Robin

Journey Road

216

I

2

3

4

5

6

7

8

G H J K L M

210

215

A B C D E F

Dungeness Road

Dungeness Road

Denge Marsh

Lane

Boulderwall Farm

Manor Farm

Brickwall Farm

Nature Reserve

Open Pits

Halfway Bush

Denge Beach

Pen Bars

1 2 3 4 5 6 7 8

A B C D E F

I grid square represents 500 metres

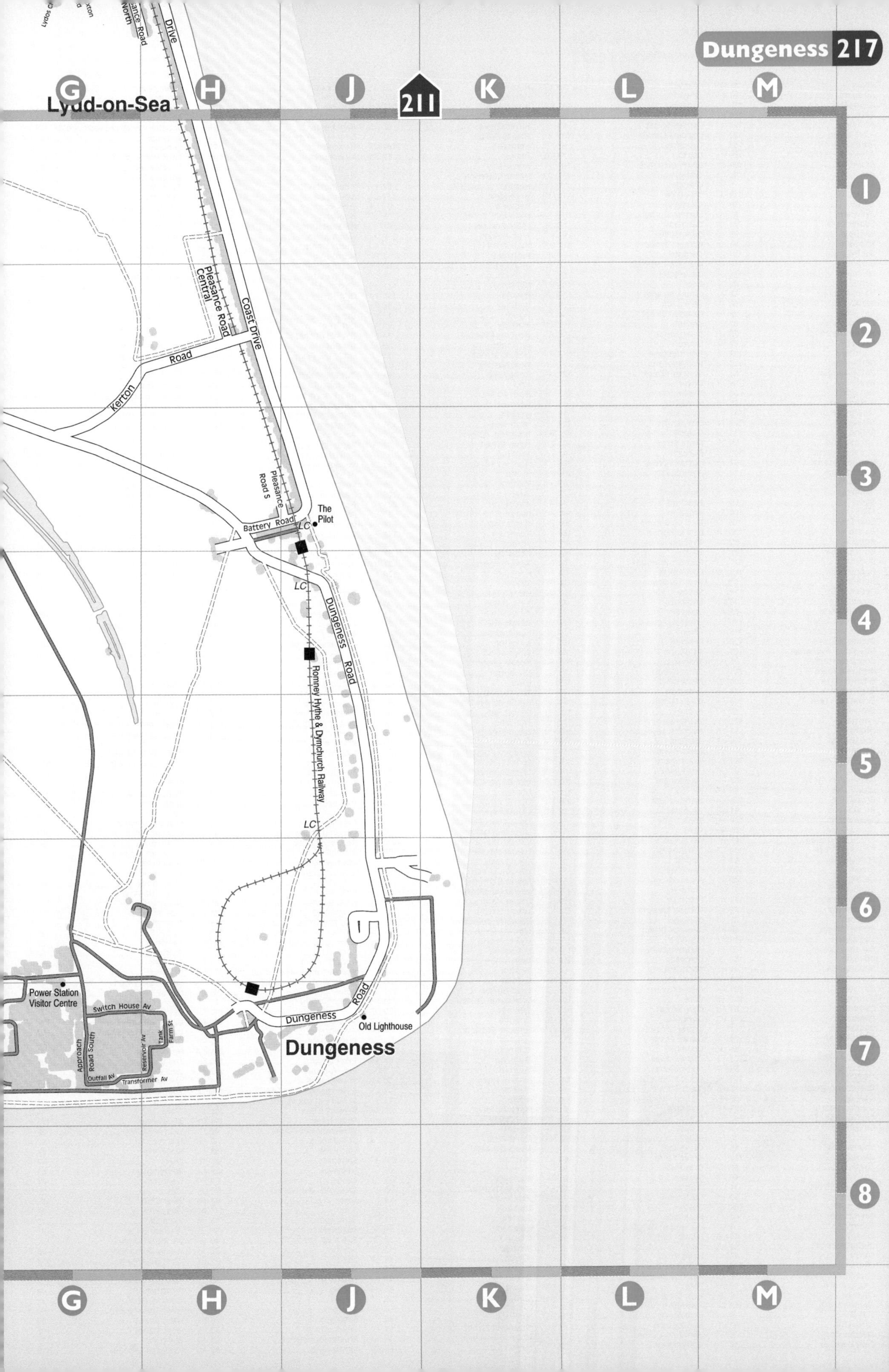

G H J **211** K L M

Lydd-on-Sea

1

Pleasance Central

Pleasance Road

Coast Drive

2

Kerton Road

3

Pleasance Road S

The Pilot

Battery Road

LC

LC

4

Dungeness Road

Romney Hythe & Dymchurch Railway

LC

5

LC

6

Power Station Visitor Centre

Switch House Av

Farm St

Tank

Reservoir Av

Approach

Road South

Outfall Av

Transformer Av

Dungeness Road

Old Lighthouse

Dungeness

7

8

G H J K L M

219

Westwood 30 D8
Westwood 115 G5
Whatsole Street 131 H7
Wheeelbarrow Town 132 C5
Whitehill 73 J2
Whitfield 137 K5
Whitstable 39 M2
Wichling 70 E8
Wickhambreaux 80 C3
Wick Hill 140 B5
Wilgate Green 73 H7
Willesborough 9 K7
Willesborough Lees 146 D3
Wingham 81 K6
Wingham Green 81 G6
Wingham Well 81 G7
Wingmore 133 K3
Winterbourne 75 J5
Wissenden 142 B6
Withersdane 129 H5
Wittersham 196 F2
Wolverton 154 B3
Womenswold 116 F3
Woodchurch 176 D4
Woodland 150 A6
Woodnesborough 83 J7
Woodside Green 88 A5
Woodstock 52 A7
Woolage Green 117 H6
Woolage Village 116 F4
Wootton 134 E4
Wormshill 69 J6
Worten 144 C2
Worth 84 D8
Wye 129 H4
Wyebanks 89 H3
Yardhurst 143 L6
Yorkletts 58 B2

USING THE STREET INDEX

Street names are listed alphabetically. Each street name is followed by its postal town or area locality, the Postcode District, the page number, and the reference to the square in which the name is found.

Example: **Abbots Wk** *RASHE* TN25 **129** G2 1

Some entries are followed by a number in a blue box. This number indicates the location of the street within the referenced grid square. The full street name is listed at the side of the map page.

GENERAL ABBREVIATIONS

ACC ACCESS
ALY ALLEY
AP APPROACH
AR ARCADE
ASS ASSOCIATION
AV AVENUE
BCH BEACH
BLDS BUILDINGS
BND BEND
BNK BANK
BR BRIDGE
BRK BROOK
BTM BOTTOM
BUS BUSINESS
BVD BOULEVARD
BY BYPASS
CATH CATHEDRAL
CEM CEMETERY
CEN CENTRE
CFT CROFT
CH CHURCH
CHA CHASE
CHYD CHURCHYARD
CIR CIRCLE
CIRC CIRCUS
CL CLOSE
CLFS CLIFFS
CMP CAMP
CNR CORNER
CO COUNTY
COLL COLLEGE
COM COMMON
COMM COMMISSION
CON CONVENT
COT COTTAGE
COTS COTTAGES
CP CAPE
CPS COPSE
CR CREEK
CREM CREMATORIUM
CRS CRESCENT
CSWY CAUSEWAY
CT COURT
CTRL CENTRAL
CTS COURTS
CTYD COURTYARD
CUTT CUTTINGS
CV COVE
CYN CANYON
DEPT DEPARTMENT
DL DALE
DM DAM
DR DRIVE
DRO DROVE
DRY DRIVEWAY
DWGS DWELLINGS
E EAST
EMB EMBANKMENT
EMBY EMBASSY
ESP ESPLANADE
EST ESTATE
EX EXCHANGE
EXPY EXPRESSWAY
EXT EXTENSION
F/O FLYOVER
FC FOOTBALL CLUB
FK FORK
FLD FIELD
FLDS FIELDS
FLS FALLS
FLS FLATS
FM FARM
FT FORT
FWY FREEWAY
FY FERRY
GA GATE
GAL GALLERY
GDN GARDEN
GDNS GARDENS
GLD GLADE
GLN GLEN
GN GREEN
GND GROUND
GRA GRANGE
GRG GARAGE
GT GREAT
GTWY GATEWAY
GV GROVE
HGR HIGHER
HL HILL
HLS HILLS
HO HOUSE
HOL HOLLOW
HOSP HOSPITAL
HRB HARBOUR
HTH HEATH
HTS HEIGHTS
HVN HAVEN
HWY HIGHWAY
IMP IMPERIAL
IN INLET
IND EST INDUSTRIAL ESTATE
INF INFIRMARY
INFO INFORMATION
INT INTERCHANGE
IS ISLAND
JCT JUNCTION
JTY JETTY
KG KING
KNL KNOLL
L LAKE
LA LANE
LDG LODGE
LGT LIGHT
LK LOCK
LKS LAKES
LNDG LANDING
LTL LITTLE
LWR LOWER
MAG MAGISTRATE
MAN MANSIONS
MD MEAD
MDW MEADOWS
MEM MEMORIAL
MKT MARKET
MKTS MARKETS
ML MALL
ML MILL
MNR MANOR
MS MEWS
MSN MISSION
MT MOUNT
MTN MOUNTAIN
MTS MOUNTAINS
MUS MUSEUM
MWY MOTORWAY
N NORTH
NE NORTH EAST
NW NORTH WEST
O/P OVERPASS
OFF OFFICE
ORCH ORCHARD
OV OVAL
PAL PALACE
PAS PASSAGE
PAV PAVILION
PDE PARADE
PH PUBLIC HOUSE
PK PARK
PKWY PARKWAY
PL PLACE
PLN PLAIN
PLNS PLAINS
PLZ PLAZA
POL POLICE STATION
PR PRINCE
PREC PRECINCT
PREP PREPARATORY
PRIM PRIMARY
PROM PROMENADE
PRS PRINCESS
PRT PORT
PT POINT
PTH PATH
PZ PIAZZA
QD QUADRANT
QU QUEEN
QY QUAY
R RIVER
RBT ROUNDABOUT
RD ROAD
RDG RIDGE
REP REPUBLIC
RES RESERVOIR
RFC RUGBY FOOTBALL CLUB
RI RISE
RP RAMP
RW ROW
S SOUTH
SCH SCHOOL
SE SOUTH EAST
SER SERVICE AREA
SH SHORE
SHOP SHOPPING
SKWY SKYWAY
SMT SUMMIT
SOC SOCIETY
SP SPUR
SPR SPRING
SQ SQUARE
ST STREET
STN STATION
STR STREAM
STRD STRAND
SW SOUTH WEST
TDG TRADING
TER TERRACE
THWY THROUGHWAY
TNL TUNNEL
TOLL TOLLWAY
TPK TURNPIKE
TR TRACK
TRL TRAIL
TWR TOWER
U/P UNDERPASS
UNI UNIVERSITY
UPR UPPER
V VALE
VA VALLEY
VIAD VIADUCT
VIL VILLA
VIS VISTA
VLG VILLAGE
VLS VILLAS
VW VIEW
W WEST
WD WOOD
WHF WHARF
WK WALK
WKS WALKS
WLS WELLS
WY WAY
YD YARD
YHA YOUTH HOSTEL

POSTCODE TOWNS AND AREA ABBREVIATIONS

ASH Ashford (Kent)
BRCH Birchington
BRDST Broadstairs
CANT Canterbury
CANTW/ST Canterbury west/Sturry
CRBK Cranbrook
DEAL Deal
DVE/WH Dover east/Whitfield
DVW Dover west
FAV Faversham
FOLK Folkestone
FOLKN Folkestone north
HAWK Hawkhurst
HB Herne Bay
HDCN Headcorn
HYTHE Hythe
IOS Isle of Sheppey
KEN/WIL Kennington/Willesborough
LYDD Lydd
MARG Margate
MSTR Minster
NROM New Romney
QBOR Queenborough
RAM Ramsgate
RASHE Rural Ashford east
RASHW Rural Ashford west
RCANTE Rural Canterbury east
RCANTW Rural Canterbury west
RDV Rural Dover
RFOLK Rural Folkestone
RMAID Rural Maidstone
RSIT Rural Sittingbourne
RYE Rye
SIT Sittingbourne
SWCH Sandwich
TENT Tenterden
WGOS Westgate on Sea
WSEA Winchelsea
WSTB Whitstable

Index - streets

Abb - Arc

A

Abbey Cl *DEAL* CT14 **103** J8
IOS ME12 **15** M7
Abbey Flds *FAV* ME13 **56** B5
Abbey Gdns *CANTW/ST* CT2 **78** C2
Abbey Gv *MSTR* CT12 **46** E8
RAM CT11 **4** C8
Abbey Pl *FAV* ME13 **55** M5
Abbey Rd *DVE/WH* CT16 **154** F1
FAV ME13 **55** M5
RDV CT15 **154** D4
Abbey St *FAV* ME13 **55** M5
Abbeyview Dr *IOS* ME12 **15** K7
Abbey Wy *KEN/WIL* TN24 **146** C3
Abbots Hl *FAV* ME13 **55** G8
RAM CT11 **5** K6
Abbots Pl *CANT* CT1 **6** F3
Abbots Rd *FAV* ME13 **56** A6
The Abbots *DVW* CT17 **10** A5
Abbots Wk *RASHE* TN25 **129** G2 1
Abbott Rd *FOLK* CT20 **13** J3
Aberdeen Cl *RCANTE* CT3 **62** F2
Abingdon Gv *RCANTE* CT3 **62** F2
Ackholt Rd *RCANTE* CT3 **99** J8
Acol Hl *BRCH* CT7 **46** D1
Acorn Cl *ASH* TN23 **163** L2
The Acorns *HDCN* TN27 **141** H4
Acorn St *IOS* ME12 **14** E4
The Acre *DVE/WH* CT16 **137** H5
Acton La *TENT* TN30 **188** C7
Acton Rd *WSTB* CT5 **39** M4
Adams Cl *TENT* TN30 **174** D4
Ada Rd *CANT* CT1 **6** B8
Addelam Cl *DEAL* CT14 **121** J1 1
Addelam Rd *DEAL* CT14 **121** J1
Addington Pl *RAM* CT11 **5** J7
Addington Rd *MARG* CT9 **3** G4
SIT ME10 **52** A2
Addington Sq *MARG* CT9 **3** G5 1
Addington St *MARG* CT9 **3** G4
RAM CT11 **5** H7
Addiscombe Gdns *MARG* CT9 **3** H7
Addiscombe Rd *MARG* CT9 **3** J6
Adelaide Dr *SIT* ME10 **51** L1
Adelaide Gdns *IOS* ME12 **14** F7
RAM CT11 **5** J7
Adelaide Pl *CANT* CT1 **6** E5
Adelaide Rd *RDV* CT15 **118** D5
Adie Rd *NROM* TN28 **210** F2
Adie Rd North *NROM* TN28 **210** F2
Adisham Downs Rd
RCANTE CT3 **98** D3
Adisham Gn *SIT* ME10 **33** H5
Adisham Rd *RCANTW* CT4 **97** M2
RCANTW CT4 **116** E3
Adisham Wy *MARG* CT9 **30** E4
Admirals Wk *IOS* ME12 **15** G7
TENT TN30 **174** E4
Admiralty Cl *FAV* ME13 **55** K5 1
Admiralty Wk *WSTB* CT5 **39** J6
Adrian Sq *WGOS* CT8 **29** G4
Adrian St *DVW* CT17 **10** D7
Aerodrome Rd *RCANTW* CT4 **98** A2
RFOLK CT18 **170** B1
Afghan Rd *BRDST* CT10 **31** H5
Agester La *RCANTW* CT4 **134** C2
Ainsdale Cl *FOLKN* CT19 **170** C6
Airedale Cl *MARG* CT9 **3** J6
Airfield Vw *IOS* ME12 **21** L5
Aisne Dr *CANT* CT1 **78** F4
Alamein Cl *DVE/WH* CT16 **156** B3
Albany Pl *DVW* CT17 **10** D6
Albany Rd *RFOLK* CT18 **171** K4
SIT ME10 **52** A2
Albemarle Rd *KEN/WIL* TN24 **9** L7
Alberta Cl *DVE/WH* CT16 **155** K2 1
Albert La *HYTHE* CT21 **183** K4
Albert Rd *BRDST* CT10 **31** G6
CANT CT1 **7** J5
DEAL CT14 **103** L7
DVE/WH CT16 **10** C3
FOLKN CT19 **13** G2
HYTHE CT21 **183** K4
KEN/WIL TN24 **8** D2
MARG CT9 **2** C5
RAM CT11 **5** M4
RFOLK CT18 **171** L4
Albert St *RAM* CT11 **5** J7
WSTB CT5 **39** M3
Albert Ter *MARG* CT9 **2** E4
Albion Cl *HB* CT6 **42** C5
Albion La *HB* CT6 **42** C5
Albion Ms *RAM* CT11 **5** L6 1
Albion Mews Rd *FOLK* CT20 **13** G6
Albion Pl *CANT* CT1 **7** H3
FAV ME13 **55** L6
IOS ME12 **14** E3 1
KEN/WIL TN24 **9** J9
RAM CT11 **5** K6
Albion Rd *BRCH* CT7 **28** C6
BRDST CT10 **31** H7
DEAL CT14 **103** M5 1
FOLKN CT19 **13** H2
MARG CT9 **3** K3
RAM CT11 **5** L4
SWCH CT13 **101** J3
Albion St *BRDST* CT10 **49** K1
Albion Vls *FOLK* CT20 **13** H6
Albuhera Sq *CANT* CT1 **78** F4 1
Aldergate La *RASHE* TN25 **181** L4
Alder Rd *FOLKN* CT19 **12** E2
Aldington Rd *HYTHE* CT21 **181** L2
Aldred Rd *FAV* ME13 **55** L7 1
Aldridge Cl *HB* CT6 **41** K2
Alexander Dr *FAV* ME13 **55** K6
Alexandra Cl *SIT* ME10 **33** G6 1
Alexandra Gdns *FOLK* CT20 **13** G6
Alexandra Pl *DVE/WH* CT16 **10** A2
Alexandra Rd *BRCH* CT7 **28** C8
BRDST CT10 **49** K1 1
DEAL CT14 **121** M3 1
IOS ME12 **14** F3
MARG CT9 **2** F8
RAM CT11 **5** H3
RFOLK CT18 **171** L3
WSTB CT5 **39** L5
Alexandra St *FOLKN* CT19 **13** J2
Alfred Cl *CANT* CT1 **77** L7
Alfred Rd *BRCH* CT7 **27** M5
CANT CT1 **77** L7 1
DVE/WH CT16 **155** K3
KEN/WIL TN24 **9** G9
MARG CT9 **3** L6
NROM TN28 **210** F2
Alicia Av *MARG* CT9 **29** J5
Alison Cl *DVE/WH* CT16 **137** J7 1
Alison Crs *DVE/WH* CT16 **137** J7
Alkham Cl *MARG* CT9 **31** H3
Alkham Rd *RDV* CT15 **154** D1
Alkham Valley Rd *RFOLK* CT18 **170** F2
Alland Grange La *MSTR* CT12 **47** G4
Allan Rd *WSTB* CT5 **39** G6
Allen Av *WGOS* CT8 **28** E6
Allenby Av *DEAL* CT14 **103** K8
Allenby Rd *MSTR* CT12 **48** D3
Allen Ct *IOS* ME12 **15** J8 1
Allendale St *FOLKN* CT19 **13** G2
Allen Fld *ASH* TN23 **145** H5
Alliance Rd *RAM* CT11 **5** L6
All Saints' Av *MARG* CT9 **2** B7
All Saints' Cl *WSTB* CT5 **40** A4
All Saints La *CANT* CT1 **6** F4 1
All Saints Rd *SIT* ME10 **52** E1
Alma Pl *CANT* CT1 **7** H2 1
RAM CT11 **5** K5
Alma Rd *FOLK* CT20 **169** M8
HB CT6 **24** D8
IOS ME12 **14** E3
MARG CT9 **3** G7
RAM CT11 **5** J4
Alma St *CANT* CT1 **7** H2
IOS ME12 **14** F3
Almond Cl *ASH* TN23 **127** H8
BRDST CT10 **48** E1
WSTB CT5 **40** F4
Almond Tree Cl *IOS* ME12 **14** C5
Almshouse Rd *FAV* ME13 **90** E7
Alpha Rd *BRCH* CT7 **28** C6
RAM CT11 **5** G6
Alsager Av *QBOR* ME11 **19** H2
Alsops Rd *KEN/WIL* TN24 **9** K9
Alston Cl *IOS* ME12 **15** L6
Alvis Av *HB* CT6 **41** J1
Amage Rd *RASHE* TN25 **129** L5
Amber Cl *RSIT* ME9 **53** M3
Ambleside *SIT* ME10 **52** E2
Amherst Cl *MARG* CT9 **30** E4 1
Amos Cl *FAV* ME13 **73** L8
HB CT6 **42** E2
Anchor La *IOS* ME12 **14** C2
Ancress Cl *CANTW/ST* CT2 **78** C1
Anna Pk *BRCH* CT7 **28** B5
Anne Boleyn Cl *IOS* ME12 **22** A2
Anne Cl *BRCH* CT7 **28** D6
Anne Roper Cl *NROM* TN28 **203** G7
Ann's Rd *RAM* CT11 **5** J3
Anselm Cl *SIT* ME10 **52** A1
Anselm Rd *DVW* CT17 **155** J5
Anson Cl *BRDST* CT10 **48** E2
Anstee Rd *DVW* CT17 **10** A3
Anthony Crs *WSTB* CT5 **39** K7
Anvil Cl *BRCH* CT7 **28** C7
Anzio Crs *DVE/WH* CT16 **156** A3
Appledore Av *IOS* ME12 **14** D5
Appledore Crs *FOLKN* CT19 **169** M6 1
Appledore Rd *RASHW* TN26 **176** E5
RASHW TN26 **189** K5
TENT TN30 **174** E6
Appledown Wy *CANT* CT1 **78** F8
Appleford Dr *IOS* ME12 **15** H6
Approach Rd *DVW* CT17 **155** J7 1
MARG CT9 **3** K5
RDV CT15 **117** M8
Approach Rd South
LYDD TN29 **217** G7
April Ri *WSTB* CT5 **39** K6 1
Apsley St *ASH* TN23 **8** C4
Aragon Cl *ASH* TN23 **145** G6
Archcliffe Rd *DVW* CT17 **155** L8
Archer Rd *FOLKN* CT19 **13** H2
Archer's Court Rd
DVE/WH CT16 **137** K6
Archery Sq *DEAL* CT14 **121** M2
Archway Rd *IOS* ME12 **14** C2
RAM CT11 **5** J6
Arcon Cl *ASH* TN23 **8** A9
Arcon Rd *ASH* TN23 **8** A9

Bredgar Cl *ASH* TN23 .... 145 H7
Bredhurst Cl *IOS* ME12 .... 14 D6
Bredlands La *RCANTE* CT3 .... 61 L4
Brenchley Av *DEAL* CT14 .... 121 H1 1
Brenchley Cl *ASH* TN23 .... 145 G7
Brenchley Rd *SIT* ME10 .... 52 B3
Brendon Dr *KEN/WIL* TN24 .... 8 D1
Brenley La *FAV* ME13 .... 74 E1
Brent Hl *FAV* ME13 .... 55 L5
Brent Rd *FAV* ME13 .... 55 L5
Brentwood *ASH* TN23 .... 145 H8 1
Brewer's Hl *FOLK* CT20 .... 184 F2
Brewer St *DEAL* CT14 .... 103 M7 2
Brewery La *RCANTW* CT4 .... 97 J4
Brewery Rd *SIT* ME10 .... 33 G7
Brewery Sq *RCANTE* CT3 .... 63 M3
Brewhouse La *RASHE* TN25 .... 128 B1
Briar Cl *DVW* CT17 .... 155 H3
KEN/WIL TN24 .... 127 L7
RCANTE CT3 .... 99 H8
Briars Rd *LYDD* TN29 .... 203 H2
Briary Cl *MARG* CT9 .... 29 H5
Brice Av *RCANTW* CT4 .... 94 E3
Brickfield La *FAV* ME13 .... 75 G3
Brickfield Rd *RCANTW* CT4 .... 116 B6
Bridewell La *TENT* TN30 .... 174 C6
Bridewell Pk *WSTB* CT5 .... 40 C4
The Bridge Ap *WSTB* CT5 .... 40 A4
Bridge Cl *HYTHE* CT21 .... 183 J3 1
RASHW TN26 .... 176 D5
Bridge Down *RCANTW* CT4 .... 97 K5
Bridgefield Rd *WSTB* CT5 .... 40 D2
Bridgeford Wy *RCANTW* CT4 .... 97 J4 1
Bridge Hl *DEAL* CT14 .... 102 E5
RCANTW CT4 .... 97 K5
Bridge Rd *ASH* TN23 .... 145 H3
DEAL CT14 .... 103 M6 1
FAV ME13 .... 55 L5
IOS ME12 .... 14 D2
MARG CT9 .... 29 J4
RASHE TN25 .... 147 M8
RCANTW CT4 .... 97 G4
Bridges Cl *BRCH* CT7 .... 45 G3
Bridgeside *DEAL* CT14 .... 103 L7
Bridge St *DVE/WH* CT16 .... 10 B3
FOLKN CT19 .... 13 J2
RASHE TN25 .... 128 F3
Bridgewater Rd *IOS* ME12 .... 14 D5
Bridle Wy *HB* CT6 .... 41 M2
HYTHE CT21 .... 184 C2
Bridleway Gdns *BRDST* CT10 .... 48 F2
Bridleway La *ASH* TN23 .... 163 K1
Brielle Wy *IOS* ME12 .... 14 C4
QBOR ME11 .... 14 C7
Brier Rd *SIT* ME10 .... 32 C8
Brightlingsea Rd *SWCH* CT13 .... 84 B5 1
Bright's Pl *RAM* CT11 .... 5 L4
Brisbane Av *SIT* ME10 .... 51 L1
Brisbane Dr *MSTR* CT12 .... 48 C4 2
Brisley La *RASHE* TN25 .... 163 M7
Brissenden Cl *NROM* TN28 .... 202 D5 1
Bristol Pl *RAM* CT11 .... 5 H5
Bristol Rd *CANT* CT1 .... 6 F7
Britannia Av *WSTB* CT5 .... 39 K6
Britannia Cl *SIT* ME10 .... 33 G6
Britannia Rd *DEAL* CT14 .... 103 M5 2
Briton Ct *IOS* ME12 .... 14 D4 1
Briton Rd *FAV* ME13 .... 55 L6
Britten Cl *HYTHE* CT21 .... 183 J2
Broadacre *RDV* CT15 .... 136 B5
RSIT ME9 .... 53 M3
Broadfield Crs *FOLK* CT20 .... 12 A4
Broadfield Rd *FOLK* CT20 .... 12 B5
Broadhurst Dr *KEN/WIL* TN24 .... 127 M6
Broadlands *CANTW/ST* CT2 .... 61 H7
Broadlands Av *NROM* TN28 .... 202 D5
Broadlands Crs *NROM* TN28 .... 202 D5
Broad La *DEAL* CT14 .... 102 C7
Broadley Av *BRCH* CT7 .... 28 B8
Broadley Rd *MARG* CT9 .... 30 F5
Broadmead *ASH* TN23 .... 145 G7 1
Broadmead Rd *FOLKN* CT19 .... 12 F4
Broadoak Rd *RSIT* ME9 .... 51 M6
Broadsole La *RDV* CT15 .... 154 A8
Broadstairs Rd *BRDST* CT10 .... 31 G8
Broad St *CANT* CT1 .... 7 G3
DEAL CT14 .... 103 M7
IOS ME12 .... 14 D3
MARG CT9 .... 2 F3
RAM CT11 .... 5 J5
Broadview *FOLK* CT20 .... 169 L7
Broadway *IOS* ME12 .... 14 E3
RCANTW CT4 .... 113 J3
The Broadway *BRDST* CT10 .... 49 H1
IOS ME12 .... 15 K6
Brockenhurst Cl *CANTW/ST* CT2 .... 78 A3
Brockenhurst Rd *RAM* CT11 .... 5 M3
Brockhill Rd *HYTHE* CT21 .... 183 K2
Brockley Rd *MARG* CT9 .... 3 H4
Brockman Crs *LYDD* TN29 .... 182 D8
Brockman Rd *FOLK* CT20 .... 12 F5
Brockman's Cl *MSTR* CT12 .... 46 D6
Brogdale Rd *FAV* ME13 .... 55 K8
Bromley Green Rd
RASHW TN26 .... 163 G7
Bromstone Rd *BRDST* CT10 .... 49 G4
Brook Cl *HB* CT6 .... 41 L2
HYTHE CT21 .... 184 D2
Brooke Av *MARG* CT9 .... 29 K6
Brooke Rd *KEN/WIL* TN24 .... 8 D1
Brookfield Pl *DVE/WH* CT16 .... 155 K3 1
Brookfield Rd *ASH* TN23 .... 145 G4
DVE/WH CT16 .... 155 J2 1
Brooklands Cl *CANTW/ST* CT2 .... 79 H1
Brook La *HB* CT6 .... 25 K8
MSTR CT12 .... 66 B1
RASHE TN25 .... 167 G3
Brook Rd *FAV* ME13 .... 55 L5
WSTB CT5 .... 40 E2
Brookside *DVE/WH* CT16 .... 136 E8
LYDD TN29 .... 194 C8
Brook St *RASHW* TN26 .... 175 L5
SWCH CT13 .... 101 L3
Brooks Wy *LYDD* TN29 .... 209 L8
Broomfield Crs *MARG* CT9 .... 31 H3
Broomfield Ga *WSTB* CT5 .... 40 F8
Broomfield Rd *FAV* ME13 .... 54 L4
FOLKN CT19 .... 170 A7
HB CT6 .... 42 D4
Broom Rd *SIT* ME10 .... 33 L8
Browning Pl *FOLKN* CT19 .... 171 G6 1
Brownings Orch *RSIT* ME9 .... 52 C6
Broxhall Rd *RCANTW* CT4 .... 114 C3
Bruce Cl *DEAL* CT14 .... 121 K1
Brunswick Fld *RSIT* ME9 .... 35 G8
Brunswick Gdns
DVE/WH CT16 .... 155 K2 3
Brunswick Rd *ASH* TN23 .... 145 G3
BRCH CT7 .... 28 C8
Brunswick Sq *HB* CT6 .... 24 A8
Brunswick St *RAM* CT11 .... 5 K5
Brymore Cl *CANT* CT1 .... 7 K1
Brymore Rd *CANT* CT1 .... 7 L1
Buckhurst Dr *MARG* CT9 .... 31 H3 1
Buckingham Rd *BRDST* CT10 .... 49 K1 2
MARG CT9 .... 2 F7
Buckland Av *DVE/WH* CT16 .... 155 K3
Buckland La *RCANTE* CT3 .... 100 B3
Bucklers Cl *IOS* ME12 .... 23 G1 1
Bucksford La *ASH* TN23 .... 144 F5
Buck St *RASHE* TN25 .... 109 L3
Buddle Dr *IOS* ME12 .... 15 G6
Budd's La *TENT* TN30 .... 197 G3
Buenos Ayres *MARG* CT9 .... 2 C5
Buffs Av *FOLK* CT20 .... 169 K7
Bugglesden Rd *HDCN* TN27 .... 158 F8
Bulleid Pl *ASH* TN23 .... 145 M6
Buller's Av *HB* CT6 .... 42 A1
Bull Hl *RMAID* ME17 .... 106 C4
Bull La *FAV* ME13 .... 57 H8
RASHW TN26 .... 160 D1
RSIT ME9 .... 50 A4
Bullockstone Rd *HB* CT6 .... 41 M3
Bullwark St *DVW* CT17 .... 155 M8 1
The Bulrushes *ASH* TN23 .... 144 E5
Bulwark Rd *DEAL* CT14 .... 103 M6 2
Bunce Court Rd *FAV* ME13 .... 89 H6
Bunker's Hl *DVW* CT17 .... 155 J3
Bunkers Hill Av *DVW* CT17 .... 155 J4
Bunkers Hill Rd *DVW* CT17 .... 155 J4
Bunkley Meadow
RASHW TN26 .... 178 C6 1
Burch Av *SWCH* CT13 .... 84 B5
Burgate *CANT* CT1 .... 7 G4 1
Burgate La *CANT* CT1 .... 7 G5 1
Burgess Cl *DVE/WH* CT16 .... 137 K6
MSTR CT12 .... 46 E6
Burgess Gn *DEAL* CT14 .... 102 E5
Burgess Rd *RCANTE* CT3 .... 99 H7
Burgoyne Hts *DVE/WH* CT16 .... 156 A3
Burkeston Cl *SIT* ME10 .... 33 J5
Burleigh Rd *HDCN* TN27 .... 107 L6
Burley Rd *SIT* ME10 .... 52 A1
Burlington Dr *HB* CT6 .... 24 F8
Burlington Gdns *MARG* CT9 .... 2 A8
Burma Crs *CANT* CT1 .... 78 F4 3
Burmarsh Rd *LYDD* TN29 .... 194 F3
Burnan Rd *WSTB* CT5 .... 40 E3
Burnham Cl *SIT* ME10 .... 33 G5
Burnt House Hl *RCANTE* CT3 .... 62 D8
Burnthouse La *HDCN* TN27 .... 140 F4
Burnt Oast Rd *FAV* ME13 .... 75 J2
Burrow Rd *FOLKN* CT19 .... 13 K3
The Burrs *SIT* ME10 .... 52 B2 1
Bursill Crs *MSTR* CT12 .... 4 C1
Bursted Hl *RCANTW* CT4 .... 114 D3
Burton Cl *FOLKN* CT19 .... 170 C6
Burton Flds *HB* CT6 .... 42 D1
Burton Rd *KEN/WIL* TN24 .... 127 M7
Bush Av *MSTR* CT12 .... 4 C1
Bush Cl *RSIT* ME9 .... 51 H8
Bushey Cl *FAV* ME13 .... 75 G2
Busheyfields Rd *HB* CT6 .... 60 C4
Bushy Hill Rd *CANTW/ST* CT2 .... 61 L6
Bushy Royds *KEN/WIL* TN24 .... 145 M7 1
Butchers La *RDV* CT15 .... 100 A8
Butchery La *CANT* CT1 .... 7 G4 2
The Butchery *SWCH* CT13 .... 84 C4 3
Butler's Hl *FAV* ME13 .... 57 M6
Buttermere *FAV* ME13 .... 56 A7 1
Buttermere Cl *FOLKN* CT19 .... 12 D2
Buttermere Gdns
RCANTE CT3 .... 99 H7 1
Butterside Rd *ASH* TN23 .... 163 L1
Butter St *RDV* CT15 .... 117 K1
Butt Field Rd *ASH* TN23 .... 145 G5
The Butts *SIT* ME10 .... 52 B1
SWCH CT13 .... 84 B4
Buxton Rd *MSTR* CT12 .... 48 D3
Bybrook Ct *KEN/WIL* TN24 .... 145 L1 1
Bybrook Fld *FOLK* CT20 .... 185 G2
Bybrook Rd *KEN/WIL* TN24 .... 127 L8
Bybrook Wy *FOLK* CT20 .... 185 G1 1
Byllan Rd *DVW* CT17 .... 155 G2
Byron Av *MARG* CT9 .... 3 H6
Byron Cl *CANT* CT1 .... 7 L7
Byron Crs *DVE/WH* CT16 .... 155 K1
Bysing Wood Rd *FAV* ME13 .... 55 J4

C

Cade Rd *ASH* TN23 .... 145 J6
Cades Orch *FAV* ME13 .... 73 G2
Cadnam Cl *CANTW/ST* CT2 .... 78 A2
Caesar's Wy *FOLKN* CT19 .... 170 A6
Cage La *HDCN* TN27 .... 141 H4
Calais Hl *CANTW/ST* CT2 .... 59 M7
Caldecot La *LYDD* TN29 .... 209 M3
Caldew Gv *SIT* ME10 .... 52 C2
Caledon Ter *CANT* CT1 .... 7 G7
Calgary Crs *FOLKN* CT19 .... 171 G5
Calland *RASHE* TN25 .... 148 A8
Calleywell La *RASHE* TN25 .... 165 J6
Callis Court Rd *BRDST* CT10 .... 31 H7
Calverden Rd *MSTR* CT12 .... 4 B1
Camber Rd *RYE* TN31 .... 206 B8
Camber Wy *DVE/WH* CT16 .... 11 M3
Cambourne Av *WGOS* CT8 .... 28 F5
Cambridge Av *SWCH* CT13 .... 85 J7
Cambridge Cl *BRCH* CT7 .... 28 D6 1
Cambridge Gdns *FOLK* CT20 .... 13 G5
Cambridge Rd *CANT* CT1 .... 6 E7
DEAL CT14 .... 121 M2 1
DVW CT17 .... 10 D8
FAV ME13 .... 55 K7
SIT ME10 .... 52 D3
Cambridge Wy *CANT* CT1 .... 6 E8 1
Camden Crs *DVE/WH* CT16 .... 10 E7
Camden Rd *BRDST* CT10 .... 31 G6
RAM CT11 .... 5 K6
Camden Sq *RAM* CT11 .... 5 K5 1
Camellia Cl *MARG* CT9 .... 29 K5 1
Campbell Cl *HB* CT6 .... 42 E2
Campbell Rd *DEAL* CT14 .... 121 M2
Canada Cl *RFOLK* CT18 .... 169 L7
Canada Rd *DEAL* CT14 .... 121 M2 2
Canberra Gdns *SIT* ME10 .... 51 L1
Cannonbury Rd *RAM* CT11 .... 5 G7
Cannongate Av *HYTHE* CT21 .... 183 M2
Cannongate Cl *HYTHE* CT21 .... 184 A3
Cannongate Gdns *HYTHE* CT21 .... 183 M2
Cannongate Rd *HYTHE* CT21 .... 183 M2
Cannon Rd *RAM* CT11 .... 5 H5
Cannon St *DEAL* CT14 .... 103 L6
LYDD TN29 .... 209 L7
NROM TN28 .... 202 D6
Canons Gate Rd *DVE/WH* CT16 .... 10 F5
Canon Woods Wy
KEN/WIL TN24 .... 128 B7 1
Canterbury Cl *BRDST* CT10 .... 30 F8 1
Canterbury Hl *CANTW/ST* CT2 .... 60 A8
Canterbury La *CANT* CT1 .... 7 G5
Canterbury Rd *BRCH* CT7 .... 45 G6
FAV ME13 .... 56 A8
FOLKN CT19 .... 13 H2
HB CT6 .... 42 C1
KEN/WIL TN24 .... 8 E2
RASHE TN25 .... 108 C4
RCANTE CT3 .... 80 A5
RCANTW CT4 .... 94 A5
RDV CT15 .... 136 A6
RFOLK CT18 .... 150 E6
SIT ME10 .... 52 D2
WSTB CT5 .... 39 M5
Canterbury Road Birchington
BRCH CT7 .... 28 C7
Canterbury Rd East *RAM* CT11 .... 48 B6
Canterbury Road Margate
MARG CT9 .... 29 K4
Canterbury Rd West *MSTR* CT12 .... 47 M6
Canterbury Road Westgate
WGOS CT8 .... 28 F5
Canute Rd *BRCH* CT7 .... 27 M5
DEAL CT14 .... 103 L4
FAV ME13 .... 55 L7
Capel Cl *BRDST* CT10 .... 31 H4
Capel Rd *FAV* ME13 .... 55 K6 1
RASHW TN26 .... 178 B2
RCANTW CT4 .... 113 H1
SIT ME10 .... 52 A3
Capel St *RFOLK* CT18 .... 171 K4
Capstan Rw *DEAL* CT14 .... 103 M6 3
Cardine Cl *SIT* ME10 .... 33 G6
Carey Cl *NROM* TN28 .... 202 D7
Carlsden Cl *DVE/WH* CT16 .... 155 J2
Carlton Av *BRDST* CT10 .... 31 J8
IOS ME12 .... 14 D4 2
RAM CT11 .... 5 H6
Carlton Hl *HB* CT6 .... 41 L1
Carlton Ri *WGOS* CT8 .... 28 E5
Carlton Rd *ASH* TN23 .... 8 A3
DEAL CT14 .... 121 L7
WSTB CT5 .... 58 F3
Carlton Rd East *WGOS* CT8 .... 28 F5 1
Carlton Rd West *WGOS* CT8 .... 28 E5
Caroland Cl *RASHE* TN25 .... 147 M8
Caroline Cl *WSTB* CT5 .... 39 K7 1
Caroline Crs *BRDST* CT10 .... 31 G7
Carriage Ms *CANTW/ST* CT2 .... 6 E3
Carroway's Pl *MARG* CT9 .... 3 G4
Carter La *LYDD* TN29 .... 200 A3
Carter's Rd *FOLK* CT20 .... 170 B8
Carter's Wd *RASHW* TN26 .... 178 C6
Caslocke St *FAV* ME13 .... 55 L6 2
Cassino Sq *DVE/WH* CT16 .... 156 A3
Castle Av *BRDST* CT10 .... 31 K7
DVE/WH CT16 .... 10 C2
HYTHE CT21 .... 183 K2
Castle Bay *FOLK* CT20 .... 184 E2
Castle Cl *HYTHE* CT21 .... 182 B3
Castle Dr *DVE/WH* CT16 .... 137 H6
Castle Hl *FOLKN* CT19 .... 170 C5
Castle Hill Av *FOLK* CT20 .... 12 E5
Castle Hill Rd *DVE/WH* CT16 .... 10 F4
Castle Mayne Av *BRCH* CT7 .... 47 H2
Castlemere Av *QBOR* ME11 .... 14 D8
Castlemount Rd *DVE/WH* CT16 .... 10 D3
Castle Rd *FOLK* CT20 .... 185 H2
HYTHE CT21 .... 183 K1
SIT ME10 .... 33 K8
WSTB CT5 .... 40 B3
Castle Rough La *SIT* ME10 .... 33 H4
Castle Rw *CANT* CT1 .... 6 E6
Castle St *CANT* CT1 .... 6 E5
DVE/WH CT16 .... 10 E6
QBOR ME11 .... 14 C8
Catherine Wy *BRDST* CT10 .... 31 J7
Catsole Hl *RCANTE* CT3 .... 99 M3
Cattle Market *SWCH* CT13 .... 84 B4 2
Catt's Hl *TENT* TN30 .... 198 B1
Catt's Wood Rd *RCANTW* CT4 .... 96 B8
Cauldham Cl *RFOLK* CT18 .... 171 J4
Cauldham La *RFOLK* CT18 .... 171 K1
The Causeway *CANTW/ST* CT2 .... 6 F2
Cave La *RCANTE* CT3 .... 99 M2
Cavell Sq *DEAL* CT14 .... 121 J2
Cavell Wy *SIT* ME10 .... 32 F8
Cavenagh Rd *RDV* CT15 .... 139 K7
Cavendish Pl *RAM* CT11 .... 5 J6 1
Cavendish Rd *HB* CT6 .... 42 C1
Cavendish St *RAM* CT11 .... 5 J5
Cavour Rd *FAV* ME13 .... 55 L6
IOS ME12 .... 14 E3
Caxton Cl *TENT* TN30 .... 174 B6 1
Cayser Dr *RMAID* ME17 .... 104 A3
Cecil Av *IOS* ME12 .... 14 D4
Cecil Ct *HB* CT6 .... 42 C1
Cecilia Gv *BRDST* CT10 .... 31 H7
Cecilia Rd *RAM* CT11 .... 5 K2
Cecil Pk *HB* CT6 .... 42 C1
Cecil Rd *DEAL* CT14 .... 121 M6 1
Cecil Sq *MARG* CT9 .... 2 F4
Cecil St *MARG* CT9 .... 2 F4 1
Cedar Cl *ASH* TN23 .... 145 G2
BRDST CT10 .... 31 H6
MARG CT9 .... 3 M6
SIT ME10 .... 52 D3 1
Cedar Crs *LYDD* TN29 .... 203 H2
Cedar Rd *CANTW/ST* CT2 .... 61 H7
Cedarview *CANTW/ST* CT2 .... 77 L4 1
Cellar Hl *RSIT* ME9 .... 53 L5
Celt Cl *SIT* ME10 .... 33 H5
Celtic Rd *DEAL* CT14 .... 121 J3
Cemetery La *KEN/WIL* TN24 .... 145 L1
Centenary Gdns *SWCH* CT13 .... 101 J3
Centenary Wk *CANTW/ST* CT2 .... 6 B3
Centenary Walk Canterbury
RCANTW CT4 .... 77 G7
Central Av *SIT* ME10 .... 52 B2
Central Pde *HB* CT6 .... 24 A8
Central Rd *RAM* CT11 .... 5 G2
Centre Rd *DVW* CT17 .... 10 B8
Centurion Wk *ASH* TN23 .... 163 K1
Century Rd *FAV* ME13 .... 56 A6
The Chain *SWCH* CT13 .... 84 C5
Chalcroft Rd *FOLK* CT20 .... 185 G1
Chalfont Dr *HB* CT6 .... 42 F3 1
Chalk Av *TENT* TN30 .... 174 D3
Chalk Cl *FOLKN* CT19 .... 170 C6
Chalk Hl *RAM* CT11 .... 48 B7
Chalk Hill Rd *DEAL* CT14 .... 121 L8
Chalkpit Hl *RCANTW* CT4 .... 97 M2
Chalk Pit La *RCANTE* CT3 .... 82 D8
Chalk Rd *QBOR* ME11 .... 14 C8
Chalksole Green La *RDV* CT15 .... 153 J3
Chalkwell Rd *SIT* ME10 .... 51 M1
Challenger Cl *SIT* ME10 .... 33 G6
Challock Ct *MARG* CT9 .... 31 H3 2
Chamberlain Dr *HB* CT6 .... 41 K1
Chamberlain Rd *DVW* CT17 .... 155 J5
Chance Meadow *RDV* CT15 .... 138 B7
Chanctonbury Cha *WSTB* CT5 .... 39 J7 1
Chandos Sq *BRDST* CT10 .... 49 K1
Channel Cl *FOLKN* CT19 .... 13 M1
Channel Lea *DEAL* CT14 .... 121 L4
Channel View Rd *DVW* CT17 .... 10 B9
Channon Rd *LYDD* TN29 .... 210 F6
Chapel Hl *MARG* CT9 .... 30 C6
RDV CT15 .... 118 E6
Chapel Hill Cl *MARG* CT9 .... 30 B6 1
Chapel La *CANTW/ST* CT2 .... 59 J6
CANTW/ST CT2 .... 60 F6
DEAL CT14 .... 120 F5
HDCN TN27 .... 123 K2
LYDD TN29 .... 193 K2
RCANTE CT3 .... 82 D7
RCANTW CT4 .... 132 E8
RDV CT15 .... 119 K7
RDV CT15 .... 139 H7
Chapel Pl *DVW* CT17 .... 10 D6
RAM CT11 .... 5 H6
Chapel Place La *RAM* CT11 .... 5 H5
Chapel Rd *DEAL* CT14 .... 119 K2 1
DVE/WH CT16 .... 137 J5 1
LYDD TN29 .... 194 E5
RAM CT11 .... 4 E5
RASHW TN26 .... 126 B4
Chapel St *DEAL* CT14 .... 103 M7 3
FAV ME13 .... 55 M7
HYTHE CT21 .... 183 K3
IOS ME12 .... 14 C2
IOS ME12 .... 15 M7
Chapmans Cl *RASHE* TN25 .... 109 L3
Chapmans Hl *RCANTE* CT3 .... 99 K8
Chappell Wy *SIT* ME10 .... 32 F7
Charing Cl *MSTR* CT12 .... 4 F2
Charing Crs *WGOS* CT8 .... 28 F6
Charing Heath Rd *HDCN* TN27 .... 107 H7
Charing Hl *HDCN* TN27 .... 108 A4
Charles Cobb Cl *LYDD* TN29 .... 194 F5
Charles Crs *FOLKN* CT19 .... 170 A6
Charles Drayson Ct *FAV* ME13 .... 56 A6 2
Charles Rd *DEAL* CT14 .... 121 K1
RAM CT11 .... 5 J2
Charles St *HB* CT6 .... 24 B8
IOS ME12 .... 14 C2
Charlesworth Dr *BRCH* CT7 .... 28 D6
Charlotte Pl *MARG* CT9 .... 3 G5
Charlotte Sq *MARG* CT9 .... 3 G5 2
Charlotte St *FOLK* CT20 .... 13 J4
SIT ME10 .... 33 G8
Charlton Av *DVE/WH* CT16 .... 10 B2
Charlton Cl *KEN/WIL* TN24 .... 146 C5
MSTR CT12 .... 48 D3 1
Charlton Gn *DVE/WH* CT16 .... 10 B2
The Charltons *FAV* ME13 .... 75 H1
Charminster *ASH* TN23 .... 145 G7 2
Charnwood *WSTB* CT5 .... 40 F4
Charnwood Rd *HB* CT6 .... 42 D4
Chart Cl *FAV* ME13 .... 55 K6
Chartham Downs Rd
RCANTW CT4 .... 94 F4
Chart Rd *ASH* TN23 .... 8 A2
FOLKN CT19 .... 170 B7
Chartwell Av *HB* CT6 .... 42 F1
Chartwell Gv *SIT* ME10 .... 51 L2 1
Chater Cl *DEAL* CT14 .... 121 L1 1
Chatham Pl *RAM* CT11 .... 5 J4
Chatham St *RAM* CT11 .... 5 H4
Chatsworth Dr *SIT* ME10 .... 32 D8
Chaucer Av *WSTB* CT5 .... 40 D4
Chaucer Cl *CANT* CT1 .... 7 M7
Chaucer Crs *DVE/WH* CT16 .... 155 K2
Chaucer Ms *CANTW/ST* CT2 .... 77 H4
Chaucer Rd *BRDST* CT10 .... 49 J2 1
CANT CT1 .... 7 L3
RDV CT15 .... 118 D4 1
SIT ME10 .... 51 M2
Cheeselands *HDCN* TN27 .... 158 B3
Cheesmans Cl *MSTR* CT12 .... 46 E8
Chegworth Gdns *SIT* ME10 .... 52 A4
Chegworth La *RMAID* ME17 .... 86 B7
Chegworth Rd *RMAID* ME17 .... 86 B6
Chelsea Rd *CANT* CT1 .... 78 E1 1
Cheney Hl *RSIT* ME9 .... 52 C8
Cheney Rd *FAV* ME13 .... 56 B6
Chennell Park Rd *TENT* TN30 .... 174 A4
Chequer La *RCANTE* CT3 .... 82 F3
Chequers Hl *RCANTW* CT4 .... 113 L2
Chequers Pk *RASHE* TN25 .... 129 G4
Chequers Rd *IOS* ME12 .... 16 A7
Cheriton Av *MSTR* CT12 .... 4 D2
Cheriton Court Rd *FOLK* CT20 .... 169 L8
Cheriton Gdns *FOLK* CT20 .... 12 F5
Cheriton High St *FOLKN* CT19 .... 169 M7
RFOLK CT18 .... 169 K7
Cheriton Int *FOLKN* CT19 .... 169 L7 1
Cheriton Pl *DEAL* CT14 .... 121 M1 1
FOLK CT20 .... 13 G6
Cheriton Rd *DEAL* CT14 .... 121 M1 2
FOLK CT20 .... 12 F5
FOLKN CT19 .... 12 B3
Cherry Av *CANTW/ST* CT2 .... 77 M3
Cherrybrook Rd *FOLK* CT20 .... 169 M7 1
Cherry Cl *SIT* ME10 .... 32 F7
Cherry Dr *CANTW/ST* CT2 .... 6 A1
Cherry Flds *SIT* ME10 .... 32 C8
Cherry Garden Av *FOLKN* CT19 .... 12 A1
Cherry Garden Crs
RASHE TN25 .... 129 H3 1
Cherry Garden La *FOLKN* CT19 .... 170 B6
RASHE TN25 .... 129 G3
RCANTE CT3 .... 83 G4
Cherrygarden La *RCANTE* CT3 .... 100 A5
Cherry Garden Rd
CANTW/ST CT2 .... 6 A1
Cherry Gdns *BRDST* CT10 .... 48 E2
HB CT6 .... 42 A1
NROM TN28 .... 202 F7
RCANTW CT4 .... 133 H8
RSIT ME9 .... 53 L3
Cherry Glebe *RASHE* TN25 .... 165 G2
Cherry Gv *RDV* CT15 .... 118 E3
Cherry La *DEAL* CT14 .... 120 F2
Cherry Orch *RASHW* TN26 .... 176 C2
RCANTW CT4 .... 93 L3
TENT TN30 .... 174 C7 1
WSTB CT5 .... 40 E5
Cherry Orchard La *RASHE* TN25 .... 180 A1
Cherry Tree Av *DVE/WH* CT16 .... 10 A2
Cherry Tree Cl *RSIT* ME9 .... 53 M3 1
Cherry Tree Rd *HDCN* TN27 .... 107 G6
Cherry Waye *RDV* CT15 .... 118 E6
Cherrywood Ri *ASH* TN23 .... 145 H1
Cherville La *RCANTE* CT3 .... 80 E6
Chessenden La *HDCN* TN27 .... 141 J4
Chester Av *RASHW* TN26 .... 142 F8
Chester Rd *WGOS* CT8 .... 29 H5 1
Chestfield Rd *WSTB* CT5 .... 40 E6
Chestnut Av *CANTW/ST* CT2 .... 59 J7
Chestnut Cl *ASH* TN23 .... 145 G2 1
DVE/WH CT16 .... 137 J5 2
HYTHE CT21 .... 183 G5 1
RMAID ME17 .... 104 B7
TENT TN30 .... 174 E4
Chestnut Ct *FAV* ME13 .... 75 H2
Chestnut Dr *BRDST* CT10 .... 48 F1
CANTW/ST CT2 .... 61 J7
DEAL CT14 .... 102 C1
HB CT6 .... 41 M3
Chestnut La *ASH* TN23 .... 163 L1
Chestnut Rd *DVW* CT17 .... 155 K6 1
Chestnuts *RASHE* TN25 .... 147 M8 1
Chestnut St *RSIT* ME9 .... 51 G1
Chestnut Wood La *RSIT* ME9 .... 51 G1
Chevalier Rd *DVW* CT17 .... 155 J6
Cheviot Ct *BRDST* CT10 .... 31 K8 1
Cheviot Wy *KEN/WIL* TN24 .... 145 L1 2
Cheyne Cl *SIT* ME10 .... 33 H5
Cheyne Rd *IOS* ME12 .... 21 M2
Chichester Cl *ASH* TN23 .... 8 C6
Chichester Rd *FOLK* CT20 .... 185 G1
MSTR CT12 .... 48 D4
Chiddingfold Cl *IOS* ME12 .... 15 M7
Chilham Av *WGOS* CT8 .... 28 F6
Chilham Cl *IOS* ME12 .... 14 D5
Chilham Rd *FOLKN* CT19 .... 170 A7
Chilston Rd *RMAID* ME17 .... 87 M8
Chiltern End *KEN/WIL* TN24 .... 8 C1
Chilton Av *RDV* CT15 .... 154 E2
SIT ME10 .... 52 C2
Chilton Fld *RCANTE* CT3 .... 82 F3
Chilton Gdns *RCANTE* CT3 .... 82 F3
Chilton La *RAM* CT11 .... 4 B7
Chilton Pl *RCANTE* CT3 .... 82 F3 1
Chilton Sq *RCANTE* CT3 .... 82 F4 1
Chilton Wy *DVW* CT17 .... 155 G2
The Chimes *KEN/WIL* TN24 .... 8 D1
Chipman's Wy *MSTR* CT12 .... 46 A6
Chippendayle Dr *RMAID* ME17 .... 86 F7
Chislett Cl *RASHE* TN25 .... 167 G3
Chisnall Rd *DVW* CT17 .... 155 G1
Chittenden's La *LYDD* TN29 .... 202 A3
Chitty La *RCANTE* CT3 .... 43 L6
Christchurch Rd *ASH* TN23 .... 8 C6
Christ Church Rd *FOLK* CT20 .... 12 F5
Christchurch Wy
DVE/WH CT16 .... 155 K2
Chrysler Av *HB* CT6 .... 41 J1
Chulkhurst *HDCN* TN27 .... 158 A3
Church Ap *NROM* TN28 .... 202 C7 1
Church Cliff *DEAL* CT14 .... 121 M7
Church Cl *RASHE* TN25 .... 165 G2
Church Court Gv *BRDST* CT10 .... 31 G7
Church Crs *RMAID* ME17 .... 87 H7 1
Church Farm Wy *SWCH* CT13 .... 83 K7
Church Fld *RASHE* TN25 .... 167 K4 1
Churchfield Pl *MARG* CT9 .... 2 F5
Churchfields *BRDST* CT10 .... 31 H6
MARG CT9 .... 2 F6
Churchfield Wy *RASHE* TN25 .... 129 G3
Church Hl *ASH* TN23 .... 163 J2
CANTW/ST CT2 .... 77 L4
DVE/WH CT16 .... 136 F8
FAV ME13 .... 57 J8
HDCN TN27 .... 106 E5
RAM CT11 .... 5 J5
RASHW TN26 .... 142 F8
RASHW TN26 .... 160 A6
RCANTW CT4 .... 93 K5
RDV CT15 .... 118 D5
RDV CT15 .... 120 C5
RDV CT15 .... 135 M1
RSIT ME9 .... 50 B6
RSIT ME9 .... 71 H6
TENT TN30 .... 198 B2
Churchill Av *DEAL* CT14 .... 121 L3
FOLKN CT19 .... 170 E5

D

K

Kake St *RCANTW* CT4 ... 112 F7
Keat Farm Cl *HB* CT6 ... 25 H8 1
Keddow's Cl *HYTHE* CT21 ... 182 F5
Keeper's Hl *RCANTW* CT4 ... 97 M3
Keith Av *MSTR* CT12 ... 4 A2
Kelvedon Rd *DEAL* CT14 ... 121 L3 1
Kemp Rd *WSTB* CT5 ... 40 E3
Kemsdale Rd *FAV* ME13 ... 57 H7
Kemsing Gdns *CANTW/ST* CT2 ... 78 D1
Kenardington Rd *RASHW* TN26 .. 189 L3
Kenbrook *KEN/WIL* TN24 ... 127 L6 1
Kendal Cl *RAM* CT11 ... 4 C6
Kendal Ri *BRDST* CT10 ... 31 J8
Kenfield Rd *RCANTW* CT4 ... 95 J7
Kenilworth Cl *RDV* CT15 ... 139 J7
Kenilworth Ct *SIT* ME10 ... 32 E8
Kennedy Cl *FAV* ME13 ... 55 M4
Kennedy Dr *DEAL* CT14 ... 121 K3
Kennel Barn Rd *RSIT* ME9 ... 68 D1
Kennel Hl *RDV* CT15 ... 119 G7
Kennelling Rd *FAV* ME13 ... 107 M1
Kennett Dr *DEAL* CT14 ... 121 J3 1
Kennett La *RASHE* TN25 ... 167 J4
Kennington Pl
KEN/WIL TN24 ... 127 M6 1
Kennington Rd *KEN/WIL* TN24 ... 146 C3
Kensington Rd *CANT* CT1 ... 78 E1
Kent Av *CANT* CT1 ... 7 M5
IOS ME12 ... 15 K7
KEN/WIL TN24 ... 8 C2
SIT ME10 ... 51 M2
Kent Gdns *BRCH* CT7 ... 28 B6
Kentmere Av *RAM* CT11 ... 48 B6
Kenton Gdns *MSTR* CT12 ... 46 D7
Kent Rd *FOLKN* CT19 ... 170 A6
IOS ME12 ... 14 D4
MARG CT9 ... 3 M8
Kent St *WSTB* CT5 ... 39 M5
Kent Ter *RAM* CT11 ... 5 L6
Kent View Dr *IOS* ME12 ... 21 M4
Kerton Rd *LYDD* TN29 ... 217 G3
Kestrel Cl *SIT* ME10 ... 52 C3
Keswick Rd *SIT* ME10 ... 52 E2
Kettle Dr *RFOLK* CT18 ... 152 D8
Kettle Hl *FAV* ME13 ... 90 B1
Kettle Hill Rd *FAV* ME13 ... 72 A8
Kevin Dr *RAM* CT11 ... 4 C7
Keycol Hl *RSIT* ME9 ... 32 A8
Keyes Pl *FOLKN* CT19 ... 171 G6
Key St *SIT* ME10 ... 32 C8
Khartoum Sq *DVE/WH* CT16 ... 137 J8
Kiln Cl *RASHE* TN25 ... 109 K4
SIT ME10 ... 52 C2
Kilndown Cl *ASH* TN23 ... 145 G7
Kilndown Gdns *CANTW/ST* CT2 ... 78 C1
MARG CT9 ... 31 G3
Kiln Dr *RYE* TN31 ... 205 K5
Kiln Fld *TENT* TN30 ... 174 E6
Kiln La *RASHW* TN26 ... 161 H1
Kiln Rd *RASHE* TN25 ... 180 B1 1
Kimberley Cl *DVE/WH* CT16 ... 155 L2
Kimberley Gv *WSTB* CT5 ... 39 H7
Kimberley Rd *MSTR* CT12 ... 48 C4
King Arthur Rd *MSTR* CT12 ... 47 M6
King Edward Av *BRDST* CT10 ... 49 J1
HB CT6 ... 42 D1
King Edward Rd *BRCH* CT7 ... 28 C8
DEAL CT14 ... 103 M5
RAM CT11 ... 4 E6
King Edward St *WSTB* CT5 ... 39 M4
Kingfisher Av *HYTHE* CT21 ... 182 F5
Kingfisher Cl *KEN/WIL* TN24 ... 146 C6
MARG CT9 ... 29 K5 3
RSIT ME9 ... 33 G1
WSTB CT5 ... 39 L6
Kingfisher Ct *HB* CT6 ... 41 M2
King Lear's Wy *DVW* CT17 ... 155 K8 1
King's Av *ASH* TN23 ... 8 A3
BRCH CT7 ... 27 M5
BRDST CT10 ... 31 K8
MSTR CT12 ... 4 D1
RYE TN31 ... 205 M7
SWCH CT13 ... 85 H6
WSTB CT5 ... 40 A4
King's Cl *DEAL* CT14 ... 121 L8
Kingsdown Hl *DEAL* CT14 ... 139 L1
Kingsdown Pk *WSTB* CT5 ... 40 B3
Kingsdown Rd *DEAL* CT14 ... 121 M5
RDV CT15 ... 139 H6
RSIT ME9 ... 70 E2
Kingsferry Br *RSIT* ME9 ... 19 J6
Kingsfield Rd *HB* CT6 ... 42 D3
Kingsford St *KEN/WIL* TN24 ... 146 F7
RASHE TN25 ... 165 G1
Kingsgate Av *BRDST* CT10 ... 31 H4
Kingsgate Bay Rd *BRDST* CT10 ... 31 J3
Kingsgate La *TENT* TN30 ... 187 L8
King's Head Aly *IOS* ME12 ... 14 C3 2
Kingsland Gdns *DEAL* CT14 ... 121 K5 1
Kingsland Hollow *LYDD* TN29 .. 203 J1 1
Kingsland La *HDCN* TN27 ... 124 A4
RASHE TN25 ... 127 H6
Kingsley Rd *WSTB* CT5 ... 40 A5 1
Kingsmarsh La *LYDD* TN29 ... 209 L1
Kingsmead *FOLKN* CT19 ... 170 D5
Kings Meadow
KEN/WIL TN24 ... 128 A6 1
Kingsmead Rd *CANT* CT1 ... 7 H1
CANTW/ST CT2 ... 7 G1
Kings Mill Cl *SIT* ME10 ... 33 G8 1
Kingsnorth Gdns *FOLK* CT20 ... 12 D5
Kingsnorth Rd *ASH* TN23 ... 145 J7
FAV ME13 ... 55 L7
King's Pk *CANT* CT1 ... 7 K3
King's Rd *BRCH* CT7 ... 28 C7
DVW CT17 ... 155 J6
FAV ME13 ... 55 L6
FOLK CT20 ... 169 M7
HB CT6 ... 42 A1
IOS ME12 ... 15 M6
RAM CT11 ... 5 G3
RCANTE CT3 ... 99 H8
Kings Ropewalk *DVW* CT17 ... 155 K8
Kingston Av *MARG* CT9 ... 29 K6
Kingston Cl *DVW* CT17 ... 155 H2
HB CT6 ... 25 G8
MSTR CT12 ... 48 D4
King St *CANT* CT1 ... 6 F3
CANTW/ST CT2 ... 79 H1
DEAL CT14 ... 103 M7
DVE/WH CT16 ... 10 D6
IOS ME12 ... 14 C3 3
LYDD TN29 ... 200 B3
MARG CT9 ... 2 F3
RAM CT11 ... 5 K5
SIT ME10 ... 33 G8
SWCH CT13 ... 84 C4
Kingsway *LYDD* TN29 ... 195 G3
Kingswood *KEN/WIL* TN24 ... 127 M8 2
Kipling Rd *ASH* TN23 ... 8 C3
Kipping Cl *RFOLK* CT18 ... 170 C1
Kirby's La *CANTW/ST* CT2 ... 6 E3
Kirkstone Av *RAM* CT11 ... 48 B6
Kirkwood Av *RASHW* TN26 ... 176 C4 1
Kitchener Cl *RCANTW* CT4 ... 116 A5
Kitchener Rd *DVW* CT17 ... 155 J6
Kitchener Sq *FOLKN* CT19 ... 171 G5 3
Kitchenour La *RYE* TN31 ... 196 A8
Kite Farm *WSTB* CT5 ... 40 F2
Kitewell La *LYDD* TN29 ... 209 M5
Kither Rd *ASH* TN23 ... 8 B9
Kit Hl *FAV* ME13 ... 74 F5
Kitsbridge La *RASHW* TN26 ... 179 H8
Knatchbull Wy *RASHE* TN25 ... 148 A8
Knight Av *CANTW/ST* CT2 ... 77 L5
Knightrider St *SWCH* CT13 ... 84 C5
Knight's Av *BRDST* CT10 ... 31 K7
Knightsfield Rd *SIT* ME10 ... 32 F7
Knight's Rd *DVE/WH* CT16 ... 10 F4
Knights Templars *DVW* CT17 ... 10 B8
Knights Wy *DVE/WH* CT16 ... 155 J2
Knock Hl *TENT* TN30 ... 198 C3
Knockholt Rd *MARG* CT9 ... 31 G2
Knock Rd *ASH* TN23 ... 145 J6
Knockwood Rd *TENT* TN30 ... 174 E4
Knold Pk *MARG* CT9 ... 2 E9
The Knole *FAV* ME13 ... 55 K6
Knoll Hl *RASHE* TN25 ... 180 E2
Knoll La *ASH* TN23 ... 145 G6
Knoll Pl *DEAL* CT14 ... 121 L4
Knoll Wy *IOS* ME12 ... 22 F1
Knott Crs *KEN/WIL* TN24 ... 146 C6 1
Knott's La *CANT* CT1 ... 7 G3
RDV CT15 ... 139 H7 2
Knowler Wy *HB* CT6 ... 24 E8
Kohima Pl *DVE/WH* CT16 ... 156 B3
Kymbeline Ct *DEAL* CT14 ... 121 K1 1

L

La Belle Alliance Sq *RAM* CT11 ... 5 L5 1
Laburnum Av *SWCH* CT13 ... 84 B5
Laburnum Cl *DVE/WH* CT16 ... 155 G1
Laburnum La *CANTW/ST* CT2 ... 61 K6
Laburnum Pl *SIT* ME10 ... 52 A1 3
Labworth Cl *IOS* ME12 ... 15 G7 2
Lacton Oast *KEN/WIL* TN24 ... 146 D5
Lacton Wy *KEN/WIL* TN24 ... 146 C5 1
Lade Fort Crs *LYDD* TN29 ... 211 G7
Ladyfields *HB* CT6 ... 42 F3
Ladyfields Cl *RSIT* ME9 ... 32 B8
Lady Garne Rd *RDV* CT15 ... 154 B8
Ladysmith Gv *WSTB* CT5 ... 39 H7
Ladysmith Rd *WSTB* CT5 ... 39 K8
Ladywell *DVE/WH* CT16 ... 10 C4
Ladywood Rd *CANTW/ST* CT2 ... 61 H6
Lady Wootton's Gn *CANT* CT1 ... 7 H4 1
Lagos Av *MSTR* CT12 ... 4 B1
Lakelands *RMAID* ME17 ... 87 G7
Lakemead *ASH* TN23 ... 145 G5
Laking Av *BRDST* CT10 ... 31 J6
Laleham Gdns *MARG* CT9 ... 3 M5
Laleham Rd *MARG* CT9 ... 3 M7
Lambden Rd *HDCN* TN27 ... 124 D7
Lamberhurst Wy *MARG* CT9 ... 31 H2 2
Lambeth Rd *CANT* CT1 ... 78 E1 2
Lamb's Wk *WSTB* CT5 ... 39 L7
Lambton Rd *DVW* CT17 ... 155 J4
Laming Rd *BRCH* CT7 ... 28 D7
Lammas Dr *SIT* ME10 ... 33 G7
Lammas Ga *FAV* ME13 ... 55 M5 2
Lancaster Av *RFOLK* CT18 ... 171 K3
Lancaster Cl *MSTR* CT12 ... 48 D4 1
RASHW TN26 ... 178 C5
Lancaster Gdns *BRCH* CT7 ... 28 B7
HB CT6 ... 24 F8
Lancaster Rd *CANT* CT1 ... 6 E8
DVW CT17 ... 10 C6
Lance Cl *SIT* ME10 ... 33 H5 2
Lanchester Cl *HB* CT6 ... 41 J2
Landbury Wk *ASH* TN23 ... 145 H1
Landgate *RYE* TN31 ... 205 L7
Landon Rd *HB* CT6 ... 24 E8
The Lanes *MSTR* CT12 ... 46 F7
The Lane *RDV* CT15 ... 138 B7
Lanfranc Gdns *CANTW/ST* CT2 ... 77 L4
Lanfranc Rd *DEAL* CT14 ... 103 L5
Lang Ct *WSTB* CT5 ... 40 E2
Langdale *ASH* TN23 ... 145 G5
Langdale Av *RAM* CT11 ... 4 B5
Langdon Av *RCANTE* CT3 ... 83 G4
Langdon Cl *RDV* CT15 ... 139 H8
Langdon Rd *FOLKN* CT19 ... 169 M6
Langham Cl *MARG* CT9 ... 29 K4
Langholm Rd *ASH* TN23 ... 8 A9
Langhorne Gdns *FOLK* CT20 ... 12 F7
Langley Gdns *MARG* CT9 ... 31 G2 2
Langley Rd *SIT* ME10 ... 33 H7
Langney Dr *ASH* TN23 ... 145 G7
Langport Rd *NROM* TN28 ... 202 E7
Langton La *CANT* CT1 ... 96 C1
Lansdown Rd *CANT* CT1 ... 7 G7
SIT ME10 ... 52 E1
Lanthorne Rd *BRDST* CT10 ... 31 J6
Lapwing Cl *IOS* ME12 ... 15 L8
Larch Cl *BRDST* CT10 ... 48 F1 1
The Larches *FAV* ME13 ... 55 J5
WSTB CT5 ... 39 L5 1
Larch Rd *RDV* CT15 ... 118 D4
Larch Wk *KEN/WIL* TN24 ... 127 L7
Larkey Vw *RCANTW* CT4 ... 95 G4 1
Larkfield Av *SIT* ME10 ... 33 G7
Larksfield Rd *FAV* ME13 ... 55 L4
Lascelles Rd *DVW* CT17 ... 155 J7
La-tene *DEAL* CT14 ... 121 K3
Latimer Cl *HB* CT6 ... 41 K3
Laundry Rd *MSTR* CT12 ... 46 F6
Laureate Cl *MARG* CT9 ... 3 M5
Laurel Av *LYDD* TN29 ... 203 H2
Laurel Cl *FOLK* CT20 ... 170 A7
Laurel Wy *RCANTW* CT4 ... 95 G4
Laureston Pl *DVE/WH* CT16 ... 10 E4
Lauriston Cl *RAM* CT11 ... 4 B8
Lauriston Mt *BRDST* CT10 ... 31 J8
Lausanne Rd *MARG* CT9 ... 3 G5
Lavender Cl *MARG* CT9 ... 2 B8
Lavender Ct *SIT* ME10 ... 52 C2
Lawley Cl *MSTR* CT12 ... 48 E4 2
Lawn Cl *TENT* TN30 ... 174 B6
Lawn Rd *BRDST* CT10 ... 49 J1
DEAL CT14 ... 121 L4
Lawrence Cl *FOLKN* CT19 ... 170 B7 1
Lawrence Ct *FOLKN* CT19 ... 13 K2
Lawrence Gdns *HB* CT6 ... 42 E1
Laws La *RASHE* TN25 ... 164 E6
Laxton Wy *CANT* CT1 ... 7 M6
FAV ME13 ... 56 A8
SIT ME10 ... 32 F7
WSTB CT5 ... 40 E4
Laylam Cl *BRDST* CT10 ... 30 F8
Lea Av *RYE* TN31 ... 205 J7
Lea Cl *HYTHE* CT21 ... 183 K1
Leacon Rd *ASH* TN23 ... 8 A5
Leafield *RASHE* TN25 ... 166 F4
Learoyd Rd *NROM* TN28 ... 202 D8
Leasam La *RYE* TN31 ... 205 K5
Leas Gn *BRDST* CT10 ... 48 F1
Leas Rd *DEAL* CT14 ... 103 K8
The Leas *DEAL* CT14 ... 139 M2
FAV ME13 ... 55 K5
FOLK CT20 ... 12 E8
IOS ME12 ... 15 K4
WSTB CT5 ... 40 E4
Leatt Cl *BRDST* CT10 ... 49 H1
Leaveland Cl *ASH* TN23 ... 145 H7
The Lees Cl *RASHE* TN25 ... 147 M8
Lees Court Rd *FAV* ME13 ... 73 L7
Lees Rd *KEN/WIL* TN24 ... 146 C4
RASHE TN25 ... 148 A6
The Lees *HB* CT6 ... 24 E8
Leicester Av *MARG* CT9 ... 30 E3
Leicester Gdns *IOS* ME12 ... 22 F2
Leigh Ct *IOS* ME12 ... 15 H8
Leigh Rd *MSTR* CT12 ... 4 A1
Leighton Rd *DVE/WH* CT16 ... 10 A2
Leighville Dr *HB* CT6 ... 41 M1
Leivers Rd *DEAL* CT14 ... 121 J2
Lenacre Av *DVE/WH* CT16 ... 137 H6
Lenacre La *DVE/WH* CT16 ... 137 H5
Lenacre St *RASHE* TN25 ... 127 J3
The Length *BRCH* CT7 ... 45 H3
Lenham Cl *BRDST* CT10 ... 49 J3 2
Lenham Forstal Rd
RMAID ME17 ... 106 D5
Lenham Gdns *MARG* CT9 ... 29 K5 4
Lenham Heath Rd *RMAID* ME17 .. 105 K2
Lenham Rd *HDCN* TN27 ... 122 C5
RMAID ME17 ... 104 B3
Lennard Rd *FOLK* CT20 ... 13 K4
Leonard Rd *LYDD* TN29 ... 211 G6
Leonard's Av *RAM* CT11 ... 5 J1
Leopold Rd *RAM* CT11 ... 5 J2
Leopold St *RAM* CT11 ... 5 J6
Le Roux Cl *RFOLK* CT18 ... 170 B1
Lerryn Gdns *BRDST* CT10 ... 31 H5
Lesley Av *CANT* CT1 ... 7 H9
Leslie Av *MARG* CT9 ... 29 K6
Leslie Crs *TENT* TN30 ... 174 D3
Leslie Rd *BRCH* CT7 ... 28 C5 2
Leslie Smith Dr *FAV* ME13 ... 55 L6
Lewd La *HDCN* TN27 ... 141 J1
Lewis Cl *FAV* ME13 ... 55 J6
Lewis Crs *MARG* CT9 ... 3 L2
Lewisham Rd *DVW* CT17 ... 155 G2
Lewson Street Rd *RSIT* ME9 ... 54 A5
Leybourne Dr *MARG* CT9 ... 29 K5
Leybourn Rd *BRDST* CT10 ... 49 K3
Leyburne Rd *DVE/WH* CT16 ... 10 D3
Leycroft Cl *CANTW/ST* CT2 ... 78 A2
Leysdown Rd *IOS* ME12 ... 22 A2
Lichfield Av *CANT* CT1 ... 7 K8
Liege Cl *SIT* ME10 ... 33 H4
Lighthouse Rd *RDV* CT15 ... 157 H1
Lillian Rd *RAM* CT11 ... 5 L3
Lime Cl *ASH* TN23 ... 145 H2
Lime Gv *IOS* ME12 ... 14 F8 1
SIT ME10 ... 52 C1
Lime Kiln Rd *CANT* CT1 ... 6 E7
Limekiln St *DVW* CT17 ... 10 B9
Limes Cl *TENT* TN30 ... 174 E6
Limes Rd *DVE/WH* CT16 ... 10 B2
FOLKN CT19 ... 170 B7
The Limes *ASH* TN23 ... 145 H8
The Linces *DVE/WH* CT16 ... 155 K1
Lincoln Av *CANT* CT1 ... 7 K7
Lincoln Gdns *BRCH* CT7 ... 28 B6
Linden Av *BRDST* CT10 ... 31 K8
HB CT6 ... 42 A1
WSTB CT5 ... 40 B5
Linden Cha *CANTW/ST* CT2 ... 6 D3
Linden Cl *SIT* ME10 ... 51 M2
WGOS CT8 ... 29 G6
Linden Crs *FOLKN* CT19 ... 13 H2
Linden Dr *IOS* ME12 ... 14 B6
Linden Gv *CANTW/ST* CT2 ... 6 D3
Linden Rd *KEN/WIL* TN24 ... 9 G4
RCANTW CT4 ... 95 G4
WGOS CT8 ... 29 H5
Lindenthorpe Rd *BRDST* CT10 ... 31 H7
Lindridge Cl *HB* CT6 ... 42 C5
Linington Rd *BRCH* CT7 ... 28 C6
Link Hill La *HDCN* TN27 ... 123 L3
Link La *CANT* CT1 ... 7 G5
Link Rd *CANTW/ST* CT2 ... 59 M7
Links Crs *LYDD* TN29 ... 203 J1
Linksfield Rd *WGOS* CT8 ... 28 F5
Links Rd *DEAL* CT14 ... 103 L5 1
Linksway *FOLKN* CT19 ... 170 C6
Links Wy *NROM* TN28 ... 202 F7
RYE TN31 ... 213 G3
Linksway Cl *FOLKN* CT19 ... 170 D5 1
The Link *RYE* TN31 ... 205 J8
Linkway *RSIT* ME9 ... 32 F1
Linley Rd *BRDST* CT10 ... 31 G6
Linnet Av *WSTB* CT5 ... 39 K7
Lion Fld *FAV* ME13 ... 55 J6
Lion's Rd *NROM* TN28 ... 202 C7
Lion St *RYE* TN31 ... 205 L8
Lion Yd *FAV* ME13 ... 55 J7 3
Lismore Rd *HB* CT6 ... 24 F8
WSTB CT5 ... 40 D5
Liss Rd *SWCH* CT13 ... 101 J4
Lister Cl *DEAL* CT14 ... 103 L8
DVW CT17 ... 155 K4 2
Lister Rd *MARG* CT9 ... 3 J8
Lister Wy *FOLK* CT20 ... 185 H2 2
The List *RCANTE* CT3 ... 80 E3
Little Av *DEAL* CT14 ... 121 H2
Littlebourne Rd *RCANTE* CT3 ... 79 G5
Littlebrook Cl *ASH* TN23 ... 8 A1
Little Brook Rd *ASH* TN23 ... 8 A1
Little Chequers *RASHE* TN25 ... 129 G3
Little Glovers *SIT* ME10 ... 52 B2
Little Meadow *CANTW/ST* CT2 ... 77 G4
Little Paddocks *WSTB* CT5 ... 40 F6
Little Robhurst *RASHW* TN26 ... 159 M6
Littlestone Rd *NROM* TN28 ... 202 F7
Little Walton *SWCH* CT13 ... 101 L2
Liverpool Lawn *RAM* CT11 ... 5 J7
Liverpool Rd *DEAL* CT14 ... 121 L5
Livingstone Cl *LYDD* TN29 ... 195 K1 1
Livingstone Rd *BRDST* CT10 ... 31 G7
Lloyds Gn *TENT* TN30 ... 196 F1
Lockholt Cl *ASH* TN23 ... 145 G2
Loder Cl *RMAID* ME17 ... 87 K8
Lodge Gdns *RMAID* ME17 ... 104 B7
Lodge Wood Dr *ASH* TN23 ... 127 G8
Lomas Rd *SIT* ME10 ... 52 F1
Lombard St *MARG* CT9 ... 2 F3
London Rd *CANTW/ST* CT2 ... 6 B3
DEAL CT14 ... 103 K8
DVE/WH CT16 ... 155 G1
DVW CT17 ... 10 B3
FAV ME13 ... 55 J7
HYTHE CT21 ... 183 H2
RAM CT11 ... 4 D7
RDV CT15 ... 136 D7
SIT ME10 ... 32 E8
London Road Temple Ewell
DVE/WH CT16 ... 136 E8
London St *FOLK* CT20 ... 13 J4
Lone Barn Rd *RMAID* ME17 ... 88 D5
Lonefield *RASHW* TN26 ... 162 D4
Longacre *WSTB* CT5 ... 40 F4
Long Acre Cl *CANTW/ST* CT2 ... 6 D1
Longacre Rd *ASH* TN23 ... 144 F6
Longage Hl *RCANTW* CT4 ... 150 C3
The Long Barrow
KEN/WIL TN24 ... 146 A8
Long Beech *ASH* TN23 ... 145 G4
Longbridge *KEN/WIL* TN24 ... 146 D4 1
Long Dr *SWCH* CT13 ... 101 L3
Longfield *TENT* TN30 ... 174 C6
Longfield Cl *WSTB* CT5 ... 40 F3
Longfield Rd *DVW* CT17 ... 155 K7
Longford Ter *FOLK* CT20 ... 13 G6
Longford Wy *FOLK* CT20 ... 13 G7
Long Hl *RCANTW* CT4 ... 93 L3
Long La *RDV* CT15 ... 117 L6
Long Length *ASH* TN23 ... 162 F2
Long Market *CANT* CT1 ... 7 G4 3
Longmead Cl *HB* CT6 ... 41 L2
Long Meadow Wy *CANTW/ST* CT2 .. 78 B1
Longmete Rd *RCANTE* CT3 ... 63 L8
Longmore Dr *IOS* ME12 ... 21 L4
Longport *CANT* CT1 ... 7 H5
Long Reach Cl *WSTB* CT5 ... 39 L7
Longridge *SIT* ME10 ... 52 D3
Long Rock *WSTB* CT5 ... 40 E2
Longsfield *RASHE* TN25 ... 165 J7
Longtye Dr *WSTB* CT5 ... 40 E6
Long Wk *ASH* TN23 ... 145 G1
Lonsdale Av *MARG* CT9 ... 30 E2
Lonsdale Dr *SIT* ME10 ... 32 E8
Lookers La *HYTHE* CT21 ... 183 K2
Loop Court Ms *SWCH* CT13 ... 84 B4 5
Loop St *SWCH* CT13 ... 84 B4
Loose Down Rd *FAV* ME13 ... 91 G6
Lords Cl *RSIT* ME9 ... 53 G3
Lord Warden Av *DEAL* CT14 ... 121 M3
Lord Warden Sq *DVW* CT17 ... 155 M8 5
Lorina Rd *MSTR* CT12 ... 4 E1
Lorne Rd *DVE/WH* CT16 ... 155 K4
RAM CT11 ... 4 F6
Loudon Ct *ASH* TN23 ... 145 G2
Loudon Wy *ASH* TN23 ... 145 G2
Lovelace Ct *RASHW* TN26 ... 142 E8
Love La *CANT* CT1 ... 7 H5
FAV ME13 ... 56 B7
HDCN TN27 ... 122 C8
IOS ME12 ... 15 M6
MARG CT9 ... 2 F3
RCANTE CT3 ... 99 G3
RYE TN31 ... 205 K7
Lovell Rd *CANTW/ST* CT2 ... 77 K2
IOS ME12 ... 15 J8
Lower Blackhouse Hl
HYTHE CT21 ... 183 M3
Lower Bridge St *CANT* CT1 ... 7 G5
Lower Chantry La *CANT* CT1 ... 7 H6
Lower Denmark Rd *ASH* TN23 ... 8 E7
Lower Ensden Rd *RCANTW* CT4 ... 93 L1
Lower Herne Rd *HB* CT6 ... 42 A5
Lower Lees Rd *RCANTW* CT4 ... 93 L3
Lower Mill La *DEAL* CT14 ... 103 L8
Lower Northdown Av *MARG* CT9 .. 3 L5
Lower Rd *DVE/WH* CT16 ... 136 F8
DVW CT17 ... 155 G1
FAV ME13 ... 55 J6
IOS ME12 ... 20 A1
RASHW TN26 ... 176 D4
RCANTE CT3 ... 82 C7
RSIT ME9 ... 53 H2
TENT TN30 ... 188 E7
Lower Sandgate Rd *FOLK* CT20 ... 12 C9
Lower Sands *LYDD* TN29 ... 195 G3
Lower Santon La *RCANTE* CT3 ... 63 M6
Lower St *DEAL* CT14 ... 119 J3
SWCH CT13 ... 101 K3
Lower Vicarage Rd
KEN/WIL TN24 ... 127 L6
Lower Wall Rd *HYTHE* CT21 ... 181 M6
RASHE TN25 ... 180 E6
Lowfield Rd *IOS* ME12 ... 15 G7 3
Lowslip Hl *RDV* CT15 ... 154 B8
Lowther Rd *DVW* CT17 ... 155 K5
Loxwood Cl *DVE/WH* CT16 ... 137 K6 2
Lucas Shadwell Wy *RYE* TN31 ... 212 B3
Lucerne Dr *WSTB* CT5 ... 39 H7
Lucerne La *RDV* CT15 ... 138 E3
Luckhurst Gdns *MARG* CT9 ... 31 G2 2
Luckhurst Rd *DVW* CT17 ... 155 G2
KEN/WIL TN24 ... 146 C6
Lucknow Cl *RDV* CT15 ... 156 B2
Lucy Av *FOLKN* CT19 ... 12 C1
Lucy's Hl *HYTHE* CT21 ... 183 K3
Luddenham Cl *ASH* TN23 ... 145 H7
Ludgate Rd *RSIT* ME9 ... 71 G1
Lukes Cl *DVW* CT17 ... 155 J4
Luton Av *BRDST* CT10 ... 49 H2
Luton Ct *BRDST* CT10 ... 49 H2 1
Luton Rd *FAV* ME13 ... 56 A6
Lydbrook Cl *SIT* ME10 ... 51 L1
Lydden Hl *RDV* CT15 ... 135 M5
Lydd Rd *NROM* TN28 ... 202 B7
RYE TN31 ... 213 G3
Lydd Town Crossing
LYDD TN29 ... 209 M5
Lydia Rd *DEAL* CT14 ... 121 J3
Lydos Cl *LYDD* TN29 ... 211 G8
Lyell Cl *HYTHE* CT21 ... 183 J4
Lyell Rd *BRCH* CT7 ... 28 B5 3
Lyminge Wy *MARG* CT9 ... 30 E4
Lymington Rd *WGOS* CT8 ... 28 F6
Lympne Hl *HYTHE* CT21 ... 182 C3
Lyndhurst Av *MARG* CT9 ... 3 L5
Lyndhurst Cl *CANTW/ST* CT2 ... 78 A2
Lyndhurst Gv *SIT* ME10 ... 52 A3
Lyndhurst Rd *BRDST* CT10 ... 31 J7
DVW CT17 ... 155 G3
LYDD TN29 ... 194 E5
RAM CT11 ... 5 M4
Lyndon Wy *RFOLK* CT18 ... 150 E6
Lyngate Ct *MARG* CT9 ... 30 F3 1
Lynmouth Dr *IOS* ME12 ... 15 L6
Lynsted Cl *ASH* TN23 ... 145 H7
Lynsted La *RSIT* ME9 ... 53 K6
Lynsted Rd *IOS* ME12 ... 15 G6
Lynton Rd *HYTHE* CT21 ... 183 L4
Lynwood *FOLKN* CT19 ... 12 E2
Lysander Cl *BRDST* CT10 ... 48 E2
RCANTW CT4 ... 98 A1 1
Lysander Wk *RFOLK* CT18 ... 170 C1 2
Lytham Aveune *HB* CT6 ... 41 M4 1

M

Mabledon Av *KEN/WIL* TN24 ... 9 H5
Mabledon Cl *NROM* TN28 ... 202 D7
Macdonald Pde *WSTB* CT5 ... 39 J6
Macdonald Rd *DVW* CT17 ... 155 J4 3
Mace La *ASH* TN23 ... 8 F3
Mackenzie Dr *FOLK* CT20 ... 170 A8
Mackerel Hl *RYE* TN31 ... 196 B8
Madeira Rd *MARG* CT9 ... 3 J4
NROM TN28 ... 203 G7
Madeira Wk *RAM* CT11 ... 5 K6
Magazine Rd *KEN/WIL* TN24 ... 8 D2
Magdala Rd *BRDST* CT10 ... 31 G7
DVW CT17 ... 155 K4
Magdalen Ct *BRDST* CT10 ... 31 J8
CANT CT1 ... 7 J7 1
Magness Rd *DEAL* CT14 ... 121 J3
Magnolia Av *MARG* CT9 ... 30 F3
Magpie Ct *IOS* ME12 ... 15 J7 3
Magpie Hall Rd *RASHW* TN26 ... 162 F3
Magpie La *RCANTW* CT4 ... 150 D2
Maiden La *CANT* CT1 ... 6 B8
Maidstone Rd *ASH* TN23 ... 8 B2
HDCN TN27 ... 107 L6
RSIT ME9 ... 50 F2
SIT ME10 ... 32 C7
Maine Cl *DVE/WH* CT16 ... 155 K2
Main Rd *IOS* ME12 ... 14 C2
QBOR ME11 ... 14 C8
Main St *RYE* TN31 ... 204 D3
Maison Dieu Pl *DVE/WH* CT16 ... 10 C4 2
Maison Dieu Rd *DVE/WH* CT16 ... 10 C4
Maitland Ct *FAV* ME13 ... 55 K4 1
Makenade Av *FAV* ME13 ... 55 M8
Malcolm Sargent Rd *ASH* TN23 .. 145 K7
Malham Dr *MARG* CT9 ... 3 K7
Mallard Ct *IOS* ME12 ... 15 J7 2
Mallards *KEN/WIL* TN24 ... 145 M6 2
Mallory Cl *MSTR* CT12 ... 48 E3
The Mall *FAV* ME13 ... 55 L7
Malmains Rd *DVW* CT17 ... 155 J6
Malthouse Cl *RMAID* ME17 ... 87 M8
Malthouse Hl *HYTHE* CT21 ... 183 K3 1
Malthouse La *RASHE* TN25 ... 128 A2
RASHW TN26 ... 177 M5
RYE TN31 ... 204 D3
Malt House La *TENT* TN30 ... 174 C6
Malthouse Rd *CANTW/ST* CT2 ... 6 F1
The Maltings *RCANTE* CT3 ... 80 B6
Malvern Meadow
DVE/WH CT16 ... 137 G8
Malvern Pk *HB* CT6 ... 42 F1
Malvern Rd *DVE/WH* CT16 ... 137 G8
KEN/WIL TN24 ... 145 K1
Manciple Cl *CANTW/ST* CT2 ... 77 L5 1
Mandeville Rd *CANTW/ST* CT2 ... 6 D1
Mangers La *DVE/WH* CT16 ... 155 J3
Mangers Pl *DVE/WH* CT16 ... 155 J2 3
Manley Cl *DVE/WH* CT16 ... 137 J6 2
Mannering Cl *DVW* CT17 ... 155 H2
Manns Hl *RCANTW* CT4 ... 114 C7
Manor Av *DEAL* CT14 ... 121 K1
Manor Cl *CANT* CT1 ... 77 L8
DEAL CT14 ... 121 J1 3
HB CT6 ... 25 H7
QBOR ME11 ... 19 H2

Manor Dr BRCH CT7 28 B7
Manorfield ASH TN23 145 G5
Manor Gv SIT ME10 52 A2
Manor House Dr ASH TN23 163 L2
Manor Lea Rd BRCH CT7 45 H4 2
Manor Leaze RASHE TN25 148 B8
Manor Ms DEAL CT14 121 H8
Manor Pound La RASHE TN25 148 A6
Manor Ri DVW CT17 155 J7
Manor Rd BRCH CT7 45 H4
DEAL CT14 121 J1
DVW CT17 155 J7
FOLK CT20 12 F5
HB CT6 25 H7
LYDD TN29 209 L8
QBOR ME11 19 H2
RSIT ME9 70 B4
WSTB CT5 40 C2
Manor Wy ASH TN23 8 A1
IOS ME12 17 L7
IOS ME12 23 J3
Manse Fld RASHE TN25 147 M8
Mansell La RDV CT15 152 D1
Mansion Gdns DVE/WH CT16 155 J1
Mansion House Cl HDCN TN27 158 B3
Manston Court Rd MARG CT9 48 A1
MSTR CT12 47 L5
Manston Rd MSTR CT12 4 B3
Mantles Hl DEAL CT14 120 F4
Manwood Av CANTW/ST CT2 78 B2
Manwood Cl SIT ME10 52 B3
Manwood Rd SWCH CT13 84 C5
Maple Cl ASH TN23 144 F3
CANTW/ST CT2 77 J3
Maple Ct RCANTE CT3 62 A4
Maple Dr LYDD TN29 203 H2
Maple Gdns RCANTE CT3 62 A5
The Maples BRDST CT10 48 E1
IOS ME12 15 K7 1
Maple St IOS ME12 14 E4
Marchants Dr RYE TN31 213 G3
Marden Av MSTR CT12 4 D3
Mardol Rd KEN/WIL TN24 127 L8
Maresfield Cl DVE/WH CT16 155 K3 2
Margarets Rd RDV CT15 139 J3
Margaret St FOLK CT20 13 J5
Margate Hl BRCH CT7 46 D2
Margate Rd BRDST CT10 48 D1
HB CT6 42 D2
Marian Av IOS ME12 15 J6
Marilyn Crs BRCH CT7 28 D6
Marina Dr IOS ME12 15 J6
Marina Esp RAM CT11 5 M5
Marina Rd RAM CT11 5 M5
The Marina DEAL CT14 103 M5
Marine Av LYDD TN29 195 H2
Marine Crs WSTB CT5 40 D2
Marine Dr BRDST CT10 31 J2
MARG CT9 2 E4
Marine Gap WSTB CT5 39 L4
Marine Gdns MARG CT9 2 E4 1
Marine Pde DVE/WH CT16 10 E7
FOLK CT20 13 H7
IOS ME12 14 F3
NROM TN28 203 G8
WSTB CT5 40 B2
Marine Rd DEAL CT14 121 M1
Mariners Lea BRDST CT10 48 F1
Marine Ter FOLK CT20 13 J6
MARG CT9 2 E5
Marine Walk St HYTHE CT21 183 L3 4
Maritime Av HB CT6 42 E1
Marjan Cl DVW CT17 155 J4
Mark Av RAM CT11 4 C8
Market Hl HYTHE CT21 183 L3 5
Market Pl HDCN TN27 107 L6
RCANTE CT3 99 H8 1
Market Rd RYE TN31 205 L8 3
Market St DEAL CT14 103 M7
FAV ME13 55 M6
HB CT6 24 B8
MARG CT9 2 F3
RYE TN31 205 L8 4
SWCH CT13 84 C4
Market Vw RCANTE CT3 99 H8
Market Wy CANTW/ST CT2 78 C3
Markland Rd DVW CT17 155 J6
RDV CT15 155 H6
Marlborough Cl BRDST CT10 49 G2 1
NROM TN28 202 F6
Marlborough Rd DEAL CT14 121 J3
DVW CT17 155 H6
MARG CT9 2 F7
RAM CT11 5 H6
RDV CT15 155 H6
WSTB CT5 39 M8
Marlborough Wy
KEN/WIL TN24 128 B6
Marler Rd FOLKN CT19 170 A7 2
Marley La DEAL CT14 102 C6
HDCN TN27 140 E1
RCANTE CT3 43 H8
RCANTW CT4 115 H5
Marley Rd RMAID ME17 87 H7
RYE TN31 205 J7
Marlow Cl WSTB CT5 40 D4 1
Marlowe Av CANT CT1 6 F6
Marlowe Rd ASH TN23 8 C3 1
DVE/WH CT16 155 K2
MARG CT9 3 M9
Marlow Mdw CANTW/ST CT2 79 H1 1
Marr Cl IOS ME12 15 H6
Marrose Av MSTR CT12 48 D2
Marshall Crs BRDST CT10 49 G1
QBOR ME11 19 H2
Marshalls Land TENT TN30 174 C2
Marshall St FOLKN CT19 13 J1
Marshborough Rd SWCH CT13 83 J6
Marsh Crs NROM TN28 202 D7
Marsh Farm Rd MSTR CT12 65 K2
Marshlands LYDD TN29 194 D7
Marshlands Cl LYDD TN29 194 D6 1
Marsh La DEAL CT14 103 J7
Marsh Vw HYTHE CT21 182 E5
Marshwood Cl CANT CT1 78 E2
Martello Dr HYTHE CT21 183 G4
Martello Rd FOLK CT20 13 K3
Marten Rd FOLK CT20 12 C5
Martha Cl FOLKN CT19 12 C1
Martindale Cl CANT CT1 6 F7
Martin Dale Crs RDV CT15 138 E3 2
Martindown Rd WSTB CT5 39 L6
Martin's Cl MSTR CT12 48 E3
TENT TN30 174 E5
The Martins RASHW TN26 160 C4
Martin's Wy HYTHE CT21 182 F5
Martyrs' Field Rd CANT CT1 6 D7
Maryland Gv CANT CT1 7 K9
Mary Rd DEAL CT14 121 J2
Mary Stamford Gn RYE TN31 212 C2 1
Mason Rd RYE TN31 205 J8
Mason's Ri BRDST CT10 31 J8
Masons Rd DVW CT17 155 J4
Matthews Cl DEAL CT14 103 L7
Matthew's Pl DVE/WH CT16 10 B3
Matthews Rd HB CT6 41 L3
Mattinson Pl RSIT ME9 69 H6
Maugham Ct WSTB CT5 39 M5
Maunsell Pl KEN/WIL TN24 9 G9
Maxine Gdns BRDST CT10 31 H8
Maxton Rd DVW CT17 155 J7
Maxwell Pl DEAL CT14 121 L1 2
Maydowns Rd WSTB CT5 40 F3
Mayers Rd DEAL CT14 121 J4
Mayfield Av DVE/WH CT16 155 K3
Mayfield Gdns DVE/WH CT16 155 L3
Mayfield Rd DVE/WH CT16 137 J6
HB CT6 42 C2
RFOLK CT18 150 E7
Mayfly Dr RFOLK CT18 170 C1
Mayforth Gdns RAM CT11 4 C7
Mayhew Cl ASH TN23 8 B8
Maynard Av MARG CT9 29 K5
Maynard Rd CANT CT1 6 B7
Maypits ASH TN23 145 H5
Maypole La RCANTE CT3 43 G7
Maypole Rd RCANTE CT3 42 F8
Mays Rd RAM CT11 4 F6
Maystreet HB CT6 43 H1
Maytham Rd CRBK TN17 186 B3
Mayton La CANTW/ST CT2 60 E4
Mayville Rd BRDST CT10 31 G7
Mccarthy Av CANTW/ST CT2 61 H6
Mcclean Wk IOS ME12 21 K5
The Meade RFOLK CT18 170 B1
Meadowbrook FOLK CT20 185 G1
Meadowbrook Cl
KEN/WIL TN24 127 M7 1
Meadowbrook Rd
KEN/WIL TN24 127 M7
Meadow Cl HB CT6 42 E1
RCANTW CT4 94 A5
RCANTW CT4 97 J4
RSIT ME9 32 F1 1
Meadow Ct RASHE TN25 167 K7
Meadow Gv RASHE TN25 166 F5
Meadow Ri RSIT ME9 32 F1
Meadow Rd ASH TN23 145 J1
CANTW/ST CT2 61 H7
MARG CT9 29 K4
The Meadows HB CT6 42 E3
HDCN TN27 158 B3 1
SIT ME10 52 B3
Meadow Vw RASHW TN26 126 D7
Meadow View Rd RDV CT15 118 A7
Meadow Wk WSTB CT5 39 L6
Meadow Wy HYTHE CT21 182 F5
Mead Rd FOLKN CT19 13 G2
KEN/WIL TN24 146 A6
The Meads Av SIT ME10 32 F6
Meads Wy LYDD TN29 203 G2
Mead Wy CANTW/ST CT2 6 D3
Meadway DVW CT17 154 F2
Medina Av WSTB CT5 39 K6
Medlar Cl RSIT ME9 51 J7
Medway Cl SIT ME10 51 M1
Medway Rd IOS ME12 14 D4
Meehan Rd NROM TN28 211 G1
Meehan Rd South NROM TN28 210 F2
Meeres Court La SIT ME10 33 L7
Meeson's Cl FAV ME13 72 A7
Meeting St RAM CT11 5 J5
Meggett La RDV CT15 153 L6
Megone Cl RFOLK CT18 170 C1
Melbourne Av DVE/WH CT16 137 K8
MSTR CT12 4 B2
Melbury Ms NROM TN28 202 E5 1
Mellanby Cl BRCH CT7 28 C7
Mellor Rw SIT ME10 33 H4 1
Melody Cl IOS ME12 23 G1
Melon La LYDD TN29 201 H1
RASHW TN26 192 D4
Melsetter Cl BRCH CT7 28 D6 5
Melville Lea SWCH CT13 83 L6
Mendfield St FAV ME13 55 L6 4
Mendip Ri KEN/WIL TN24 145 K1
Menin Rd SIT ME10 33 H4
Mentmore Rd MSTR CT12 48 E2
Menzies Av DEAL CT14 121 K4
Menzies Ct IOS ME12 15 J8 3
Mercer Dr RMAID ME17 87 H7
Mercery La CANT CT1 6 F4 6
Merchants Wy CANTW/ST CT2 77 L6
Mere Ga MARG CT9 2 E7
Merleburgh Dr SIT ME10 33 H5 3
Merlin Cl SIT ME10 52 C2
Mermaid St RYE TN31 205 K8
Merritt Rd NROM TN28 210 F3
Merrivale Hts BRDST CT10 49 J2
Merton La CANT CT1 96 B2
Meryl Gdns DEAL CT14 121 L4
Meteor Av WSTB CT5 39 K6
Meteor Cl SIT ME10 33 G5
Metropole Rd East FOLK CT20 12 C8
Metropole Rd West FOLK CT20 12 C8
Meverall Av MSTR CT12 47 M8
The Mews SIT ME10 52 B2
Meyrick Rd IOS ME12 14 E3
Michael Av RAM CT11 49 J5
Michelle Gdns MARG CT9 29 J5
Mickleburgh Av HB CT6 42 D2
Mickleburgh Hl HB CT6 42 D1
Middelburg Sq FOLK CT20 13 G6
Middle Cl ASH TN23 144 E4 1
Middle Deal Rd DEAL CT14 103 K8
Middle Md FOLKN CT19 12 C1
Middle Rw FAV ME13 55 M6
Middle St ASH TN23 8 D4 2
DEAL CT14 103 M7 4
Middletune Av SIT ME10 33 G6
Middle Wall WSTB CT5 39 M3
Middle Wy SIT ME10 52 D2
Midsummer Hl
KEN/WIL TN24 127 M7 2
Milbourne Gv SIT ME10 33 G6
Mile Rd RCANTE CT3 45 H7
Miles Ct RCANTE CT3 81 J5 2
Milestone Cl FOLKN CT19 170 C6
Milestone Rd DEAL CT14 103 K8 2
Miles Wy BRCH CT7 28 B6
Military Rd CANT CT1 7 J2
DVW CT17 10 C6
FOLK CT20 185 H2 3
HYTHE CT21 183 J3
RAM CT11 5 J7
RYE TN31 205 M4
Millais Rd DVE/WH CT16 10 A2
Millbank La LYDD TN29 201 H6
Millbank Rd ASH TN23 145 H8
Mill Bay FOLK CT20 13 H5
Millbrook Meadow ASH TN23 145 G4
Mill Cl DVW CT17 155 H3
RMAID ME17 105 L1
SWCH CT13 84 A3
Mill Cottages RAM CT11 5 G7
Mill Ct KEN/WIL TN24 9 G4
Milldale Cl DEAL CT14 121 K1
Millennium Wy BRDST CT10 48 E1
Millen Rd SIT ME10 33 G8
Miller Av CANTW/ST CT2 6 A4
Miller Cl KEN/WIL TN24 9 G4
SIT ME10 33 J5
Miller Ct IOS ME12 15 J8 4
Millers Ct WSTB CT5 39 M6
Millers La MSTR CT12 45 L6
Millfield ASH TN23 144 F4
Mill Fld BRDST CT10 31 H8
Millfield FOLK CT20 12 F6
RASHW TN26 159 M6
Mill Fld RCANTE CT3 83 G4
Millfield RDV CT15 139 H7
RFOLK CT18 152 E7
SIT ME10 52 B2
Millfield Cl RFOLK CT18 152 D8
Millfield Mnr WSTB CT5 40 A4 1
Millfield Rd FAV ME13 56 A6
MSTR CT12 48 D2
Millfields RDV CT15 136 A1
Mill Fields Rd HYTHE CT21 183 H3
Mill Gn SWCH CT13 101 J3
Mill Hl DEAL CT14 121 J2
Mill La BRCH CT7 28 B7
CANT CT1 6 F3 1
CANTW/ST CT2 77 L5
DEAL CT14 102 B1
DEAL CT14 120 B1
DVE/WH CT16 10 E6
DVE/WH CT16 137 J5
HB CT6 42 D2
HDCN TN27 141 H3
KEN/WIL TN24 146 C4
LYDD TN29 209 L6
MARG CT9 2 F5
RASHE TN25 165 G8
RCANTE CT3 63 L7
RCANTW CT4 93 M6
RCANTW CT4 97 H4
RCANTW CT4 132 B3
RDV CT15 118 A1
RDV CT15 118 B3
RFOLK CT18 152 D8
RSIT ME9 53 K8
RYE TN31 204 B2
SWCH CT13 101 J3
TENT TN30 174 D4
Millmead Av MARG CT9 30 F4
Millmead Gdns MARG CT9 30 F4
Millmead Rd MARG CT9 3 M7
Mill Ms DEAL CT14 121 K1 2
Mill Rd CANTW/ST CT2 79 G1
DEAL CT14 121 K1
HYTHE CT21 183 M3
LYDD TN29 194 D6
LYDD TN29 209 M7
RASHW TN26 143 G8
RCANTE CT3 43 H8
RCANTE CT3 81 G7
RCANTE CT3 82 C7
RYE TN31 205 L6
Mill Rw BRCH CT7 28 B7
Mills Cl IOS ME12 15 H7
Millstream Cl FAV ME13 55 L6 5
WSTB CT5 40 A4
Mill St DVE/WH CT16 136 F8 3
SIT ME10 33 G8
Millstrood Rd WSTB CT5 40 A5
Mill Vw KEN/WIL TN24 9 L8
RASHW TN26 176 C2
Mill View Rd HB CT6 42 C4
Mill Wall Pl SWCH CT13 84 C5
Mill Wy SIT ME10 33 H7
Milner Cl RDV CT15 118 D4
Milner Crs RCANTE CT3 99 G8
Milne Rd KEN/WIL TN24 9 M8
Milner Rd RDV CT15 118 D4
WSTB CT5 39 J7
Milstead Cl IOS ME12 14 D5 2
Milton Av MARG CT9 3 H6
Milton Cl CANT CT1 7 L9
DVE/WH CT16 155 K1
Milton Rd ASH TN23 8 C3
CANT CT1 7 G8
DVE/WH CT16 155 K1
SIT ME10 52 A1
Minerva Av DVE/WH CT16 10 A1
Minnis La RDV CT15 154 D4
Minnis Rd BRCH CT7 27 M5
Minnis Wy DEAL CT14 84 D8
Minster Dr HB CT6 41 M1
IOS ME12 15 K5
Minster Rd BRCH CT7 46 D3
FAV ME13 56 A6 3
IOS ME12 15 K7
MSTR CT12 46 E5
RAM CT11 4 D8
WGOS CT8 29 H6
Mintching Wood La RSIT ME9 70 B3
Minter Av RFOLK CT18 152 C6
Minter Cl RFOLK CT18 152 B6
Minterne Av SIT ME10 51 L1
The Mint RYE TN31 205 K8 4
Miranda Ct IOS ME12 14 D4
Misling La RCANTW CT4 131 L7
Mitcham Rd LYDD TN29 194 E5
Mitchell Av RFOLK CT18 152 D8
Mitchell Cl RMAID ME17 87 L8
Mitchell St FOLKN CT19 169 M7 2
Moat Farm Rd FOLKN CT19 12 F1
Moatfield Meadow ASH TN23 163 K1
Moat La CANTW/ST CT2 77 K1
CANTW/ST CT2 79 H2
RCANTE CT3 82 F4
Moat Sole SWCH CT13 84 B4
The Moat HDCN TN27 107 L6
Moat Wy QBOR ME11 14 C8
Mockett Dr BRDST CT10 31 H6 1
Mock La ASH TN23 144 D7
Molehill Rd WSTB CT5 40 F6
Molineux Rd MSTR CT12 46 D7
Molland Cl RCANTE CT3 82 E3
Molland La RCANTE CT3 64 F8
Molland Lea RCANTE CT3 82 E3
Molloy Rd RASHW TN26 162 D4
Monastery Av DVE/WH CT16 10 D3
Monastery St CANT CT1 7 H5
Mongeham Church Cl
DEAL CT14 120 F1
Mongeham Rd DEAL CT14 120 F3
Monica Cl FAV ME13 75 G7
Monins Rd DVW CT17 155 K6
Monkery La RASHE TN25 108 E3
Monks Cl CANTW/ST CT2 78 C3
FAV ME13 55 K5
Monkshill Rd FAV ME13 57 J3
Monks Wk HDCN TN27 107 L6
Monks Wy DVE/WH CT16 155 J2
Monkton Court La RDV CT15 118 F6
Monkton Gdns MARG CT9 31 G2 3
Monkton Pl RAM CT11 5 H5
Monkton Rd MSTR CT12 46 C7
Monkton St MSTR CT12 45 L6
Mons Ct SIT ME10 33 H4
Montague Ct IOS ME12 14 D4
Montague Rd RAM CT11 5 K3
Montefiore Av RAM CT11 5 M1
Montefiore Cottages RAM CT11 5 L3
Montfort Cl ASH TN23 145 H6
CANTW/ST CT2 78 C1
Montgomery Wy FOLKN CT19 170 F5
Montpelier Av WSTB CT5 39 M7
Montreal Cl DVE/WH CT16 155 K2 6
Monument Wy KEN/WIL TN24 146 B8
Monypenny CRBK TN17 186 B2
Moon Hl RDV CT15 136 A1
Moore Cl LYDD TN29 200 C2
Moorfield CANTW/ST CT2 78 B1
The Moorings RSIT ME9 35 G7
Moorland Rd RDV CT15 135 M1
Moor La LYDD TN29 200 F2
RASHW TN26 176 B6
Moorstock La RASHE TN25 166 F3
Moorwell Dr RDV CT15 117 M8
Moray Av BRCH CT7 28 B5
Mordaunt Av WGOS CT8 29 G5
Morehall Av FOLKN CT19 170 B7
Morello Cl RSIT ME9 53 L3 1
Morgan Kirby's Gdn FAV ME13 73 M8
Morris Av HB CT6 41 H1
Morris Court Cl RSIT ME9 52 F3
Morrison Rd FOLK CT20 13 K3
Mortimer Cl ASH TN23 145 K6 2
Mortimer Rd DVE/WH CT16 11 G4
Mortimer St HB CT6 24 B8
Mossend Ms RAM CT11 49 G3
Mountain St RCANTW CT4 93 K7
Mountbatten Wy RASHE TN25 148 A7
Mount Castle La RMAID ME17 106 B4
Mount Fld FAV ME13 55 K7
QBOR ME11 14 C8 1
Mountfield Rd NROM TN28 202 E7 1
Mountfield Wy WGOS CT8 28 F7
Mount Green Av MSTR CT12 47 M8
Mount Pleasant CANTW/ST CT2 59 J7
TENT TN30 174 E5 1
Mountpleasant Cl RFOLK CT18 150 E6
Mount Pleasant Rd FOLK CT20 13 H4
Mount Rd CANT CT1 7 L8
DVW CT17 155 J8
Mounts Cl DEAL CT14 103 J8
Mounts La CRBK TN17 186 C3
Mount St HYTHE CT21 183 L3 6
Mountview RSIT ME9 51 K3
Mount View Rd HB CT6 42 C3
Moyes Cl MSTR CT12 47 M8
Muir Rd RAM CT11 5 M2
Mulberry Cl RAM CT11 5 L3
Mulberry Ct CANT CT1 6 E5
Mulberry Fld SWCH CT13 84 B4 5
Mulberry Hl RCANTW CT4 93 M4
Munday Bois Rd HDCN TN27 124 A4
Munsgore La RSIT ME9 51 G3
Murston Rd SIT ME10 52 D2
Murthwaite Ct IOS ME12 15 J8 5
Murton Pl FAV ME13 57 G4
Musgrave Cl MSTR CT12 47 H3 1
Musgrave Rd SIT ME10 33 H7
Musgrove ASH TN23 8 B7 1
Mustards Rd IOS ME12 22 F3
Mutrix Gdns MARG CT9 29 J4
Mutrix Rd MARG CT9 29 J5
Mutton La FAV ME13 55 J8
Mymms Cl WSTB CT5 40 E5
Myrtle Rd FOLKN CT19 13 K2
Mystole La RCANTW CT4 94 E5
Mystole Rd RCANTW CT4 94 C5

N

Nackington Rd RCANTW CT4 96 C4
Nailbourne Cl RCANTW CT4 115 M2
Naildown Cl HYTHE CT21 184 C2
Naildown Rd HYTHE CT21 184 C2
Nairne Cl RASHW TN26 162 C5
Namur Pl RDV CT15 156 B2
Napchester Rd DVE/WH CT16 137 J5
Napier Cl SIT ME10 51 L1
Napier Gdns HYTHE CT21 183 L4
Napier Rd BRDST CT10 31 G7 2
DVE/WH CT16 155 K2
Napleton Rd FAV ME13 55 L6
RAM CT11 4 E6
Nargate St RCANTE CT3 80 C5
Narrabeen Rd FOLKN CT19 170 A7
Narrowbush La LYDD TN29 200 C6
Naseby Av FOLK CT20 169 M8
Nash Court Gdns MARG CT9 2 F9
Nash Court Rd MARG CT9 3 G9
Nash Gdns BRDST CT10 49 K1 3
Nash Hl RFOLK CT18 150 E7
Nash La MARG CT9 30 B6
Nash Rd MARG CT9 2 F9
Nasmyth Rd BRCH CT7 28 C5 3
Natal Rd DVE/WH CT16 155 L1
Nativity Cl SIT ME10 52 A1
Nat's La RASHE TN25 129 J8
Nautilus Cl IOS ME12 15 J8 6
Nautilus Dr IOS ME12 15 J8
Naylands MARG CT9 2 C6
Neal's Place Rd CANTW/ST CT2 77 L3
Neame Rd BRCH CT7 28 C6
Neason Wy FOLKN CT19 13 L2
Neath Rd LYDD TN29 214 B4
Nelson Av IOS ME12 15 M7
Nelson Cl IOS ME12 14 C5
KEN/WIL TN24 146 D5 1
Nelson Ct BRCH CT7 28 A5
Nelson Crs RAM CT11 5 J7
Nelson Park Rd RDV CT15 139 G5
Nelson Pl BRDST CT10 31 K8
Nelson Rd WSTB CT5 39 L4
Nelson St DEAL CT14 103 M6
FAV ME13 55 L7
Nesbit Rd LYDD TN29 203 H1
Ness Rd LYDD TN29 209 L7
The Ness CANT CT1 78 C8
Nether Av NROM TN28 202 F8
Nethercourt Farm Rd RAM CT11 4 C5
Nethercourt Gdns RAM CT11 4 C6
Nethercourt Hl RAM CT11 4 C6
Nethergong Hl RCANTE CT3 62 F1
Netherhale Farm Rd BRCH CT7 45 K1
Nethersole Cl CANTW/ST CT2 78 C1 3
Nethersole Rd RCANTW CT4 117 G4
Nettlefield KEN/WIL TN24 128 A8
Nettlepole La HDCN TN27 125 G4
Nevill Gdns DEAL CT14 121 K4
Newbridge Av SIT ME10 33 G6
Newbury Cl BRCH CT7 28 D7 1
FOLK CT20 169 M8
Newcastle Hl RAM CT11 5 K5
Newchurch La LYDD TN29 192 A7
Newcomen Rd IOS ME12 14 E3
New Cross St MARG CT9 2 F4 2
New Cut Rd FAV ME13 93 J1
New Dover Rd CANT CT1 7 J7
RFOLK CT18 171 K4
Newenden Cl ASH TN23 145 H7
New Forest La RCANTW CT4 93 J1
New Gardens Rd RSIT ME9 53 L3
Newgate Gap MARG CT9 3 J2
Newgate Lower Prom MARG CT9 3 J2
Newgate Prom MARG CT9 3 J2
New Hall Cl LYDD TN29 194 E5
New House Cl CANT CT1 95 M1
Newhouse La FAV ME13 73 L6
New House La RCANTW CT4 95 L3
Newing Cl RCANTE CT3 80 A5
Newington Rd MSTR CT12 48 D3
RAM CT11 4 E4
RFOLK CT18 169 J5
Newland Green La HDCN TN27 123 M5
Newland Rd IOS ME12 14 B6 1
Newlands ASH TN23 144 F7
DVE/WH CT16 137 K7
LYDD TN29 203 H2
Newlands Av SIT ME10 51 K1
Newlands Dr DEAL CT14 121 K5
Newlands La MSTR CT12 48 F3
Newlands Rd HDCN TN27 107 H8
MSTR CT12 5 G1
New La LYDD TN29 209 L7
New Lydd Rd RYE TN31 212 F2 1
Newlyn's Meadow RDV CT15 153 L4
Newman Dr SIT ME10 33 H5
Newman Rd RCANTE CT3 99 G8
Newnham La FAV ME13 72 A6
New Rectory La ASH TN23 163 K1
New Rd CANTW/ST CT2 60 B2
CANTW/ST CT2 76 E2
HDCN TN27 124 C3
HYTHE CT21 183 K1
IOS ME12 14 C5
IOS ME12 15 L7
RCANTW CT4 151 H1
RDV CT15 118 E6
RYE TN31 205 M7
New Road Hl RASHE TN25 180 B1
New Romney Pl SWCH CT13 84 B5 4
New Ruttington La CANT CT1 7 H2
New St CANT CT1 6 D7
CANTW/ST CT2 6 C2
DEAL CT14 103 M6 12
DVE/WH CT16 10 D6
FOLK CT20 13 H4
IOS ME12 14 D4
KEN/WIL TN24 8 C2
LYDD TN29 209 L7
MARG CT9 2 F4
RCANTE CT3 83 G4
SWCH CT13 84 C5
Newton Rd FAV ME13 55 M6
WSTB CT5 40 D3
New Town Gn KEN/WIL TN24 9 G8
Newtown Rd ASH TN23 8 F6
New Town Rd KEN/WIL TN24 9 G8
New Town St CANT CT1 7 H1
RCANTW CT4 76 E8
Nicholas Dr MSTR CT12 47 M8

Pleasance Road Central
LYDD TN29 217 H2
Pleasance Rd North
LYDD TN29 211 G8
Pleasance Rd South
LYDD TN29 217 H3
Pleasent Pl IOS ME12 15 G7 4
Pleydell Gdns FOLK CT20 13 G7
Plimsoll Av FOLKN CT19 170 F5
Plough Ct HB CT6 42 F3 5
Plough Hl RDV CT15 172 D1
Plough La WSTB CT5 40 F2
Plough Rd IOS ME12 16 C8
Plover Rd IOS ME12 15 J8
Pluckley Gdns MARG CT9 31 G3
Pluckley Rd HDCN TN27 107 K8
HDCN TN27 141 K3
RASHW TN26 125 J8
Plumford Rd FAV ME13 73 J3
Plummer La TENT TN30 174 B7
Plumpudding La FAV ME13 57 M5
Plumstone Rd BRCH CT7 46 C3
Plum Tree Gdns
RASHW TN26 176 D4 1
Plurenden Rd RASHW TN26 161 G6
Poets Cnr MARG CT9 3 H6
Poets Wk DEAL CT14 121 K4
Pollard Cl ASH TN23 145 H5 2
Polo Wy WSTB CT5 40 E4
Pomfret Rd RCANTW CT4 94 F4
Pommeus La DEAL CT14 120 F6
Poncia Rd ASH TN23 145 J6 3
Pond Dr SIT ME10 52 C3
Pond Farm Rd RSIT ME9 51 H4
Pond Hl RCANTE CT3 98 F4
Pond Hill Rd FOLK CT20 169 L8
Pond La RCANTE CT3 116 F2
RDV CT15 138 F6
Ponycart La RCANTW CT4 132 A2
Pook La HDCN TN27 158 E1
Poorhole La BRDST CT10 30 C8
Pope House La TENT TN30 174 D1
Popes La CANTW/ST CT2 61 G6
Pope St RCANTW CT4 112 A1
Poplar Cl ASH TN23 145 H2
Poplar Dr HB CT6 41 L3
RDV CT15 118 D3 3
Poplar La LYDD TN29 209 M6
Poplar Rd BRDST CT10 31 G7
RAM CT11 5 G5
TENT TN30 196 F1
The Poplars RCANTE CT3 62 B4
Popsal La RCANTE CT3 81 K7
Porter Cl IOS ME12 15 J7
Porter's La FAV ME13 73 K3
Portland Av SIT ME10 52 E1
Portland Cl HYTHE CT21 183 K3
KEN/WIL TN24 127 K6
Portland Ct RAM CT11 5 K4
Portland Rd HYTHE CT21 183 K3
Postling ASH TN23 145 G4 5
Postling Rd FOLKN CT19 170 A6
Pot Kiln La RASHW TN26 159 M2
Potten Street Rd BRCH CT7 44 F2
Potters Cl KEN/WIL TN24 127 G7
Potter St SWCH CT13 84 C4 5
Pottingfield Rd RYE TN31 205 J7
Poulders Rd SWCH CT13 83 M5
Poulton Cl DVW CT17 155 H5
Poulton La RCANTE CT3 82 E4
Pound Ct ASH TN23 163 J2
Poundhurst Rd RASHW TN26 178 D1
Pound La ASH TN23 163 H1
CANTW/ST CT2 6 E3
RASHE TN25 148 B8
RCANTW CT4 110 B1
RCANTW CT4 151 H1 3
Power Station Rd IOS ME12 15 G6
Prentis Cl SIT ME10 32 E8
Prentis Quay SIT ME10 33 G8 2
Prescott Cl RDV CT15 138 A8
Prestedge Av RAM CT11 49 G3
Preston Av FAV ME13 56 A8
Preston Gv FAV ME13 55 L7
Preston Hall Gdns IOS ME12 22 F1
Preston Hl RCANTE CT3 81 K4
Preston La FAV ME13 55 L7
RCANTE CT3 81 K1
Preston Pde WSTB CT5 39 H6
Preston Pk FAV ME13 55 M7
Preston Rd MSTR CT12 47 M2
RCANTE CT3 81 K1
Preston St FAV ME13 55 M7
Pretoria Rd CANT CT1 7 K4
Price's Av MARG CT9 3 K5
RAM CT11 4 E6
Priest Av CANTW/ST CT2 77 L5
Priest Flds HB CT6 25 H8
Priest Wk WSTB CT5 40 D2
Primrose Dr ASH TN23 163 K2
Primrose Hl RCANTW CT4 76 C6
Primrose La RSIT ME9 51 J7
Primrose Rd DVW CT17 155 J4
Primrose Wy MSTR CT12 47 L8 1
WSTB CT5 40 E4
Prince Andrew Rd BRDST CT10 31 G6
Prince Charles Av IOS ME12 15 L7
SIT ME10 52 D3
Prince Charles Rd BRDST CT10 31 G6
Prince of Wales Rbt DVW CT17 10 C8
Prince of Wales Ter DEAL CT14 103 M8
Princes Av IOS ME12 15 M6
MSTR CT12 4 D1
Princes Cl BRCH CT7 27 M6 1
Princes Crs MARG CT9 3 G5
Princes Dr SWCH CT13 85 J4
Prince's Gdns MARG CT9 30 E3
Princes Pde HYTHE CT21 184 B3
Prince's Rd RAM CT11 5 G3
Princess Anne Rd BRDST CT10 31 G6
Princess Cl WSTB CT5 40 E2
Princess Margaret Av MARG CT9 30 F3
MSTR CT12 4 B1
Princess Rd WSTB CT5 40 E2
Princess St FOLKN CT19 13 J2
Princes St DEAL CT14 103 M6
DVW CT17 10 D6
MARG CT9 2 F4
RAM CT11 5 J6
Prince's Wk MARG CT9 30 E2
Princes Wy CANTW/ST CT2 6 C3
Prioress Rd CANTW/ST CT2 6 A4
Prior Rd LYDD TN29 210 F6
Priory Cl NROM TN28 202 B7
Priory Gdns FOLK CT20 13 H6
Priory Gate Rd DVW CT17 10 B5
Priory Gv DVW CT17 10 B5
Priory Hl DVW CT17 10 A5
Priory La RASHE TN25 166 E1
Priory of St Jacob CANT CT1 6 B8
Priory Rd DVE/WH CT16 10 C5
DVW CT17 10 C5
FAV ME13 55 K5
RAM CT11 5 H7
RASHE TN25 164 E7
Priory Rw FAV ME13 55 L4
Priory Station Approach Rd
DVW CT17 10 B5
Priory St DVE/WH CT16 10 C5
Priory Wy TENT TN30 174 E6
Promenade BRCH CT7 28 B5
DEAL CT14 121 M2
The Promenade IOS ME12 23 J3
Prospect Cl WGOS CT8 29 G6 1
Prospect Gdns MSTR CT12 46 D6
Prospect Pl BRDST CT10 49 K1 6
CANT CT1 7 G7
DVW CT17 155 K4
Prospect Rd BRCH CT7 28 B6
BRDST CT10 49 K1
FOLK CT20 184 F2 1
HYTHE CT21 183 L3 7
MSTR CT12 46 D7
Prospect Ter RAM CT11 5 J7
Prospect Wy RASHE TN25 148 A7
Provender Rd FAV ME13 54 B7
Providence St ASH TN23 8 E8
Puckle La CANT CT1 7 G8
Pudding La RCANTE CT3 82 F4
Pullman Cl MSTR CT12 4 F1
Pump La MARG CT9 3 G4
Purchase La RASHW TN26 144 A6
Puttney Dr SIT ME10 33 J5
Pye Alley La WSTB CT5 58 D2
Pyson's Rd MSTR CT12 48 E3

Q

Quantock Dr KEN/WIL TN24 8 D1
Quantock Gdns MSTR CT12 48 D2
Quarrington La RASHE TN25 147 H5
Quarry Rd HYTHE CT21 183 K2
Quarry Vw ASH TN23 144 F6
Quarry Wk HYTHE CT21 184 C2
Quarry Wd RASHE TN25 165 J7
Quay La SWCH CT13 84 C4 6
Queen Bertha Rd RAM CT11 4 E7
Queen Bertha's Av BRCH CT7 28 E5
Queenborough Dr IOS ME12 15 K6
Queenborough Rd IOS ME12 15 J8
Queendown Rd BRCH CT7 47 H1
Queen Elizabeth Av MARG CT9 30 F4
Queen Elizabeth Rd
DVE/WH CT16 11 G5
Queen's Av BRCH CT7 27 M6
BRDST CT10 31 K7
CANTW/ST CT2 6 B3
DVW CT17 155 H6
FOLK CT20 169 K7
HB CT6 24 F8
MARG CT9 2 F6
MSTR CT12 4 D2
Queens Ct MARG CT9 3 K2 2
Queensdown Rd DEAL CT14 139 L1
Queen's Gdns DVE/WH CT16 10 D5
HB CT6 24 B8
Queen's Gate Rd RAM CT11 4 F4
Queens Ms DEAL CT14 103 M7 5
Queens Pde MARG CT9 3 K2
Queen's Prom MARG CT9 3 L2
Queen's Ri DEAL CT14 121 H8
Queen's Rd BRDST CT10 49 K1
FAV ME13 55 K6
IOS ME12 15 M6
KEN/WIL TN24 8 D2
KEN/WIL TN24 146 C4 3
LYDD TN29 209 L7
NROM TN28 202 F7
RAM CT11 5 M4
RCANTE CT3 82 F3
RCANTE CT3 99 H8
WGOS CT8 29 H5 3
WSTB CT5 40 B3
Queen St ASH TN23 8 D4
DEAL CT14 103 L7 1
DVE/WH CT16 10 D6
FOLK CT20 13 J4
HB CT6 24 B8
MARG CT9 2 F4
RAM CT11 5 J7
Queen's Wy IOS ME12 14 C5
Queensway LYDD TN29 194 F3
LYDD TN29 209 L7
Quern Rd DEAL CT14 121 J3
Querns Pl CANT CT1 7 K4
Querns Rd CANT CT1 7 L4
Quested Rd FOLKN CT19 170 A7
Quested Wy RMAID ME17 86 E7
Quetta Rd MSTR CT12 48 B4
Quex Rd WGOS CT8 29 H5
Quex View Rd BRCH CT7 28 C8
Quince Orch RASHW TN26 178 C5 1
Quinton Rd RSIT ME9 32 E6

R

Rabbit Hole RCANTW CT4 116 C6
Radfall Ride WSTB CT5 40 E8
Radfall Rd WSTB CT5 40 E7
Radley Cl BRDST CT10 31 J7
Radnor Bridge Rd FOLK CT20 13 J4
FOLKN CT19 13 K4
Radnor Cliff FOLK CT20 12 A9
Radnor Cliff Crs FOLK CT20 185 H2
Radnor Cl HB CT6 42 D4
Radnor Park Av FOLKN CT19 12 D3
Radnor Park Crs FOLKN CT19 12 F4
Radnor Park Gdns FOLKN CT19 12 F3
Radnor Park Rd FOLKN CT19 12 F3
Radnor Pk West FOLKN CT19 12 D4
Radnor St FOLKN CT19 13 K5 1
Ragstone Hollow RASHE TN25 165 J7
Railway Av WSTB CT5 40 A4
Railway Hl RCANTW CT4 116 A5
Railway Rd IOS ME12 14 D3
Railway Ter QBOR ME11 14 C8
Raleigh Cl KEN/WIL TN24 146 C5
Raleigh Wy IOS ME12 15 G7
Ram La RASHW TN26 125 L5
Rampart Rd HYTHE CT21 183 K3
Ramsey Cl CANTW/ST CT2 6 C2
Ramsgate Rd BRDST CT10 49 H2
MARG CT9 3 G9
SWCH CT13 66 C6
Ramstone Cl RASHE TN25 148 A8
Rancorn Rd MARG CT9 2 A6
Randolph Cl CANT CT1 7 H8
Randolph Gdns
KEN/WIL TN24 128 A8 5
Randolph La RYE TN31 205 J2
Randolph Rd DVW CT17 155 K4
Ranelagh Gdns BRDST CT10 31 G8 2
Ranelagh Gv BRDST CT10 31 G8
Ranelagh Rd DEAL CT14 103 M8 4
IOS ME12 14 E3
Range Rd HYTHE CT21 183 K5
IOS ME12 21 M4
Raspberry Hill La RSIT ME9 18 E7
Ratling Rd RCANTE CT3 99 J7
Rattington St RCANTW CT4 94 F3
Ravenlea Rd FOLK CT20 12 B5
Ravenscourt Rd CANTW/ST CT2 77 K2
DEAL CT14 103 L8
Rawdon Rd RAM CT11 4 D6
Rawling St RSIT ME9 70 B1
Rayham Rd WSTB CT5 40 C5
Raymond Av CANT CT1 7 G7
Raymond Fuller Wy
KEN/WIL TN24 146 A1
Raymoor Av LYDD TN29 203 J1
Rayners Hl RMAID ME17 88 E7
Reach Cl RDV CT15 139 H8
Reachfields HYTHE CT21 183 J4
Reach Rd HYTHE CT21 181 M3
RDV CT15 139 H8
Reader's Bridge Rd TENT TN30 174 B1
Readers La RYE TN31 197 H8
Reading Cl DEAL CT14 121 K4
Reading Rd DVW CT17 155 H6
Reading St BRDST CT10 31 H5
TENT TN30 188 D2
Reading Street Rd MARG CT9 31 G4
Recce La RFOLK CT18 152 C1
Recreation Ground Rd
TENT TN30 174 D6
Rectory Cl RASHW TN26 176 C3
Rectory Gdns WSTB CT5 40 F3
Rectory La HYTHE CT21 168 D8
RCANTW CT4 116 C4
RFOLK CT18 150 E7
RMAID ME17 87 G8
RYE TN31 205 K5
Rectory Rd BRDST CT10 31 K8
DEAL CT14 121 H1
LYDD TN29 193 K8
SIT ME10 52 D2
Rectory Wy KEN/WIL TN24 127 L8
Reculver Av BRCH CT7 28 A6
Reculver Cl HB CT6 25 H7 1
Reculver Dr HB CT6 25 G8
Reculver La HB CT6 25 J8
Reculver Rd HB CT6 25 G8
Reculvers Rd WGOS CT8 29 H6
Redberry Rd ASH TN23 145 K8
Redbrook St RASHW TN26 160 E6
Redbrooks Wy HYTHE CT21 183 H2
Redcot La RCANTE CT3 61 K6
Redhill Rd WGOS CT8 28 F5
Redhouse La RCANTW CT4 96 A5
Redhouse Wall DEAL CT14 103 K4
Redmill Cl FOLK CT20 170 A8
Redoubt Wy LYDD TN29 195 J1
Red Rd FAV ME13 57 M8
Redsull Av DEAL CT14 121 J2
Red Tree Orch ASH TN23 145 G6 1
Redwood Cl CANTW/ST CT2 6 C1
CANTW/ST CT2 78 A3 1
Reed Av CANT CT1 78 E3
Reedland Crs FAV ME13 55 L5
Reedmace Cl ASH TN23 144 F5 3
Reeds Cl HB CT6 42 D1
Reeves Wy WSTB CT5 40 E4
Regency Ct SIT ME10 51 M1
Regency Pl CANT CT1 7 K1
Regents Pl ASH TN23 8 C3
Regent St CRBK TN17 186 A2
WSTB CT5 39 M3
Regis Crs SIT ME10 33 H6
Rendezvous St FOLK CT20 13 H5
The Rendezvous MARG CT9 2 F3
Rentain Rd RCANTW CT4 94 F3
Repton Cl BRDST CT10 31 H7 2
Repton Manor Rd ASH TN23 8 A1
Reservoir Av LYDD TN29 217 H7
Reservoir Rd WSTB CT5 40 A3
Rest Harrow FAV ME13 73 L8
The Retreat BRCH CT7 28 D5 3
MSTR CT12 4 C2
Reynolds Cl HB CT6 42 D1
Rhee Wall RASHW TN26 189 M6
Rheims Ct CANTW/ST CT2 6 A3
Rheims Wy CANT CT1 6 D5
CANTW/ST CT2 6 B3
Rhodaus Cl CANT CT1 6 F6
Rhodaus Town CANT CT1 6 F6
Rhodes Gdns BRDST CT10 31 H7
Richardson Wy MSTR CT12 47 M7 1
Richborough Rd SWCH CT13 66 A8
WGOS CT8 29 H6
Richbourgh Rd SWCH CT13 84 A2
Richdore Rd RCANTW CT4 112 E6
Richmond Av MARG CT9 3 L6
Richmond Dr HB CT6 43 G1
NROM TN28 202 E5
SIT ME10 33 G6
Richmond Gdns CANTW/ST CT2 77 L3
Richmond Rd RAM CT11 5 G6
WSTB CT5 40 D4
Richmond St FOLKN CT19 169 M7
HB CT6 24 B8
IOS ME12 14 F3
Riddles Rd SIT ME10 51 L2
The Ridge KEN/WIL TN24 128 A8 4
Ridgeway HYTHE CT21 182 C2
WSTB CT5 40 E4
Ridgeway Rd HB CT6 42 C6
The Ridgeway BRDST CT10 49 G2
DVW CT17 155 G3
FAV ME13 75 J2
MARG CT9 3 M6
RASHE TN25 147 K8
Ridgeway Wk HB CT6 42 C6
Ridham Av SIT ME10 33 J4
Riding Gate Rbt CANT CT1 6 F6
Riding Hl KEN/WIL TN24 127 L7 1
The Ridings MARG CT9 31 G2
WSTB CT5 40 F4
Ridley Cl HB CT6 42 C5
Rigden Rd ASH TN23 145 K6
Rigshill Rd FAV ME13 89 K8
Riley Av HB CT6 41 H1
Ringlestone Rd RMAID ME17 86 E1
Ringold Av MSTR CT12 4 B2
Ring Wall DEAL CT14 103 G3
Ringwood Cl CANTW/ST CT2 78 A2
Ringwould Rd DEAL CT14 121 K8
RDV CT15 138 F1
Ripley Rd KEN/WIL TN24 146 C5
Ripple Rd DEAL CT14 121 H7
Risborough La FOLK CT20 169 M8
Risborough Wy FOLK CT20 170 A7
Risdon Cl CANTW/ST CT2 61 H7
The Rise ASH TN23 145 G6
DEAL CT14 121 L8
IOS ME12 14 E8
RDV CT15 139 K7
RSIT ME9 51 K3
Rising Rd ASH TN23 8 A6
River Ct RCANTW CT4 94 F2
River Dl DVW CT17 155 H2
Riverdale Rd CANT CT1 78 D2
River Dr DVW CT17 155 H3
Riverhead Cl MARG CT9 3 M7
SIT ME10 51 L2
River Meadow DVW CT17 155 H2
Riversdale Rd ASH TN23 8 E8
MSTR CT12 4 C1
Riverside RCANTW CT4 94 E2
Riverside Cl ASH TN23 163 J2
RCANTW CT4 97 J4
Riverside Ms RCANTW CT4 97 J4 5
Riverside Rd MSTR CT12 66 C4
Rivers Rd RSIT ME9 53 M3
River St DVW CT17 155 G2
Riverview ASH TN23 145 G4 4
River Vw CANTW/ST CT2 61 H6
QBOR ME11 19 H2
Riviera Rd FOLK CT20 12 A9
Riverside DVE/WH CT16 136 E8
Road of Remembrance
FOLK CT20 13 H6
Roberts Cl SIT ME10 32 F6
Roberts Rd NROM TN28 211 G4
WSTB CT5 39 H7
Robert St DEAL CT14 103 M6
Robin Hood La LYDD TN29 209 L8
Robin La LYDD TN29 209 L7
Robins Av RMAID ME17 105 L1
Robin's Cl HYTHE CT21 182 E5
RMAID ME17 105 L1
Robus Cl RFOLK CT18 150 E6
Rochester Av CANT CT1 7 K7
Rock Channel RYE TN31 205 L8
Rock Hill Rd HDCN TN27 124 A3
Rockingham Pl HB CT6 42 D3
Rock Rd SIT ME10 52 A1
Rockstone Wy MSTR CT12 48 B4
Rocky Bourne Rd RASHE TN25 164 F8
Rodmer Cl IOS ME12 15 L5
Rodney St RAM CT11 5 H7
Roebuck Rd FAV ME13 55 J6
Rogersmead TENT TN30 174 B6
Rokesley Rd DVE/WH CT16 137 K8
Rolfe La NROM TN28 202 C7
Roll's Av IOS ME12 21 M4 1
Rolvenden Dr SIT ME10 32 D8
Roman Cl DEAL CT14 103 K7
Roman Rd FAV ME13 55 L6
MSTR CT12 48 D3
RDV CT15 119 L8
Roman Sq SIT ME10 52 B2
Roman Wy ASH TN23 163 K1
FOLKN CT19 169 L7
RDV CT15 118 D3
RDV CT15 139 H8
Romden Rd HDCN TN27 142 A3
Rome Rd NROM TN28 202 C7 2
Romilly Gdns MSTR CT12 48 E3 2
Romney Av FOLK CT20 170 B8
Romney Ct SIT ME10 32 F8
Romney Marsh Rd ASH TN23 8 E6
Romney Rd KEN/WIL TN24 9 K6
LYDD TN29 202 A8
RASHW TN26 178 C6
Romney Wy HYTHE CT21 183 G4
Romsey Cl KEN/WIL TN24 146 C3 1
Rookery Cl KEN/WIL TN24 127 M6
RSIT ME9 51 J7
Rook La RSIT ME9 32 B7
Roonagh Ct SIT ME10 52 A3
Roosevelt Rd DVE/WH CT16 155 K2
Roper Cl CANTW/ST CT2 6 D2
Roper Rd CANTW/ST CT2 6 D2
RSIT ME9 53 M2
Rope Wk RYE TN31 205 L7
Roseacre Cl CANTW/ST CT2 6 D2
Roseacre Ct MARG CT9 31 G3 5
Rose Acre Rd RCANTE CT3 80 B6
Rosebery Av HB CT6 25 G8
RAM CT11 5 L1
Rosebery Cl SIT ME10 52 F1
Rosedale Rd MARG CT9 3 J6
Rose Gdns BRCH CT7 28 B7 1
HB CT6 42 E1
MSTR CT12 46 D7
RDV CT15 118 F6
Rose Hl RAM CT11 5 J6
TENT TN30 188 D8
Roselands DEAL CT14 121 K4
Roselands Gdns
CANTW/ST CT2 77 M3 1
Rose La CANT CT1 6 F5 1
RCANTW CT4 97 L8
RMAID ME17 106 D4
Roselawn Gdns MARG CT9 29 K5
Roselea Av HB CT6 42 B2
Roseleigh Rd SIT ME10 51 M4
Rosemary Av BRDST CT10 49 H3
IOS ME12 14 F7
Rosemary Gdns BRDST CT10 49 H3
WSTB CT5 40 B5
Rosemary La CANT CT1 6 E5
HDCN TN27 123 G8
Rose St IOS ME12 14 D3
Rosetower Ct BRDST CT10 31 H5
Rose Wk RFOLK CT18 170 C1
Rossendale Gdns FOLK CT20 13 K3
Rossendale Rd FOLK CT20 13 K3
Rossetti Rd BRCH CT7 28 B5
Ross Gdns CANTW/ST CT2 77 J2
Rossland Rd MSTR CT12 4 A2
Ross Wy FOLK CT20 185 G1
Rothbrook Dr KEN/WIL TN24 127 L6
Rothley Cl TENT TN30 174 D5
Rough Common Rd
CANTW/ST CT2 77 J3
Roundel Cl RSIT ME9 53 M3
The Roundel SIT ME10 52 A3
Rowan Cl ASH TN23 145 G3
CANTW/ST CT2 61 H7
RCANTE CT3 82 C7 1
Rowe Cl MARG CT9 30 B6
Rowena Rd WGOS CT8 29 G4
Rowetts Wy IOS ME12 21 L2
Rowland Crs HB CT6 25 G8 3
Rowland Dr HB CT6 41 L3
The Row RCANTW CT4 151 H1
Roxburgh Rd WGOS CT8 29 H4
Royal Av WSTB CT5 39 L8
Royal Cl BRDST CT10 49 G1
Royal Esp MARG CT9 29 J4
RAM CT11 4 D9
Royal Military Av FOLK CT20 169 M8
Royal Military Canal Pth
RASHE TN25 179 J5
RASHW TN26 190 A4
TENT TN30 198 C5
Royal Military Rd HYTHE CT21 181 M4
Royal Pde RAM CT11 5 J8
Royal Rd IOS ME12 14 E3 4
RAM CT11 5 H7
Royds Rd KEN/WIL TN24 145 M7
Royston Gdns RDV CT15 139 H7
Royton Av RMAID ME17 87 M8
Rubery Dro RCANTE CT3 65 L7
Ruckinge Rd RASHW TN26 178 C6
Rugby Cl BRDST CT10 31 H8
Rugby Gdns ASH TN23 8 F8
Rugby Rd DVW CT17 155 J7
Ruins Barn Rd RSIT ME9 69 L1
SIT ME10 52 A5
Rumfields Rd BRDST CT10 48 F1
Runham La RMAID ME17 105 G2
Runnymede Ms FAV ME13 55 L6 6
Rusham Rd RCANTE CT3 81 L4
Rush Cl LYDD TN29 194 D7
Rushenden Rd QBOR ME11 19 J1
Rushmead Cl CANTW/ST CT2 77 M3
Russell Cl SIT ME10 51 L2
Russell Dr WSTB CT5 40 F2
Russell Pl FAV ME13 55 K2
Russell Rd FOLKN CT19 12 F2
Russell St DVE/WH CT16 10 E5
IOS ME12 14 D3
Russet Av FAV ME13 56 A8
Russet Rd CANT CT1 7 M6
The Russets WSTB CT5 40 F4
Rutherford Rd KEN/WIL TN24 127 K8
Rutland Av MARG CT9 30 E3 1
Rutland Cl CANT CT1 78 F6
Rutland Gdns BRCH CT7 28 B6
MARG CT9 30 E3
Rutland Rd DVE/WH CT16 155 K2
Rydal Av RAM CT11 4 B5
Ryder's Av WGOS CT8 28 F5
Ryde St CANTW/ST CT2 6 C3
Rye Rd LYDD TN29 199 M5
RYE TN31 205 H3
TENT TN30 197 J3
Rye Wk HB CT6 42 E3
Ryland Pl FOLK CT20 13 K4
Rylands Rd KEN/WIL TN24 145 M1
Rype Cl LYDD TN29 209 L8
Ryswick Ms NROM TN28 202 E5 3

S

Sackett's Gap MARG CT9 30 E2 4
Sacketts Hl BRDST CT10 30 D7
Sackville Cl RASHW TN26 126 C6 2
Sackville Crs ASH TN23 8 A3
Saddlers Hl RCANTE CT3 99 M3
Saddlers Ms WSTB CT5 40 F4 1
Saddler's Wall La LYDD TN29 199 K4
Saddlers Wy ASH TN23 163 K1
Saddleton Rd WSTB CT5 39 M5
Saffron's Pl FOLK CT20 13 J5
Saffron Wy SIT ME10 33 H6
St Agnes Gdns IOS ME12 14 E4
St Alban's Rd RCANTE CT3 62 A4
St Alphege Cl WSTB CT5 39 K6 2
St Alphege La CANT CT1 6 F3 3
St Alphege Rd DVE/WH CT16 10 B2
St Ambrose Gn RASHE TN25 129 G3 5

St Andrews Cl CANT CT1 6 D6
FOLKN CT19 170 D6
HB CT6 42 B1
MARG CT9 30 B6
WSTB CT5 40 A6
St Andrews Gdns DVW CT17 155 K3 3
RDV CT15 118 A8
St Andrew's Lees SWCH CT13 84 C5
St Andrew's Rd DEAL CT14 103 L7
NROM TN28 202 F7
RAM CT11 5 L2
St Andrews Wy DEAL CT14 119 J2
St Anne's Dr HB CT6 41 M1
St Anne's Gdns MARG CT9 3 C9
St Anne's Rd ASH TN23 145 H6
WSTB CT5 40 B2
St Ann's Rd FAV ME13 55 K7
LYDD TN29 194 D6
St Anthony's Wy MARG CT9 30 E4
St Augustine's Av MARG CT9 3 C9
St Augustine's Crs WSTB CT5 40 F2
St Augustine's Pk RAM CT11 4 F7
St Augustine's Rd CANT CT1 7 J6
DEAL CT14 121 H1 2
RAM CT11 5 C8
St Bart's Rd SWCH CT13 84 A5
St Benedict's Lawn RAM CT11 5 G8 1
St Benet's Rd WGOS CT8 29 G6
St Benets Wy TENT TN30 174 D5
St Catherine's Dr FAV ME13 55 M7
St Catherine's Gv MSTR CT12 47 M4
St Christopher Cl MARG CT9 30 F5 2
St Christophers Gn
BRDST CT10 31 H8 3
St Clare Rd DEAL CT14 121 L4
St Clements SWCH CT13 84 C4 7
St Clements Cl IOS ME12 22 F3
St Clements Ct BRDST CT10 31 G8 3
St Clements Rd IOS ME12 23 G2 1
WGOS CT8 29 G4
St Cosmus Cl RASHE TN25 109 K4
St Crispin's Rd WGOS CT8 29 G5
St Davids Av DVW CT17 173 J1
St David's Cl BRCH CT7 28 D5
WSTB CT5 40 A6
St David's Rd DEAL CT14 103 L7 2
RAM CT11 5 L1
St Denys Rd RFOLK CT18 152 D8
St Dunstan's Cl CANTW/ST CT2 6 C2
St Dunstan's Rd MARG CT9 3 K5
St Dunstan's St CANTW/ST CT2 6 D2
St Dunstan's Ter CANTW/ST CT2 6 C3
St Eanswythe Wy FOLK CT20 13 H5
St Edmunds Rd CANT CT1 6 E5
DEAL CT14 121 G1
St Francis Cl DEAL CT14 121 G1
MARG CT9 30 F5 3
St Francis Rd FOLKN CT19 170 B7 2
St George's Av IOS ME12 14 D5
IOS ME12 21 L3
St George's Cl WSTB CT5 40 A6
St Georges Crs DVW CT17 155 K8
St Georges La CANT CT1 6 F5 2
St George's Lees SWCH CT13 84 C5 5
St George's Pl CANT CT1 7 G5
HYTHE CT21 182 F5
RDV CT15 139 H7
SWCH CT13 84 D5
St George's Rd BRDST CT10 49 J1
DEAL CT14 103 M7 5
FOLKN CT19 170 B7 3
RAM CT11 5 L2
SWCH CT13 84 C5
St George's Rbt CANT CT1 7 G5
St George's St CANT CT1 7 G5 2
St Giles Rd DVW CT17 155 K8 2
St Gregory's CANT CT1 7 H3 3
St Gregory's Cl DEAL CT14 121 H1 3
St Gregory's Rd CANT CT1 7 J3
St Helen's Rd IOS ME12 14 F4
St Hilda Rd FOLKN CT19 170 A7 3
St Hilda's Rd HYTHE CT21 183 K4
St Jacob's Pl CANT CT1 6 B8
St James' Av BRDST CT10 31 G8
MSTR CT12 48 D4
St James Cl IOS ME12 22 F1
St James' Gdns WSTB CT5 39 M5 1
St James La DVE/WH CT16 10 E6
St James' Park Rd MARG CT9 29 J5 2
St James Rd DEAL CT14 121 L8
St James's Terrace BRCH CT7 28 D5
St James St DVE/WH CT16 10 E6
St Jean's Rd WGOS CT8 29 G6
St John's Av MSTR CT12 4 B1
SIT ME10 52 D2
St John's Church Rd
FOLKN CT19 12 F3
St John's Cl RFOLK CT18 152 C6
St Johns Crs CANTW/ST CT2 59 M6
St John's La ASH TN23 8 E4
CANT CT1 6 E5
St John's Pl CANT CT1 7 G2
St John's Rd DVW CT17 10 B6
FAV ME13 55 M6
HYTHE CT21 183 J2
MARG CT9 3 G5
NROM TN28 202 C7
RDV CT15 118 D3
WSTB CT5 40 F2
St John's St FOLK CT20 13 H4
MARG CT9 3 G5 3
St John's Wy RFOLK CT18 152 B6
St Julien Av CANT CT1 78 F4
St Katherine Rd IOS ME12 15 G6
St Laurence Cl RSIT ME9 52 F3
St Lawrence Av RAM CT11 4 D9
St Lawrence Cl CANT CT1 7 J8
St Lawrence Forstal CANT CT1 7 J9
St Lawrence Rd CANT CT1 7 K8
St Leonard's Rd DEAL CT14 121 K1 3
HYTHE CT21 183 K4
St Louis Gv HB CT6 41 L1
St Luke's Av RAM CT11 5 K3
St Luke's Cl WGOS CT8 29 G5
WSTB CT5 40 A6
St Luke's Rd RAM CT11 5 K3
St Luke's Wk RFOLK CT18 170 A1
St Margaret's Cl WSTB CT5 39 J7 3
St Margarets Dr DEAL CT14 121 K5 2
St Margarets Rd BRCH CT7 47 H2
RDV CT15 139 J8
WGOS CT8 29 G6
St Margaret's St CANT CT1 6 F5 3
St Mark's Cl FOLK CT20 169 M8
WSTB CT5 40 A5
St Martins Av CANT CT1 7 K4
St Martins Cl CANT CT1 7 K4
DVW CT17 155 K8
St Martin's Hl CANT CT1 7 K5
St Martin's Pl CANT CT1 7 K4
St Martin's Rd CANT CT1 7 J4
DEAL CT14 121 H1
FOLK CT20 169 M7
NROM TN28 202 D7
RDV CT15 156 A1
St Martin's Vw HB CT6 42 C5
St Mary's SWCH CT13 84 B4 3
St Mary's Av MARG CT9 30 F4
St Mary's Cl RASHW TN26 178 C5
RDV CT15 99 L8
SWCH CT13 83 K7
SWCH CT13 101 K3
St Mary's Gdns LYDD TN29 194 C8
RCANTE CT3 63 G2 1
St Marys Gn KEN/WIL TN24 128 A6 2
St Mary's Gv DEAL CT14 119 J1
WSTB CT5 39 H7
St Mary's Meadow RCANTE CT3 81 J5
St Marys Ms KEN/WIL TN24 9 M8
St Mary's Rd BRDST CT10 49 K1 2
DEAL CT14 121 L4
FAV ME13 55 M7
HYTHE CT21 182 D4
MSTR CT12 46 D7
NROM TN28 202 D5
RCANTW CT4 97 K2
St Mary's St CANT CT1 6 E5
St Michaels Av MARG CT9 30 F5
St Michaels Cl CANTW/ST CT2 77 J4
St Michael's Pl CANTW/ST CT2 78 A3
St Michael's Rd CANTW/ST CT2 78 A3
SIT ME10 52 A1
St Michael's St FOLK CT20 13 J4
St Michael's Wk RFOLK CT18 170 B1 1
St Mildred's Av BRCH CT7 28 A6
BRDST CT10 49 J1
RAM CT11 4 E7
St Mildred's Cl TENT TN30 174 C6 2
St Mildreds Ct DEAL CT14 121 L4 1
St Mildred's Gdns WGOS CT8 29 H4 3
St Mildreds Pl CANT CT1 6 D7
St Mildred's Rd MARG CT9 3 K5
MSTR CT12 46 D8
RAM CT11 4 E7
WGOS CT8 29 G5
St Monicas Rd DEAL CT14 121 M7
St Nicholas Cl CANTW/ST CT2 61 H6
DEAL CT14 121 H1
St Nicholas Rd CANT CT1 77 L7
FAV ME13 55 J6
HYTHE CT21 183 K3
NROM TN28 202 F7
St Patrick's Cl DEAL CT14 103 L7 3
WSTB CT5 40 A6
St Patrick's Rd DEAL CT14 103 L7
DVW CT17 173 J1
RAM CT11 5 L2
St Paul's Av FAV ME13 55 J6
St Pauls Crs FAV ME13 75 J2
St Pauls Rd FAV ME13 75 J2
MARG CT9 3 K3
St Paul's St SIT ME10 33 G8 3
St Pauls Ter CANT CT1 7 H5 1
St Paul's Wy FOLK CT20 185 G1
St Peter's Cl IOS ME12 14 E7
St Peter's Ct BRDST CT10 31 H8
FAV ME13 55 J6
St Peter's Footpath MARG CT9 3 J7
St Peter's Gv CANT CT1 6 E4
St Peter's La CANT CT1 6 E3 1
CANTW/ST CT2 6 F3 4
St Peter's Park Rd BRDST CT10 31 H8
St Peter's Pl CANT CT1 6 D4
St Peter's Rd BRDST CT10 31 G8
FAV ME13 75 J2 2
MARG CT9 3 J8
WSTB CT5 39 M3
St Peter's Rbt CANTW/ST CT2 6 D4
St Peter's St CANT CT1 6 E3 2
SWCH CT13 84 C4 3
St Radigund's Pl CANT CT1 7 G2 1
St Radigund's Rd DVW CT17 155 J4
St Radigunds St CANT CT1 6 F3
St Richard's Rd DEAL CT14 121 H1
St Saviour's Cl FAV ME13 56 A6
FOLKN CT19 13 H1
St Stephen's Cl CANTW/ST CT2 6 F1
St Stephen's Ct CANTW/ST CT2 6 F1
St Stephen's Flds
CANTW/ST CT2 6 F2 1
St Stephen's Gn CANTW/ST CT2 78 B2
St Stephen's Hl CANTW/ST CT2 60 A8
St Stephen's Rd CANTW/ST CT2 6 F2
St Stephen's Wk ASH TN23 145 H6
St Swithin's Rd WSTB CT5 40 D3
St Theresa's Cl KEN/WIL TN24 8 C2
St Thomas Hl CANTW/ST CT2 77 L2
St Vincent Rd RDV CT15 139 G6
St Vincent's Cl RCANTE CT3 80 B5
WSTB CT5 40 A6
St Welcume's Wy RMAID ME17 87 G7
St Winifred Rd FOLKN CT19 170 B7 4
Salisbury Av BRDST CT10 49 H2
RAM CT11 5 L3
Salisbury Cl SIT ME10 52 E1
Salisbury Rd CANTW/ST CT2 78 A3
DEAL CT14 121 K3
DVE/WH CT16 10 C3
FOLKN CT19 170 A6
HB CT6 24 D8
RDV CT15 139 K7
WSTB CT5 39 M5 2
Salmestone Ri MARG CT9 2 F9
Salmestone Rd MARG CT9 2 F9
Salmon Crs IOS ME12 15 H7
Saltcote St RYE TN31 205 L5
Salters La FAV ME13 55 M8
LYDD TN29 199 L5
Salthouse Cl LYDD TN29 199 M5
The Saltings NROM TN28 203 G8 1
Salts Cl WSTB CT5 39 M4
Salt's Dr BRDST CT10 31 G8
Saltwood Gdns MARG CT9 31 G3
Samian Crs FOLKN CT19 169 L7
Sancroft Av CANTW/ST CT2 77 L4
Sanctuary Cl BRDST CT10 49 H3
DVW CT17 154 F1
Sandbanks Rd FAV ME13 56 D3
Sandford Rd SIT ME10 32 D8
Sandgate Esp FOLK CT20 184 E3
Sandgate Hl FOLK CT20 185 H2
Sandgate Rd FOLK CT20 12 D7
Sandhurst Cl CANTW/ST CT2 78 C1 3
Sandhurst Rd MARG CT9 31 H3
Sandilands KEN/WIL TN24 9 K5
Sandle's Rd BRCH CT7 28 B6 4
Sandlewood Dr BRCH CT7 45 H4 3
Sandling Rd HYTHE CT21 168 B7
Sandown Cl DEAL CT14 103 M4 1
Sandown Dr HB CT6 41 M1
Sandown Lees SWCH CT13 84 E6
Sandown Rd DEAL CT14 103 M4
SWCH CT13 84 E5
Sandpiper Rd WSTB CT5 39 K7
Sandpit Hl RCANTE CT3 43 L8
Sandstone Dr SIT ME10 33 G5
Sandway Rd RMAID ME17 105 J2
Sandwich Cl FOLK CT20 170 B8
Sandwich Hl RCANTE CT3 81 K5
Sandwich Rd DVE/WH CT16 137 J6
MSTR CT12 66 D2
RCANTE CT3 83 J4
RDV CT15 100 A8
RDV CT15 137 J3
SWCH CT13 101 L2
Sandwood Rd BRDST CT10 49 H4
SWCH CT13 84 B5
Sandyhurst La KEN/WIL TN24 127 G7
Sandy La HYTHE CT21 184 D2
KEN/WIL TN24 146 D4
RASHW TN26 143 M6
TENT TN30 174 D6
Sandy Pl RASHE TN25 147 M8
Sanger Cl MARG CT9 2 E7
Sangro Pl CANT CT1 78 F4 2
Sanspareil Av IOS ME12 15 H7
Santon La RCANTE CT3 63 M5
Sark Cl LYDD TN29 194 E5
Sarre Pl SWCH CT13 84 B5 3
Satis Av SIT ME10 33 G6
Satmar La RFOLK CT18 171 M2
Satmore La RFOLK CT18 171 L1
Saunders La RCANTE CT3 83 H4
Saunders Wy RYE TN31 213 J3 1
Savernake Dr HB CT6 42 D3
Saw Lodge Fld ASH TN23 163 L1
Sawpit Rd RSIT ME9 70 C2
Saxon Av IOS ME12 15 K7
Saxon Cl HYTHE CT21 184 A3
Saxon Rd FAV ME13 55 L7
RAM CT11 4 C7
RCANTW CT4 97 J4
WGOS CT8 29 H4
Saxon Shore Wy DEAL CT14 121 M5
DVE/WH CT16 10 E7
FAV ME13 56 B4
HB CT6 25 H7
HYTHE CT21 181 L4
RASHE TN25 178 F3
RASHW TN26 177 L7
RCANTE CT3 43 L2
RCANTE CT3 63 G1
RDV CT15 139 L7
RFOLK CT18 168 E1
RSIT ME9 18 E4
RYE TN31 198 B8
SWCH CT13 83 M1
WSTB CT5 40 D2
Saxon St DVW CT17 10 C5
Saxton Rd LYDD TN29 211 G8
Sayer Rd HDCN TN27 107 L5
Scanlons Bridge Rd
HYTHE CT21 183 J3
Scarborough Dr IOS ME12 15 K4
Sceales Dr MSTR CT12 47 M7 2
Sceptre Wy WSTB CT5 39 K6 3
The School Cl WGOS CT8 29 G4 2
School Hl RCANTW CT4 93 K6
School La CANTW/ST CT2 59 J6
FAV ME13 89 M7
HB CT6 42 C5
RAM CT11 5 J5
RCANTE CT3 43 G7
RCANTE CT3 64 A3
RCANTE CT3 80 E5
RCANTE CT3 81 J6
RCANTE CT3 82 C7
RCANTE CT3 99 L3
RCANTW CT4 96 D8
RCANTW CT4 97 K1
RFOLK CT18 169 J6
RMAID ME17 105 H3
RSIT ME9 32 E2
RSIT ME9 51 H2
RSIT ME9 52 F3
RYE TN31 204 C4
RYE TN31 205 L4
School Rd DEAL CT14 119 J2
FAV ME13 55 K7
HDCN TN27 107 L5
HYTHE CT21 183 K1
RASHW TN26 126 C6
RASHW TN26 160 F1
RASHW TN26 189 K4
RCANTE CT3 82 E3
RFOLK CT18 152 A6
SIT ME10 52 D2
SWCH CT13 84 B4
Scocles Rd IOS ME12 20 D1
Scoggers Hl FAV ME13 75 J6
Scot's La RASHE TN25 148 F5
Scotton St RASHE TN25 129 H3
Scotts Acre RYE TN31 213 G2
Scrapsgate Rd IOS ME12 15 J6
Scraps Hl RSIT ME9 53 G1
Sea Ap IOS ME12 22 F1
Seabourne Wy LYDD TN29 194 D6
Seabrook Ct HYTHE CT21 184 D2
Seabrook Gdns HYTHE CT21 184 C3
Seabrook Gv HYTHE CT21 184 C3
Seabrook Rd HYTHE CT21 184 A3
Seabrook V HYTHE CT21 184 D1
Seacroft Rd BRDST CT10 49 J4
Seadown Cl HYTHE CT21 184 C1 1
Seafield Rd BRDST CT10 49 H1
RAM CT11 4 E5
WSTB CT5 40 D2
Seagar Rd FAV ME13 55 K4
Seager Rd IOS ME12 15 G3
Seagrave Crs FOLKN CT19 13 L4
Seamark Cl MSTR CT12 45 M7
Seamark Rd MSTR CT12 45 M5
Seapoint Rd BRDST CT10 49 K2
Sea Rd BRCH CT7 28 D5
DEAL CT14 121 L7
HYTHE CT21 184 C3
RYE TN31 213 H3
WGOS CT8 28 E4
Seasalter Beach WSTB CT5 39 J6
Seasalter Cl IOS ME12 23 G1
Seasalter Cross WSTB CT5 39 H7
Seasalter La WSTB CT5 58 B1
Seasalter Rd FAV ME13 57 G3
Seaside Av IOS ME12 15 L5
Sea St HB CT6 41 K2
RDV CT15 139 J7
Seathorpe Av IOS ME12 15 L6
Seaton Av HYTHE CT21 183 K2
Seaton Rd RCANTE CT3 80 E3
Sea View Av BRCH CT7 28 A5
Seaview Av IOS ME12 23 K4
Sea View Cl RFOLK CT18 171 K4 1
Sea View Gdns IOS ME12 23 G2
Sea View Rd BRCH CT7 28 A5
BRDST CT10 31 J7
HB CT6 24 E8
MSTR CT12 47 M7
RDV CT15 157 H1
Seaview Rd NROM TN28 210 F4
Sea View Sq HB CT6 24 B8 1
Sea View Ter MARG CT9 2 B5
Seaville Dr HB CT6 25 G8
Sea Wall LYDD TN29 194 F5
WSTB CT5 39 M3
Seaway Crs LYDD TN29 203 H1
Seaway Gdns LYDD TN29 203 J1
Seaway Rd LYDD TN29 203 H1
Second Av BRDST CT10 31 J3
IOS ME12 14 D4
IOS ME12 17 H8
MARG CT9 3 L2
QBOR ME11 19 H2
RYE TN31 213 H3
Segrave Rd FOLKN CT19 13 L4
Selbey Cl HB CT6 42 E1
Selborne Rd MARG CT9 3 M8
Selkirk Rd DVE/WH CT16 155 K2
Selling Ct FAV ME13 74 E7
Selling Rd FAV ME13 74 B3
RCANTW CT4 93 K2
Selway Ct DEAL CT14 121 K2
Selwood Cl IOS ME12 15 G7
Selwyn Dr BRDST CT10 31 G8
Semaphore Rd BRCH CT7 28 B5 3
Semple Cl MSTR CT12 46 E6 1
Sene Pk HYTHE CT21 183 M2
Senlac Cl RAM CT11 4 C7
Serene Ct BRDST CT10 49 K1 3
Setterfield Rd MARG CT9 3 G7
Sevastopol Pl CANT CT1 78 F4 3
Sevenacre Rd FAV ME13 55 L4
Seven Stones Dr BRDST CT10 49 J4
Sevington La KEN/WIL TN24 9 M8
Sewell Cl BRCH CT7 28 C7
Sexburga Dr IOS ME12 15 K5
Seymour Av MARG CT9 29 H4
WSTB CT5 40 A4
Seymour Cl HB CT6 42 D4
Seymour Pl CANT CT1 6 C7
Seymour Rd RDV CT15 139 H5
Shadoxhurst Rd RASHW TN26 176 E1
Shaftesbury Av FOLKN CT19 170 A6
Shaftesbury Rd
CANTW/ST CT2 78 B2 1
RCANTE CT3 62 A4 1
WSTB CT5 39 M4 1
Shaftsbury St RAM CT11 5 L5
Shah Pl RAM CT11 5 H4 1
Shakespeare Rd BRCH CT7 28 C5
DVW CT17 155 K7 1
MARG CT9 3 H6 2
SIT ME10 52 C1
Shakespeare Ter FOLK CT20 12 F6
Shalloak Rd CANTW/ST CT2 60 F8
Shallows Rd BRDST CT10 30 E7
Shalmsford Ct RCANTW CT4 94 D4
Shalmsford Rd RCANTW CT4 94 A3
Shalmsford St RCANTW CT4 94 C3
Shamrock Av WSTB CT5 39 K6
Shapland Cl HB CT6 42 E2
Share & Coulter Rd WSTB CT5 40 F4
Sharp's Fld HDCN TN27 122 A8
Sharsted Hl RSIT ME9 71 L5
Shaw Cross KEN/WIL TN24 127 M8 3
Shawdon Av SWCH CT13 85 J6
Shearwater Av WSTB CT5 39 L6
Shearwater Ct IOS ME12 14 D5 3
Shear Wy LYDD TN29 181 L8
Shearway Rd FOLKN CT19 170 B5
Sheepfold La ASH TN23 163 L1
Sheerstone RSIT ME9 32 F2
Sheerwater Rd RCANTE CT3 64 A8
Sheerways FAV ME13 55 J7 2
Sheet Glass Rd QBOR ME11 19 J2
Sheldon Cl RCANTE CT3 99 J7 1
Sheldwich Cl ASH TN23 145 H7
Shelley Av CANT CT1 78 E3
Shellness Rd IOS ME12 23 K4
Shellons St FOLK CT20 13 H5
Shelvin La RCANTW CT4 134 E1
Shepherd Dr KEN/WIL TN24 146 C5 3
Shepherd's Close Rd
RCANTW CT4 98 A4
Shepherdsgate CANTW/ST CT2 6 E2 2
Shepherdsgate Dr HB CT6 42 C5 1
Shepherds Wk HYTHE CT21 183 G5
WSTB CT5 40 E5
Shepherds Wy WSTB CT5 40 E5
Shepherdswell Rd RDV CT15 118 B6
Sheppey Cl BRCH CT7 28 C6 3
Sheppey St IOS ME12 14 C3 4
Sheppey Vw WSTB CT5 39 K7
Sheppey Wy IOS ME12 19 M2
RSIT ME9 19 J6
SIT ME10 32 C8
Shepway KEN/WIL TN24 128 A8
Shepway Cl FOLKN CT19 13 G3
Sheridan Rd DVE/WH CT16 155 K2
Sheron Cl DEAL CT14 103 J8
Sherriffs Court La MSTR CT12 46 B7
Sherway Cl HDCN TN27 122 A8
Sherway Rd HDCN TN27 122 F6
Sherwood Cl FAV ME13 55 K5
HB CT6 42 E3
KEN/WIL TN24 127 M6 2
WSTB CT5 39 L7 1
Sherwood Dr WSTB CT5 39 L7
Sherwood Gdns RAM CT11 49 G4
Sherwood Rd BRCH CT7 28 B8
Ship Cl LYDD TN29 194 E5
Shipley Mill Cl ASH TN23 163 L1
Shipman Av CANTW/ST CT2 77 L5
Shipmans Wy DVE/WH CT16 155 J2
Ship St FOLKN CT19 13 G4
Shire La FAV ME13 89 L7
Shireway Cl FOLKN CT19 12 B1
Shirley Av RAM CT11 49 G3
Sholden Bank DEAL CT14 121 G1
Sholden New Rd DEAL CT14 103 H8
Shooter's Hl DVW CT17 10 A3
RDV CT15 118 E5
Shore Cl HB CT6 41 K2
Shoreham La TENT TN30 174 C2
Shorncliffe Crs FOLK CT20 170 A8
Shorncliffe Rd FOLK CT20 12 A5
FOLK CT20 170 A8 3
Shortlands Rd SIT ME10 52 C1
Short La LYDD TN29 190 F7
RDV CT15 153 M4
Short's Prospect IOS ME12 21 K5
Short St IOS ME12 14 D3 1
RCANTE CT3 100 C5
SWCH CT13 84 C4 9
Shottendane Rd BRCH CT7 46 F1
Shottenden Rd FAV ME13 91 L6
Shrimpton Cl RCANTW CT4 93 K2
The Shrubbery DEAL CT14 121 L4
Shrubcote TENT TN30 174 E6 1
Shrub Hill Rd WSTB CT5 40 F6
Shrubsole Av IOS ME12 14 E4 1
Shuart La BRCH CT7 45 H2
Shurland Av IOS ME12 15 K7
IOS ME12 23 K4
SIT ME10 52 B4
Shuttle Rd BRDST CT10 49 K1
Shuttlesfield La RCANTW CT4 150 F4
Sibert's Cl RDV CT15 118 B8
The Sidings RFOLK CT18 150 E6
Sidney St FOLKN CT19 13 J2
Silver Av BRCH CT7 28 D7
Silver Birch Gv ASH TN23 163 K1
Silverdale Av IOS ME12 15 J7
Silverdale Dr HB CT6 42 F3
Silverdale Gv SIT ME10 51 L2
Silverdale Rd RAM CT11 4 B8
Silver Hl TENT TN30 174 D4
Silver Hill Gdns
KEN/WIL TN24 146 C4 4
Silver Hill Rd KEN/WIL TN24 146 C4
Silverlands Rd RFOLK CT18 150 D6
The Silvers BRDST CT10 48 E1 1
Silver St DEAL CT14 103 M6 13
RSIT ME9 51 H8
Simmonds Rd CANT CT1 6 C7
Simon Av MARG CT9 30 F3
Simone Weil Av KEN/WIL TN24 145 K1
Simon's Av ASH TN23 145 H6
Simpson Rd SIT ME10 32 E8
Singledge La RDV CT15 136 D2
Singleton Cl MSTR CT12 46 D7 3
Singleton Hl ASH TN23 144 F4
Singleton Rd ASH TN23 144 E4
Sion Hl RAM CT11 5 J7
Sir John Moore Av HYTHE CT21 183 J3
Siskin Cl RFOLK CT18 170 A1
Six Fields Pth TENT TN30 174 C6
Sixth Av IOS ME12 17 J8
Skeete Rd RFOLK CT18 150 B6
Skinner Rd LYDD TN29 209 L8 1
Slade Rd RMAID ME17 88 F5
Slades Cl WSTB CT5 40 E5
Sleigh Rd CANTW/ST CT2 61 H7
Slip La RDV CT15 153 K3
Sloe La BRDST CT10 30 D7
Slough Rd RSIT ME9 70 C1
Smallhythe Rd TENT TN30 174 B6 3
Smarden Rd HDCN TN27 124 C8
HDCN TN27 140 A1
HDCN TN27 158 C1
Smeed Cl SIT ME10 52 D1 2
Smiths Orch RSIT ME9 51 H8
Smithy Dr ASH TN23 163 L1
Smuggler's Wy BRCH CT7 28 C5
Snakes Hl RCANTE CT3 81 J8
Snargate La LYDD TN29 190 F8
Snargate St DVW CT17 10 C8
Snell Gdns HB CT6 41 K3
Snowbell Rd ASH TN23 163 K1
Snowdrop Cl FOLKN CT19 170 E5
Snughorne La HDCN TN27 140 E5
Sobraon Wy CANT CT1 78 F4
Soleshill Rd RCANTW CT4 93 G4
Solomons La FAV ME13 55 M6 3
Somerset Cl SIT ME10 51 L1
WSTB CT5 39 K6
Somerset Rd CANT CT1 7 M5
DEAL CT14 121 K2
FOLKN CT19 170 A7
KEN/WIL TN24 8 E3

The Tram Rd FOLKN CT19 13 K3
Transformer Av LYDD TN29 217 G7
Travers Gdns RSIT ME9 51 H8 1
Travers Rd DEAL CT14 103 J8
Treasury Vw RCANTE CT3 80 E5
Tribune Ct IOS ME12 14 D5 4
Tribune Dr SIT ME10 33 H7
Trimworth Rd FOLKN CT19 170 B7
Trinity Crs FOLK CT20 12 D7
Trinity Gdns FOLK CT20 12 E7
Trinity Pl DEAL CT14 121 J1
RAM CT11 5 L4
Trinity Rd FOLK CT20 12 D6
IOS ME12 14 E3
KEN/WIL TN24 127 L6
SIT ME10 33 H6
Trinity Sq BRDST CT10 31 H6
MARG CT9 3 G3
Trinty Hl MARG CT9 2 F3
Tritton Cl KEN/WIL TN24 128 B6
Tritton Flds KEN/WIL TN24 128 A6 3
Tritton Gdns LYDD TN29 194 F4
Tritton La NROM TN28 202 D7 2
Troubridge Cl KEN/WIL TN24 146 C6 2
Troughton Ms MARG CT9 2 D6
Troy Town La RASHE TN25 129 K7
Trueman Cl CANTW/ST CT2 59 J6
Truro Rd RAM CT11 5 L5
Tudor Av LYDD TN29 194 F4
Tudor Byway KEN/WIL TN24 127 M7 3
Tudor Cl BRCH CT7 28 D5 1
Tudor End KEN/WIL TN24 127 M8
Tudor Rd CANT CT1 6 D7
FOLKN CT19 169 M7
KEN/WIL TN24 127 M8
Tufton Rd KEN/WIL TN24 9 G4
Tufton St ASH TN23 8 D4
Tunis Ct CANT CT1 78 F4
Tunis Rw BRDST CT10 31 K8
Tunstall Rd CANTW/ST CT2 78 C1
RSIT ME9 51 L5
Turketel Rd FOLK CT20 12 B5
Turmine Ct IOS ME12 15 J8 7
Turnagain La CANT CT1 6 F4 2
Turnden Gdns MARG CT9 31 G3
Turner Cl SIT ME10 33 J6
Turners Av TENT TN30 174 D5
Turner St RAM CT11 5 K5
Turnpike Cl HYTHE CT21 183 J3 3
Turnpike Hl HYTHE CT21 183 J2
Twelve Acres KEN/WIL TN24 9 K8
Twiss Av HYTHE CT21 183 M3
Twiss Gv HYTHE CT21 183 M3
Twiss Rd HYTHE CT21 183 M3
Twyne Cl CANTW/ST CT2 61 J7
Tyler Cl CANTW/ST CT2 78 B2
Tyler Hill Rd CANTW/ST CT2 59 J7
Tyler Wy WSTB CT5 41 G2
Tyndale Pk HB CT6 42 D1
Tysoe Ct IOS ME12 15 H8
Tyson Av MARG CT9 29 J4
Tyson Rd FOLKN CT19 13 K1

U

Uden Rd LYDD TN29 195 J1
Udimore Rd RYE TN31 205 J8
Uffington Ct RCANTE CT3 99 J3
Ufton La SIT ME10 52 A2
Ulcombe Gdns CANTW/ST CT2 78 C2
Ulcombe Hl RMAID ME17 104 B4
Ulley Rd KEN/WIL TN24 127 M6
Ullswater Gdns RCANTE CT3 99 H7 6
Ulster Rd MARG CT9 3 G8
Undercliff FOLK CT20 185 G2
Undercliffe Rd DEAL CT14 121 M8
Underdown La HB CT6 42 B3
Underdown Rd DVW CT17 155 K6 4
HB CT6 42 B1
Underhill Rd FOLK CT20 169 K8
Underwood RFOLK CT18 152 D7
Underwood Cl CANT CT1 78 C8
KEN/WIL TN24 127 M7 4
Union Crs MARG CT9 3 G4
Union Pl CANT CT1 7 H2
Union Rd DEAL CT14 103 M7
IOS ME12 15 M6
RAM CT11 5 L2
RCANTW CT4 97 H4
Union Rw MARG CT9 3 G4
Union St CANT CT1 7 H2
DVW CT17 10 D8
FAV ME13 55 L6
IOS ME12 14 C3 5
RAM CT11 5 K5 3
Unity Pl RAM CT11 5 L4
Unity St IOS ME12 14 F3
SIT ME10 52 A2
University Rd CANTW/ST CT2 77 M2
Upchurch Wk MARG CT9 31 G3 7
Uphill RFOLK CT18 170 D1
Uplands CANTW/ST CT2 78 B1
Uplands Wy IOS ME12 14 E8
Uplees Rd FAV ME13 36 B7
Upper Approach Rd
BRDST CT10 49 J2 3
Upper Brents FAV ME13 55 M4
Upper Bridge St CANT CT1 7 G6
RASHE TN25 129 H3
Upper Chantry La CANT CT1 7 H6
Upper Dane Rd MARG CT9 3 K6
Upper Denmark Rd ASH TN23 8 D8
Upper Dumpton Park Rd
RAM CT11 5 J4
Upper Field Rd SIT ME10 33 K8
Upper Free Down HB CT6 42 C3
Upper Gv MARG CT9 3 G4
Upper Malthouse Hl
HYTHE CT21 183 K3 2
Upper Rd DVE/WH CT16 11 K2
Upper St Ann's Rd FAV ME13 55 K7
Upper Strand St SWCH CT13 84 C4 11
Upper St DEAL CT14 119 J2
DEAL CT14 121 M8
RMAID ME17 86 A2
Upper Vicarage Rd
KEN/WIL TN24 127 M6
Upton Cl FOLKN CT19 12 B1
Upton Rd BRDST CT10 31 H8
Ursuline Dr WGOS CT8 28 F6

V

Valebrook Cl FOLK CT20 169 L8
Valenciennes Rd SIT ME10 52 A2
Vale Pl RAM CT11 5 G6
Vale Rd BRDST CT10 49 H1
RAM CT11 4 F6
RDV CT15 120 D6
WSTB CT5 39 M5
Vale Sq RAM CT11 5 H6
Valestone Cl HYTHE CT21 184 D1
The Vale BRDST CT10 49 H1
Vale View Rd DVW CT17 155 K6
RCANTE CT3 99 G8
Valkyrie Av WSTB CT5 39 K5
The Vallance RSIT ME9 53 J7
Valley Rd CANT CT1 6 C8
DVW CT17 155 G2
FOLK CT20 185 G1
MARG CT9 48 A1
RCANTW CT4 116 A3
Valley Wk HYTHE CT21 184 D2
Vanity Rd IOS ME12 23 H4
Varne Pl FOLKN CT19 13 M4
Varne Rd FOLKN CT19 13 M4
Vaughan Dr SIT ME10 33 H5
Vauxhall Av CANT CT1 78 E2
HB CT6 41 J2
Vauxhall Crs CANT CT1 78 E2 1
Vauxhall Industrial Rd
CANT CT1 78 E1
Vauxhall Rd CANTW/ST CT2 78 E1
Vectis Dr SIT ME10 33 H5
Venture Cl LYDD TN29 194 F4
Vere Rd BRDST CT10 49 J1
Vereth Rd RAM CT11 5 G7
Vernon Pl CANT CT1 7 G6
DEAL CT14 103 M5 4
Vesper Ct HDCN TN27 141 J4
Vestey Ct WGOS CT8 29 G4
Viaduct Cl MSTR CT12 4 F2
The Viaduct DVW CT17 155 M8 6
Viburnum Cl ASH TN23 145 G3
Vicarage Gdn MSTR CT12 45 L6
Vicarage Gdns RCANTE CT3 81 J6 2
Vicarage Hl RCANTW CT4 113 J1
Vicarage La ASH TN23 8 E4
DEAL CT14 103 H8
DEAL CT14 119 J2
FAV ME13 55 J8
FAV ME13 74 E7
RCANTW CT4 151 H1
RDV CT15 99 L8
RDV CT15 139 H7
SWCH CT13 84 B4 10
Vicarage Pl MARG CT9 2 F6
Vicarage Rd FOLK CT20 185 H2
IOS ME12 15 M6 3
SIT ME10 32 F6
Vicarage St BRDST CT10 30 F8
FAV ME13 55 M5
Vickers Cl RFOLK CT18 170 C1
Victor Av MARG CT9 30 F3
Victoria Av BRDST CT10 31 G5
HYTHE CT21 183 K3
MARG CT9 3 L7
RDV CT15 139 K7
WGOS CT8 29 H6
Victoria Cl RMAID ME17 105 G6
Victoria Crs ASH TN23 8 D6
DVE/WH CT16 10 C4 3
Victoria Gv FOLK CT20 13 G5
HYTHE CT21 184 D3
Victoria Pde RAM CT11 5 M4
Victoria Pk DVE/WH CT16 10 F4
HB CT6 24 B8
Victoria Pl FAV ME13 55 L6
Victoria Rd ASH TN23 8 D5
BRDST CT10 31 G7
CANT CT1 6 D7
DEAL CT14 103 M8
DEAL CT14 139 L1
FOLKN CT19 12 F4
HYTHE CT21 183 L4
MARG CT9 3 G5
NROM TN28 203 G8
RAM CT11 5 L4
RFOLK CT18 171 K3
SIT ME10 51 M1
Victoria Rd West NROM TN28 202 F8
Victoria Rw CANT CT1 7 G3 3
CANT CT1 7 H2 3
Victoria St DVW CT17 155 K4
IOS ME12 14 D4
NROM TN28 202 C7 3
SIT ME10 52 D3 1
Victory St IOS ME12 14 D3 2
Viking Cl BRCH CT7 27 M5
Village Wy RASHW TN26 178 C6
Villiers Rd CANT CT1 78 F4
Vincent Cl BRDST CT10 48 E2
FOLK CT20 185 G1
Vincent Gdns IOS ME12 14 E4
Vincent Pl KEN/WIL TN24 146 B1
Vincent Rd MARG CT9 47 L1
SIT ME10 52 E2
Vine Cl RAM CT11 49 G3
Vine Lands LYDD TN29 209 K7
Viners Cl SIT ME10 52 A4
Viney's Gdns TENT TN30 174 E4
Vinson Cl FAV ME13 56 F4
Vinten Cl HB CT6 42 D5
Violet Av MSTR CT12 48 E3
Virginia Rd WSTB CT5 40 C5
Vlissingen Dr DEAL CT14 103 L5
Volante Dr SIT ME10 33 G6
Vulcan Cl WSTB CT5 39 L6

W

Wacher Cl CANTW/ST CT2 78 B3
Waddington Dr RFOLK CT18 170 C1
Wades Cl LYDD TN29 193 K8
Wadham Pl SIT ME10 52 D3
Wain Ct IOS ME12 15 J8
Wainwright Pl KEN/WIL TN24 9 G8
Wakefield Wy HYTHE CT21 183 K4
Walcheren Cl DEAL CT14 103 L5 3
The Waldens RMAID ME17 104 A3
Waldershare Av SWCH CT13 85 J6
Waldershare Rd RDV CT15 119 J8
Waldron Rd BRDST CT10 49 K3
Walker La BRCH CT7 27 M5 4
Wallace Ms FOLKN CT19 170 F6
Wallace Wy BRDST CT10 49 G1
Waller Rd LYDD TN29 211 G6
Wallers Rd FAV ME13 55 J6
Wallis Rd KEN/WIL TN24 9 H3
Wall Rd KEN/WIL TN24 8 D2
The Wall SIT ME10 33 G8
Wallwood Rd RAM CT11 5 M3
Walmer Castle Rd DEAL CT14 121 L4
Walmer Gdns DEAL CT14 121 J3
MSTR CT12 47 L8
SIT ME10 32 F8
Walmer Rd WSTB CT5 40 A5
Walmer Wy DEAL CT14 121 J3
Walmsley Rd BRDST CT10 31 H8
Walner Gdns NROM TN28 202 D6
Walner La NROM TN28 202 D6
Walnut Cl KEN/WIL TN24 127 M7
Walnut Tree Dr SIT ME10 51 M1 1
Walnut Tree La CANTW/ST CT2 61 L6
Walpole Rd MARG CT9 3 G3
Walsby Dr SIT ME10 33 J5
Waltham Cl KEN/WIL TN24 9 M4
MARG CT9 31 G3 8
Waltham Rd RCANTW CT4 113 H4
Walton Gdns FOLKN CT19 13 G1
Walton Manor Cl FOLKN CT19 170 F5
Walton Rd FOLKN CT19 13 G2
The Waltons FOLKN CT19 170 E5
Wanden La HDCN TN27 123 K4
Wantsum Cl HB CT6 25 H8
Wantsume Lees SWCH CT13 84 A3
Wantsum Wk BRCH CT7 27 L6
BRCH CT7 44 F6
HB CT6 25 J8
Wantsum Wy BRCH CT7 45 G3
Warden Bay Rd IOS ME12 23 G2
Warden House Ms
DEAL CT14 121 J1 2
Warden Rd IOS ME12 22 A1
Warden View Gdns IOS ME12 22 E4
Wardour Cl BRDST CT10 49 K1 3
Wards Hill Rd IOS ME12 15 K5
Warehorne Rd RASHW TN26 178 B6
Warre Av RAM CT11 4 E8
Warren Cl FOLKN CT19 13 M2
SIT ME10 52 D3 3
Warren Dr BRDST CT10 31 G8
The Warren Dr WGOS CT8 28 F6
Warren La KEN/WIL TN24 145 J1
RDV CT15 135 M6
Warren Rd FOLKN CT19 13 L3
NROM TN28 202 F7
Warren St RMAID ME17 88 F7
The Warren RASHE TN25 148 A8
WSTB CT5 39 L7
Warren Vw ASH TN23 145 H1
Warren Wy FOLKN CT19 13 L3
Warten Rd RAM CT11 49 H4
Warwick Crs SIT ME10 32 E8
Warwick Dr RAM CT11 4 C8
Warwick Rd CANT CT1 7 M5
DEAL CT14 121 M3
KEN/WIL TN24 128 A7
MARG CT9 3 J6
WSTB CT5 39 M3
Washford Farm Rd ASH TN23 145 G8
Washington Cl DVE/WH CT16 155 K2 6
Washington La LYDD TN29 200 D6
Wassall La CRBK TN17 186 A6
Wass Dro RCANTE CT3 64 D6
Watchbell La RYE TN31 205 L8 6
Watchbell St RYE TN31 205 K8
Watchester Av RAM CT11 4 F8
Watchester La MSTR CT12 46 D8
Waterbrook Av KEN/WIL TN24 146 B8
Watercress La ASH TN23 145 G5
Waterditch La RMAID ME17 88 F7
Waterfall Rd RASHW TN26 126 C7
Water Farm RCANTW CT4 151 H1
Waterham Rd FAV ME13 57 L4
Water La CANT CT1 6 E4 2
FAV ME13 55 L6 7
HDCN TN27 141 G3
RMAID ME17 104 B2
Waterloo Crs DVE/WH CT16 10 E7
DVW CT17 10 D8
Waterloo Hl IOS ME12 15 M7 1
Waterloo Pl RAM CT11 5 L5
Waterloo Rd FOLK CT20 169 M8 2
SIT ME10 32 F8
WSTB CT5 39 M3
Water Mdw CANTW/ST CT2 79 H1 2
Watersend DVE/WH CT16 136 E8
Waterside KEN/WIL TN24 9 M6
Waterside Dr WGOS CT8 29 H4 6
Waterside Vw IOS ME12 23 G1
Water St DEAL CT14 103 M6
Waterworks Hl RDV CT15 138 D2
Waterworks La RDV CT15 138 D2
Watkin Rd FOLKN CT19 12 F2
Watling Pl SIT ME10 52 C2
Watling St CANT CT1 6 F5
Watsons Cl RASHE TN25 127 L5
Watson's Hl SIT ME10 33 G8
Wauchope Rd WSTB CT5 39 H7
Waverley Av IOS ME12 15 K6
Waverley Rd MARG CT9 2 A7
Wayborough Hl MSTR CT12 46 F5
Way Hl MSTR CT12 47 G6
Wayne Cl BRDST CT10 31 G8
Wayside TENT TN30 174 D3 1
Wayside Av TENT TN30 174 D2
Weald Ct SIT ME10 51 M3
Wealden Av TENT TN30 174 D3
Wealdhurst Pk BRDST CT10 30 F8
The Weald KEN/WIL TN24 8 E1
Wear Bay Crs FOLKN CT19 13 L4
Wear Bay Rd FOLKN CT19 13 M4
Weatherall Cl FAV ME13 75 K3
Weatherly Dr BRDST CT10 49 H3
The Weavers HDCN TN27 158 C4
Weavers Wy ASH TN23 145 G6
DVE/WH CT16 155 J2
Webb Cl FOLKN CT19 170 C6
Weddington La RCANTE CT3 83 G3
Weeks Ct QBOR ME11 14 C8 2
Weeks La HDCN TN27 140 C8
Weigall Pl RAM CT11 4 E5
Well Cl CANTW/ST CT2 61 J7
Wellesley Av DEAL CT14 121 L3
Wellesley Cl BRDST CT10 49 G2
WGOS CT8 29 G6 2
Wellesley Rd ASH TN23 8 E3
DVE/WH CT16 10 E6
IOS ME12 14 F4
KEN/WIL TN24 8 E3
MARG CT9 3 L6
WGOS CT8 29 G6 3
Wellfield Rd FOLK CT20 12 A5
Wellington Cl WGOS CT8 29 G4 3
Wellington Crs RAM CT11 5 L6
Wellington Gdns MARG CT9 3 H3 1
Wellington Pde DEAL CT14 121 M6
Wellington Pl FOLK CT20 184 F2 2
Wellington Rd DEAL CT14 103 M8
DVE/WH CT16 136 F8
FOLK CT20 169 M8
SIT ME10 32 D8
WGOS CT8 29 G6
Wellington St WSTB CT5 39 M8
Wellis Gdns MARG CT9 2 B7
Well La CANTW/ST CT2 79 J2
FAV ME13 72 D2
RDV CT15 139 H7
Well Rd QBOR ME11 14 C8 3
RFOLK CT18 150 E7
Wells Av CANT CT1 7 K7
Wells Cl NROM TN28 202 E7
TENT TN30 174 C5
Wells Rd FOLKN CT19 170 A7
Wells Wy FAV ME13 55 K4
Well Winch Rd SIT ME10 32 F8
Welsdene Rd MARG CT9 29 K5 5
Welson Rd FOLK CT20 12 A5
Wemyss Wy CANT CT1 7 M3
Wenham's La LYDD TN29 201 G3
Wentworth Av MARG CT9 29 J4
Wentworth Cl RFOLK CT18 150 E7 1
Wentworth Dr MSTR CT12 4 A1
SIT ME10 32 E8 2
Wentworth Gdns HB CT6 41 M3
Wesley Ter RFOLK CT18 150 E6 1
Westbere La CANTW/ST CT2 61 K7
Westbourne ASH TN23 144 F7 3
Westbourne Gdns FOLK CT20 12 C7
Westbourne St SIT ME10 33 G8
Westbrook Av MARG CT9 29 J4
Westbrook Cottages
MARG CT9 2 B6 1
Westbrook Gdns MARG CT9 2 A6
Westbrook La HB CT6 41 K2
Westbrook Prom MARG CT9 29 K3
Westbrook Rd MARG CT9 2 B6 2
Westbury Crs DVW CT17 155 K7
Westbury Rd DVW CT17 155 K7
WGOS CT8 29 H5
West Cliff WSTB CT5 39 L5
West Cliff Ar RAM CT11 5 J7 1
West Cliff Dr HB CT6 41 K1
Westcliff Dr IOS ME12 15 M6
West Cliff Gdns FOLK CT20 13 H6
HB CT6 41 K2
Westcliff Gdns MARG CT9 2 A6
West Cliff Prom RAM CT11 5 G9
West Cliff Rd BRDST CT10 49 J2
RAM CT11 5 G7
Westcliff Rd MARG CT9 2 A6
Westcourt La RCANTW CT4 117 H6
West Cross TENT TN30 174 B6
West Cross Gdns TENT TN30 174 B6
Westdean Cl DVW CT17 155 G3
West Dumpton La RAM CT11 49 G3
Westerham Cl CANTW/ST CT2 78 C1 7
MARG CT9 31 H3 8
Westerham Rd SIT ME10 51 L2
Westerhout Cl DEAL CT14 103 L5
Western Av ASH TN23 8 B3
HB CT6 41 M1
IOS ME12 14 F6
RCANTW CT4 97 H4
Western Esp BRDST CT10 49 K3
Western Gdns KEN/WIL TN24 9 J8
Western Link FAV ME13 55 J5
Western Rd DEAL CT14 103 L7
MARG CT9 30 E5
Western Undercliff RAM CT11 4 D9
Westfield CANTW/ST CT2 59 J7
Westfield La RFOLK CT18 168 F2
Westfield Rd BRCH CT7 28 B6
MARG CT9 29 K5
Westfields HDCN TN27 124 F5
Westgate Av BRCH CT7 47 J1
Westgate Bay Av WGOS CT8 28 F4
Westgate Cl CANTW/ST CT2 77 L4
Westgate Court Av
CANTW/ST CT2 6 A3
Westgate Gv CANTW/ST CT2 6 E3 5
Westgate Hall Rd CANT CT1 6 E3 4
Westgate Rd FAV ME13 56 A6
Westgate Rbt CANTW/ST CT2 6 D3
Westgate Ter WSTB CT5 39 M3
West Gn SIT ME10 33 H4
West Hythe Rd HYTHE CT21 182 C5
Westlands Av SIT ME10 51 K1
Westlands Rd HB CT6 41 K2
Westland Wy RFOLK CT18 170 D2
West La IOS ME12 14 C3 6
SIT ME10 52 C1
West Lawn Gdns FOLK CT20 184 F2
West Lea DEAL CT14 103 L6
Westleigh Rd WGOS CT8 28 F5 2
Westmarsh Dr MARG CT9 31 G3 9
Westmeads Rd WSTB CT5 40 A3
Westminster Rd CANT CT1 78 E1
Westmoors ASH TN23 144 F7
West Norman Rd DVE/WH CT16 10 F4
Westonville Av MARG CT9 29 K4
Westover Gdns BRDST CT10 31 G6
Westover Rd BRDST CT10 31 G6
West Pde HYTHE CT21 183 K5
West Park Av MARG CT9 30 F4
West Pas IOS ME12 14 C3 7
West Pl LYDD TN29 199 M5
West Rdg SIT ME10 51 M3
West Rd FOLK CT20 184 E1
MSTR CT12 66 C5
West Side RDV CT15 138 C4
West St ASH TN23 8 C3
DEAL CT14 103 L6
DVW CT17 10 A4
FAV ME13 55 L5
IOS ME12 14 C2
NROM TN28 202 C7
QBOR ME11 14 B8
RASHW TN26 126 A6
RMAID ME17 86 E7
RMAID ME17 88 A5
RYE TN31 205 L8
SIT ME10 52 A1
West Ter FOLK CT20 13 G6
West Undercliff RYE TN31 205 J8
West View Cl HB CT6 41 L3
Westwell Ct TENT TN30 174 B6
Westwell La KEN/WIL TN24 127 G7
RASHE TN25 126 C3
Westwood Pl FAV ME13 55 M8
Westwood Rd BRDST CT10 48 E1
Weyburn Dr MSTR CT12 4 B1
Weymouth Cl FOLKN CT19 169 M7
Weymouth Rd FOLKN CT19 169 M7
Wey St RASHW TN26 191 M2
Wharfedale Rd MARG CT9 3 J6
Wharton Gdns KEN/WIL TN24 9 K7
Whatmer Cl CANTW/ST CT2 61 J7
Wheatcroft Cl SIT ME10 52 D1
Wheatley Rd MSTR CT12 48 E4 3
WSTB CT5 40 A3
Wheatsheaf Cl FAV ME13 75 J2 3
Wheatsheafe La RDV CT15 138 D3
Wheatsheaf Gdns IOS ME12 14 D4
Wheelwrights Wy SWCH CT13 101 K3
Wheler Rd HDCN TN27 107 L5 2
Whimbrel Cl SIT ME10 33 H5
Whinfell Av RAM CT11 48 B6
Whinless Rd DVW CT17 155 J5
Whiston Av RASHW TN26 160 E1
Whitby Rd FOLK CT20 169 M7
White Acre Dr DEAL CT14 121 K5
Whiteacre La RCANTW CT4 131 H1
White Cliffs Country Trail
RDV CT15 120 C4
SWCH CT13 84 E4
Whitecliff Wy FOLKN CT19 13 M2
Whitefriars Meadow
SWCH CT13 84 C5 4
Whitefriars Wy SWCH CT13 84 B4 11
Whitehall LYDD TN29 199 M5
Whitehall Bridge Rd
CANTW/ST CT2 6 C3
Whitehall Cl CANTW/ST CT2 6 D4
Whitehall Gdns CANTW/ST CT2 6 D4
Whitehall Rd CANTW/ST CT2 6 D4
MSTR CT12 4 D2
SIT ME10 52 A3
Whitehall Wy RASHE TN25 166 F4
White Hl RASHE TN25 110 A4
White Hill Cl RCANTW CT4 96 C5
White Horse Hl RFOLK CT18 170 E3
White Horse La CANT CT1 6 F4 8
RCANTW CT4 150 C2
Whitehouse Dro RCANTE CT3 65 M6
Whitelocks Cl RCANTW CT4 115 M2
Whitenbrook HYTHE CT21 184 C2
Whiteness Gn BRDST CT10 31 H4
Whiteness Rd BRDST CT10 31 J4
White Post Gdns RCANTE CT3 82 F4
Whites Hl DEAL CT14 119 J3
Whiteway Rd QBOR ME11 14 B7
White Wood Rd SWCH CT13 101 K4
Whitfeld Rd ASH TN23 8 D8
Whitfield Av BRDST CT10 31 G6
DVE/WH CT16 155 K3
Whitfield Ct DVE/WH CT16 137 J7
Whitfield Hl DVE/WH CT16 155 G1
Whiting Crs FAV ME13 55 J5
Whitstable Rd CANTW/ST CT2 6 B1
FAV ME13 56 A6
HB CT6 41 J2
Whybornes Cha IOS ME12 15 L6
Whytecliffs BRDST CT10 49 J3 3
Wichling Cl CANTW/ST CT2 78 C2
Wickenden Crs KEN/WIL TN24 146 C5
Wicken La HDCN TN27 108 A7
Wickham Av RAM CT11 49 J5
Wickham Court La RCANTE CT3 80 D2
Wickham La RCANTE CT3 80 D3
Wickham Rd RCANTE CT3 80 D4
Wick La RCANTW CT4 116 F6
Widgeon Wk RFOLK CT18 170 D2
Widred Rd DVW CT17 10 A4
Wife of Bath Hl CANTW/ST CT2 77 L5
Wigmore La RDV CT15 118 E5
Wigwam Paddocks BRCH CT7 28 C5 4
Wihtred Rd RSIT ME9 52 F3
Wilberforce Rd FOLK CT20 185 G2
Wilbrough Rd BRCH CT7 28 C6
Wilcox Cl RCANTE CT3 116 F1
Wilderness Hl MARG CT9 3 J4
Wildish Rd FAV ME13 55 J5
Wildwood Cl RMAID ME17 104 A3
Wiles Av NROM TN28 202 D7
Wilfred Rd RAM CT11 4 F4
Wilgate Green Rd FAV ME13 73 G6
Wilkes Rd BRDST CT10 49 G2
Wilkie Rd BRCH CT7 28 C5 5